PSYCHOTHERAPY
THE TOP 50
THEORISTS & THEORIES

DAVID E. MALOCCO

B.C.L., B.Sc. (Psych), Dip. F. Sc. Dip. P.C.P.

ISBN: 1505487374
ISBN-13: 978-1505487374

ACKNOWLEDGEMENTS

Thanks to Gary Power for his work on the cover.

DEDICATION

To Colette.

CONTENTS

DAVID ELIO MALOCCO

SIGMUND FREUD (1856-1939)

"The great question that has never been answered, and which I have not yet been able to answer, despite my thirty years of research into the feminine soul, is 'What does a woman want?'"

The Founder of Psychoanalysis

Sigmund Freud was an Austrian neurologist and the founder of psychoanalysis. He can rightly be called the most influential intellectual legislator of his age.

His contributions to psychology are enormous. It has been said that his creation of psychoanalysis was not just a theory of the human psyche and a therapy for the relief of mental illness, it was an optic for the interpretation of human behavior, culture and society.

His enduring legacy has influenced not only psychology, but also art and literature. He created a whole new lexicon in his theories and these words like anal (in relation to personality), denial, cathartic, libido, repression and neurotic are used today by everyday people.

His revolutionary theory of psychoanalysis is often known as the talking cure. Freud employed psychoanalysis by encouraging his patients to talk freely, usually on his famous couch, regarding their symptoms and to describe exactly what was in their mind.

Freud became famous through the publication of his treatment of a patient he referred to as Anna O. Her real name was Bertha Pappenheim and his treatment of her went on to influence the future direction of psychology as a whole. Anna suffered from hysteria. Her condition was such that she exhibited physical symptoms like paralysis, convulsions, hallucinations, and speech loss, without any apparent physical cause.

Initially, her doctor, Josef Breuer, succeeded in treating Anna by helping her to recall forgotten memories of traumatic events. Breuer then discussed the case with his friend neurologist Dr. Sigmund Freud. From these discussions the germ of an idea emerged that the young Freud was to pursue for the rest of his life.

Sigmund Freud was born on the 6 May 1856 to Jewish Galician parents in the Moravian town of Příbor (German: Freiberg in Mähren), in the then Austrian Empire, which is now part of the Czech Republic. He was the first of their eight children. His father, Jakob Freud, was a Jewish wool merchant who had two sons, Emanuel and Philipp, from his first marriage.

Jakob's family were Hasidic Jews, and though Jakob himself had moved away from the tradition, he came to be known for his Torah study. His mother was Amalie Nathansohn who was twenty years her husband's junior and his third wife. When Sigmund was born his father was forty and the family were struggling financially and living in a rented room, in a locksmith's house at Schlossergasse 117. His father was a relatively remote and authoritarian figure, while his mother appears to have been more nurturing and emotionally available. Although he had two older half-brothers, his strongest bond seems to have been with his nephew, John, one year his senior, who provided the model of intimate friend and hated rival that Freud reproduced often at later stages of his life.

In 1859, the Freuds were compelled, for economic reasons, to move to Leipzig and then a year after to Vienna, where Freud remained until the Nazi annexation of Austria seventy eight years later.

In 1873, Freud graduated from the Sperl Gymnasium and, apparently inspired by a public reading of an essay by Goethe on nature, turned to medicine as a career. At the University of Vienna he worked with one of the leading physiologists of his day, Ernst von Brücke, an exponent of the materialist, antivitalist science of Hermann von Helmholtz. In 1882 he entered the General Hospital in Vienna as a clinical assistant to train with the psychiatrist Theodor Meynert and the professor of internal medicine Hermann Nothnagel.

In 1885, Freud was appointed lecturer in neuropathology. Around this time he developed an interest in the pharmaceutical benefits of cocaine, which he pursued for several years. His advocacy of the drug lead not only to a mortal addiction in another close friend, Ernst Fleischl von Marxow, but it also tarnished his medical reputation for a time.

In late 1885, Freud left Vienna to continue his studies of neuropathology at the Salpêtrière clinic in Paris, where he worked under the guidance of Jean-Martin Charcot. His nineteen weeks in the French capital proved a turning point in his career. At the time, Charcot was working with patients classified as "hysterics." He introduced Freud to the possibility that psychological disorders might have their source in the mind rather than the brain. Freud returned to Vienna in February 1886 with the seed of his revolutionary psychological method firmly implanted in his head.

Several months after his return, Freud married Martha Bernays, the daughter of a prominent Jewish family. She was to bear six children, one of whom, Anna Freud, was to become a distinguished psychoanalyst in her own right. Shortly after his marriage, Freud began his closest friendship, with the Berlin physician, Wilhelm Fliess, whose role in the development of psychoanalysis has occasioned widespread debate. Throughout the fifteen years of their intimacy, Fliess stimulated Freud's belief in human bisexuality, his idea of erotogenic zones on the body, and perhaps even his imputation of sexuality to infants.

Freud's partnership with the physician Josef Breuer, after his return from Paris, was far less complicated and uncontroversial. Freud turned to a clinical practice in neuropsychology, and the office he established at Berggasse 19 was to remain his consulting room for almost half a century. Enter Anna O.

Anna was suffering from a variety of hysterical symptoms. Rather than using hypnotic suggestion, as had Charcot, Breuer allowed her to lapse into a state resembling autohypnosis, in which she would talk about the initial manifestations of her symptoms. Much to his surprise, Breuer noticed that the very act of verbalization seemed to provide some relief from their hold over her. This verbalization referred to as the "talking cure" by Breuer and "chimney sweeping" by Anna, appeared to act cathartically to produce a discharge of the pent-up emotional blockage at the root of the pathological behavior.

Freud failed to understand the full implications of Breuer's experience until a decade later, when he developed the technique of **free association.** This revolutionary method was announced in the work Freud published jointly with Breuer in 1895, *Studien über Hysterie* (Studies in Hysteria). By encouraging the patient to express any random thoughts that came associatively to mind, the technique aimed at uncovering hitherto unarticulated material from the realm of the psyche that Freud called the unconscious. Because of its incompatibility with conscious thoughts or conflicts with other unconscious ones, this material was normally hidden, forgotten, or unavailable to conscious reflection.

Freud thought that the difficulty in freely associating, the sudden silences, stuttering, or the like, had something to do with the importance of the material struggling to be expressed, as well as the power of what he called the patient's defenses against that expression. Freud called these blockages **resistance.** This resistance had to be broken down in order to reveal hidden conflicts.

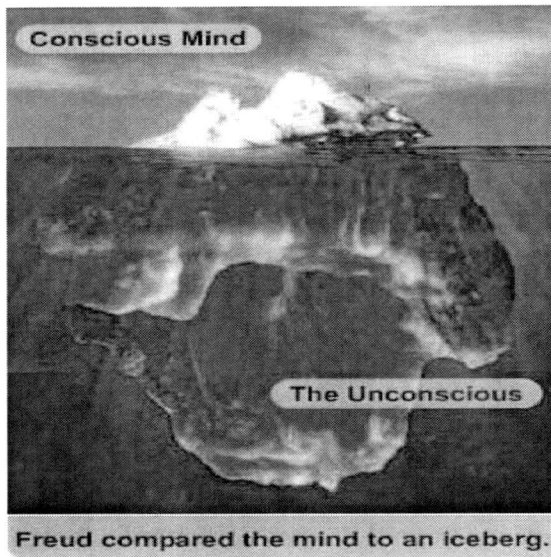

Conscious Mind

The Unconscious

Freud compared the mind to an iceberg.

In this 1895 book Freud was not just advancing an explanation of a particular illness. Implicitly, he was proposing a revolutionary new theory of the human psyche itself. This theory emerged "bit by bit" as a result of

Freud's clinical investigations. Eventually, it caused him to propose that there were at least three levels to the mind. Freud went on to develop a topographical model of the mind, whereby he described the features of the mind's structure and function. In this model the **conscious mind**, that is, everything we are aware of, is seen as the tip of the iceberg. While the unconscious mind is a repository of a 'cauldron' of primitive wishes and impulse, kept in check and mediated by the preconscious area.

But Freud believed that some events and desires were often too frightening or painful for his patients to acknowledge. These painful events were hidden, through the process of repression, in an area he called the **unconscious mind**. Freud emphasized the importance of the unconscious mind. A primary assumption of his theory is that the unconscious mind governs behavior to a greater degree than people suspect. Accordingly, the primary aim of psychoanalysis is to make the unconscious conscious.

Freud later developed a more structural model of the mind comprising of what he called the **psychic apparatus** which we now know as the entities **id**, **ego** and **superego**. These are not physical areas within the brain. They are, in fact, hypothetical conceptualizations of important mental functions.

Freud assumed the id operated at an unconscious level according to the pleasure principle. The **id** contains two kinds of biological instincts which Freud called Eros and Thanatos. **Eros**, or life instinct, helps the individual to survive. Eros directs life-sustaining activities such as respiration, eating and sex. The energy created by the life instincts is known as **libido**. In contrast, **Thanatos** or death instinct, is viewed as a set of destructive forces present in all human beings. When this energy is directed outward onto others, it is expressed as aggression and violence.

The **ego** develops from the id during infancy. The aim of the ego is to satisfy the demands of the id in a safe and socially acceptable way. In contrast to the id the ego follows the reality principle as it operates in both the conscious and unconscious mind.

The **superego** develops during early childhood when the child identifies with the same sex parent. The superego is responsible for ensuring moral standards are followed. The superego operates on the morality principle and motivates us to behave in a socially responsible and acceptable manner. The superego can make a person feel guilty if rules are not followed. When there is conflict between the goals of the id and superego the ego must act as a referee and mediate this conflict. The ego can deploy various defense mechanisms to prevent it from becoming overwhelmed by anxiety.

The defense mechanisms employed are repression, denial, projection, displacement, regression and sublimation. **Repression** is an unconscious mechanism employed by the ego to prevent disturbing or threatening thoughts from becoming conscious. An example is when we repress complex aggressive thoughts about the same sex during the Oedipus complex.

Denial is where we block external events from our awareness in situations where it is simply too painful to acknowledge them. An example would be where alcoholics refuse to admit to themselves that their continued drinking is harmful to their health.

Projection is where we attribute our own unacceptable thoughts, feelings and motives to another person. For example, you might hate your mother but your superego tells you that such behavior is unacceptable. You can "solve" the problem by trying to believe that it is your mother who hates you.

Displacement is where we satisfy an impulse such as aggression with a substitute object. An employee, frustrated and angered by his employer, might go home and take out his frustrations and anger on his wife.

Regression is a movement back in psychological time when we are faced with stress. A child may re-start a former practice of sucking their thumb or wetting their bed when they need to spend time in hospital.

Sublimation is somewhat similar to displacement in that it is satisfying an impulse like aggression with a substitute object but in a socially acceptable way. An example would be sport where we channel our aggressive emotions into something constructive. Freud also delved headlong into the area of psychosexual stages.

Freud lived in a highly repressive "Victorian" society where people in general and women in particular were forced to repress their sexual needs. In many cases, this repression resulted in some form of neurotic illness. Freud endeavored to understand the nature and variety of these illnesses by retracing the sexual history of his patients. But he was not primarily interested in investigating their sexual experiences as such.

He was far more interested in the patient's wishes and desires, their experience of love, hate, shame, guilt and fear, and how they handled these powerful emotions. It was this interest which led to the most controversial part of Freud's work, his theory of psychosexual development and of the Oedipus complex.

Freud believed that children are born with a sexual pleasure urge which he termed a libido. There are a number of stages of childhood, and during these different stages the child seeks pleasure from a different 'object'.

In order for us to be psychologically healthy it is necessary for us to successfully complete each stage. If any stage is not completed successfully then that failure might result in mental abnormality in that the person becomes 'fixated' in a particular stage. This particular theory shows how adult personality is determined by childhood experiences.

Freud was also heavily involved with the concept of **dream analysis**. He considered dreams to be the '**royal road to the unconscious.**' This is because it is in dreams that the ego's defenses are lowered. Accordingly, some of the repressed material filters through, in a distorted form, to awareness. Freud believed that dreams perform important functions for the unconscious mind and serve as valuable clues to how the unconscious mind operates.

Freud wrote about the famous dream he had on the 24 July 1895, a dream that actually formed the basis of his theory. He had been worried about one of his patients called Irma. Irma was not responding as well to treatment as he had hoped. Freud blamed himself for this and was feeling guilty. Freud had a dream that he met Irma at a party and examined her. He then saw a chemical formula for a drug that another doctor had given Irma flash before his eyes and realized that her condition was caused by a dirty syringe used by the other doctor. Freud's guilt was thus relieved.

Freud interpreted this dream as **wish-fulfillment**. He had wished that Irma's poor condition was not his fault and the dream had fulfilled this wish by informing him that another doctor was at fault. Based primarily on this dream, Freud went on to propose that a major function of dreams was the fulfillment of wishes.

He distinguished between what the dreamer remembers (often based on the events of the day) which he called the **manifest content of a dream** and the underlying wish or symbolic meaning of the dream which he called the **latent content of the dream.** The process in which the underlying wish is translated into the manifest content is called **dream-work,** the purpose of which is to transform the forbidden wish into a non-threatening form. This has the effect of reducing our anxiety and allowing us to continue to sleep.

Dream work involves the three processes of condensation, displacement, and secondary elaboration.

Condensation is the joining of two or more ideas or images into one. For example, a dream about a woman may be a dream about both one's mother and one's lover.

Displacement occurs when we transform the person or object we are really concerned about to someone else. For example, one of Freud's patients who was extremely resentful of his sister-in-law and used to refer to her as a dog, dreamed of strangling a small white dog. Freud interpreted this as representing his wish to kill his sister-in-law. If the patient would have really dreamed of killing his sister-in-law, he would have felt guilty. The unconscious mind transformed her into a dog to protect him.

Secondary elaboration occurs when the unconscious mind strings together wish-fulfilling images in a logical order of events. The result is that latent content is further obscured. This is the reason why the manifest content of dreams can be in the form of believable events.

In later years, Freud explored the possibility of **universal symbols** in dreams. Some of these were sexual in nature, including poles, guns and swords representing the penis and horse riding and dancing representing sexual intercourse.

Certain problems have been identified with Freud's theories. While they are excellent at explaining behavior they are not very good at predicting it. And predicting behavior is one of the goals of psychotherapy. Accordingly, his critics claim that Freud's theories are falsifiable, in that they can neither be proved true or refuted. How can you test or objectively measure the unconscious mind? To this extent his theories are considered unscientific.

Secondly, the majority of the empirical evidence for Freud's theories is extrapolated from a very unrepresentative sample. He mostly studied himself, his patients who were in the main middle aged women from Vienna and only one child. This makes generalizations to the wider population extremely difficult. However, Freud thought this unimportant, believing in only a qualitative difference between people.

Critics also point out that Freud may also have shown research bias in his interpretations. They claim that he may have only paid attention to information which supported his theories, and that he may have ignored information and other explanations that did not fit them. Others, like

Fisher & Greenberg (1996) argue that Freud's theory should be evaluated in terms of specific hypotheses rather than as a whole.

They like others concluded that there is ample evidence to support Freud's concepts of oral and anal personalities and some aspects of his ideas on depression and paranoia. But they found little evidence for the Oedipal conflict and no support for Freud's views on women's sexuality and how their development differs from men's. Freud died in London on the 23 September 1939 at the age of 83. In the words of W. H. Auden's poetic tribute, he had, by that time, become "a whole climate of opinion under whom we conduct our different lives".

ALFRED ADLER (1870-1936)

"A simple rule in dealing with those who are hard to get along with is to remember that this person is striving to assert his superiority; and you must deal with him from that point of view."

Inferiority Complex
Individual Psychology
Vienna Psychoanalytical Society

Alfred W. Alder was an Austrian psychotherapist best known for founding the school of individual psychology and his concept of the inferiority complex. His emphasis on the importance of the inferiority complex is recognized as isolating an element which plays a key role in personality development.

He was born at Mariahilfer Straße 208 in Rudolfsheim, a village on the western fringes of Vienna, on the 5 February 1870. His father was a Hungarian-born, Jewish grain merchant. He was the third of seven children. A sickly child he developed rickets and didn't walk until he was four. He then contracted pneumonia and overheard a doctor tell his father he wouldn't survive. It was then he decided to be a physician. He was an active and popular child and known for his competitive attitude toward his older brother, Sigmund. He was an average student and attended the University of Vienna where he attached himself to a group of socialist students.

It was in this group that he met his future wife, Raissa Timofeyewna Epstein, who was a Russian intellectual and social activist studying in Vienna. He received his medical degree in 1895 and began his career as an ophthalmologist. Soon afterwards, he switched to general practice. He set up office in a poor part of Vienna across from the Prater. The area was known for its combination of amusement parks and circuses. Many of his clients included the circus fraternity and it was from them that he developed his insights into "organ inferiorities" and "compensation".

In 1902, Sigmund Freud extended to him an invitation to join the **Wednesday Society** *(Mittwochsgesellschaft.)* This was an informal discussion group that met every Wednesday evening at Freud's house. Its members included Rudolf Reitler and Wilhelm Stekel. It soon expanded and became the basis for the psychoanalytic movement.

In 1910, Adler became president of the *Vienna Psychoanalytic Society* but he and a number of other members split a year later becoming the first of the great dissenters from Freud's orthodox psychoanalysis. (Carl Jung left three years later in 1914). By the time of this departure Freud and Adler had grown to dislike each other. Adler had always maintained his own views on psychoanalysis. He later made it clear that he was a colleague of Freud rather than his pupil.

In 1912, he founded the *Society for Individual Psychology*. Among his earlier members were a group which included orthodox Nietzschean adherents who maintained that Adler's ideas on power and inferiority were closer to Nietzsche than Freud. While Adler retained a lifelong admiration for Freud's ideas on dreams and credited him with creating a scientific approach to their clinical utilization he had his own theoretical and clinical approach. Adler believed that the social realm (**exteriority**) is as important to psychology as is the internal realm (**interiority**). For him the dynamics of power and compensation extend beyond sexuality, and gender and politics can be as important as libido.

Following his break from Freud, Adler enjoyed considerable success and celebrity in building an independent school of psychotherapy and a unique personality theory. His goal was to create a psychological movement that strived for the holistic view of an individual as well as social equality. In this, his theory of personality and humanity significantly differed from Freud's. He believed that the social and community realm is equally as important to psychology as the internal realm of the individual.

In the 1930s, he established a number of child guidance clinics. From 1921 onwards, he was a frequent lecturer in Europe and the United States, becoming a visiting professor at Columbia University in 1927. His clinical treatment methods for adults were aimed at uncovering the hidden purpose of symptoms using the therapeutic functions of insight and meaning. He was concerned with the overcoming of the superiority/inferiority dynamic and was one of the first psychotherapists to discard the analytic couch in favor of two chairs, encouraging the clinician and patient to sit together more or less as equals.

Clinically, his methods are not limited to treatment after-the-fact but extend to the realm of prevention by pre-empting future problems in the child. His prevention strategies include encouraging and promoting social interest, belonging, and a cultural shift within families and communities that leads to the eradication of pampering and neglect. He always retained a pragmatic approach that was task-oriented.

He identified his "**Life tasks**" as occupation/work, society/friendship, and love/sexuality. Their success depends on cooperation. The tasks of life are not to be considered in isolation since, according to Adler, "they all throw cross-lights on one another".

Adler was influenced by the mental construct ideas of Hans Vaihinger, the philosophies of Rudolf Virchow, Immanuel Kant, Friedrich Nietzsche; the literature of Dostoevsky; and the statesman Jan Smuts (who coined the term "holism"). His own concept "Individual Psychology" often called Adlerian Psychology is both a social and community psychology as well as a depth psychology. He was an early advocate in psychology for prevention.

He was also unique in emphasizing the training of parents, teachers, and social workers in approaches that permit children to exercise their power through reasoned decision making whilst co-operating with others. A pragmatic psychologist Adler believed that lay people could make practical use of the insights of psychology.

Adler engaged in innovative thinking, for example, he was an early supporter of feminism in psychology and the social world. He believed that feelings of superiority and inferiority were often gendered and expressed symptomatically in characteristic masculine and feminine styles. These styles could form the basis of psychic compensation and lead to mental health difficulties. In his book, *Über den nervösen Charakter* (1927) (The Neurotic Character) Alder argued that human personality could be explained teleologically: parts of the individual's unconscious self ideally work to convert feelings of inferiority to superiority (or rather completeness). If you ignore the corrective factors and the individual overcompensated, then an inferiority complex would occur. This could result in the individual becoming egocentric, power-hungry and aggressive.

He held that human psychology is psychodynamic in nature. But his type of approach differed from Freud's metapsychology that emphasizes instinctual demands. For Adler, human psychology is guided by goals (largely unconscious) and fueled by a yet unknown creative force. These goals have a "teleological" function. Usually there is a fictional final goal which can be deciphered alongside of innumerable sub-goals.

Part of Adler's theory is similar to the principles developed in Rational Emotive Behavior Therapy (REBT) and Cognitive Therapy (CT) with both Albert Ellis and Aaron T. Beck crediting Adler as a major precursor to REBT and CT.

As a psychodynamic system, Adlerian theory excavates the past of a client in order to alter their future and increase integration into community in the 'here-and-now'. The 'here-and-now' aspects are especially relevant to those Adlerians who emphasize humanism and/or existentialism in their approaches.

Meanwhile, metaphysical Adlerians emphasize a spiritual holism in keeping with what Jan Smuts articulated, that is, the spiritual sense of one-ness that holism usually implies. Adlerian psychology, unlike community psychology, is holistically concerned with both prevention and clinical treatment after-the-fact. Accordingly, Adler is often referred to as the "first community psychologist".

Adlerian psychology, Carl Jung's analytical psychology, Gestalt therapy and Karen Horney's psychodynamic approach are all holistic schools of psychology.

Although strictly speaking, Adler did not actually believe in personality types he did develop a scheme of so-called provisional or heuristic personality types. He believed that the danger with typology was to lose sight of the individual's uniqueness. American Adlerians such as Harold Mosak have made use of Adler's typology in this provisional sense:

The Getting or Leaning: These are sensitive people who have developed a shell around themselves which protects them, but they must rely on others to carry them through life's difficulties. **The Avoiding Types**: These are people that hate being defeated. They may be successful, but have not taken any risks getting there. They are likely to have low social contact in fear of rejection or defeat in any way. **The Ruling or Dominant Type**: They strive for power and are willing to manipulate situations and people, anything to get their way. These 'types' are typically formed in childhood and are expressions of the Style of Life.

Adler wrote about the importance of the interpretation of early memories in working with patients and school children. He said: "Among all psychic expressions, some of the most revealing are the individual's memories." For him memories are expressions of "private logic" and as metaphors for an individual's personal philosophy of life or "lifestyle." They are never incidental or trivial; rather, they are chosen reminders: "A person's memories are the reminders she carries about with her of her limitations and of the meanings of events. There are no "chance" memories. Out of the incalculable number of impressions that an individual receives, she chooses to remember only those which she considers, however dimly, to have a bearing on her problems."

For Adler **Birth Order** had an influence on the style of life and the strengths and weaknesses in everyone's psychological make-up. By Birth Order he meant the placement of siblings within the family. In his opinion the firstborn child would be in a favorable position, enjoying the full attention of the eager new parents until the arrival of a second child. This second child would then cause the first born to suffer feelings of dethronement. This is because the first child would no longer be the center of attention.

So, in a three-child family, the oldest child would be the most likely to suffer from neuroticism and substance addiction which he reasoned was a compensation for the feelings of excessive responsibility, for example, in having to look after the younger ones and the sadness of losing that once supremely pampered position. As a result, he predicted that this child was the most likely to end up in jail or an asylum. Youngest children would tend to be overindulged, leading to poor social empathy. Consequently, the middle child would not experience dethronement nor overindulgence and was most likely to develop into a successful individual. However, they are also most likely to be rebellious in nature and feel some form of abandonment.

Through his theory of Birth Order Adler showed that children do not grow up in the same family. The eldest grows up in a family where they have younger siblings, the middle child with older and younger siblings, and the youngest with older siblings. The position in the family constellation, Adler said, is the reason for these differences in personality and not genetics. This theory was later developed by Eric Berne. Unfortunately, Adler never produced any scientific support for his interpretations on birth order roles.

On May 1937 Adler died suddenly in Aberdeen, Scotland, during a three-week visit to the University of Aberdeen. He was cremated at Warriston Crematorium in Edinburgh. In 2007, his ashes were rediscovered in a casket at Warriston Crematorium and returned to Vienna for burial in 2011.

With Sigmund Freud and a small group of Freud's colleagues, Adler was among the co-founders of the psychoanalytic movement and a core member of the *Vienna Psychoanalytic Society*. He was the first major figure to break away from psychoanalysis to form an independent school of psychotherapy and personality theory, which he called individual psychology because he believed a human to be an indivisible whole, an individuum. Following his split from Freud, Adler would come to have an enormous, independent effect on the disciplines of counseling and psychotherapy as they developed over the course of the twentieth century.

He influenced notable figures in subsequent schools of psychotherapy such as Albert Ellis, Viktor Frankl, Abraham Maslow and Rollo May. Adler's most famous concept is the inferiority complex which speaks to the problem of self-esteem and its negative effects on human health (e.g. sometimes producing a paradoxical superiority striving). His emphasis on power dynamics is rooted in the philosophy of Nietzsche but his conceptualization of the "Will to Power" focuses on the individual's creative power to change for the better.

Some commentator's suggest that Adler's most influential concept and the one that drives Adlerian Psychology today, is that of social interest, that is, the individual's personal interest in furthering the welfare of others. Adler believed that collaborating and cooperating with one another as individuals and communities can progress to benefit society as a whole. Adler is considered, along with Freud and Jung, to be one of the three founding figures of depth psychology, which emphasizes the unconscious and psychodynamics.

E. L. THORNDIKE (1874-1949)

"Whatever exists at all exists in some amount. To know it thoroughly involves knowing its quantity as well as its quality"

Educational Psychology & Connectionism

Edward Lee Thorndike was an American psychologist whose

work on animal behavior and the learning process led to the theory of connectionism.

Connectionism states that behavioral responses to specific stimuli are established through a process of trial and error that affects neural connections between the stimuli and the most satisfying responses.

Through his work and theories, Thorndike became strongly associated with the American school of thought known as functionalism. Other prominent functionalist thinkers included Harvey Carr, James Rowland Angell and John Dewey. Thorndike is also often referred to as the father of modern day educational psychology, and published several books on the subject.

Edward Lee Thorndike, known affectionately as Ted, was born on the 31 August, 1874 in Williamsburg, Massachusetts, America to Edward Roberts Thorndike and Abbie Ladd. His father was a Methodist minister. In 1891, he graduated from The Roxbury Latin School in West Roxbury, Massachusetts before entering Wesleyan University from which he received a B.Sc. in 1895.

He then went on to Harvard where he obtained a masters in 1897. It was here that he became interested in ethology, how animals learn. Later, he became interested in the animal 'man'. After graduation Thorndike returned to his initial interest, educational psychology. In 1898, he completed his Ph.D. at Columbia University under the supervision of James McKeen Cattell, who was one of the pioneers of psychometrics.

In 1899, he joined Teachers College at Columbia University as an instructor in psychology. He remained at Teachers College for the rest of his career, studying human learning, education, and mental testing. His work on Comparative psychology and the learning process which led to the theory of connectionism helped lay the scientific foundation for modern educational psychology.

He also worked on solving industrial problems, such as employee exams and testing. In 1900, he married Elizabeth Moulton with whom he had five children. He was a member of the board of the Psychological Corporation and in 1912 served as president of the *American Psychological Association*. Thorndike died of a massive cerebral hemorrhage on the 9 August, 1949.

Thorndike was a pioneer not only in behaviorism and learning, but also in using animals in psychology experiments. His doctoral dissertation, *Animal Intelligence: An Experimental Study of the Associative Processes in Animals*, has the distinction of being the first dissertation in psychology where the subjects tested were non-humans. He was interested in whether animals could learn tasks through imitation or observation so he created puzzle boxes for them. In fact, Thorndike is perhaps best-known for the theory he called the **law of effect**, which emerged from his research on how cats learn to escape from these puzzle boxes.

The puzzle boxes were approximately 20 inches long, 15 inches wide, and 12 inches tall. He invented them in order to study instrumental or operant conditioning in cats. Each box had a door that was pulled open by a weight attached to a string that ran over a pulley and was attached to the door. The string attached to the door led to a lever or button inside the box. When the animal pressed the bar or pulled the lever, the string attached to the door would cause the weight to lift and the door to open. Thorndike's puzzle boxes were arranged so that the animal would be required to perform a certain response (pulling a lever or pushing a button), while he measured the amount of time it took them to escape. Once the animal had performed the desired response they were allowed to escape and were also given a reward, usually food (a positive reinforcer). Thorndike primarily used cats in his puzzle boxes.

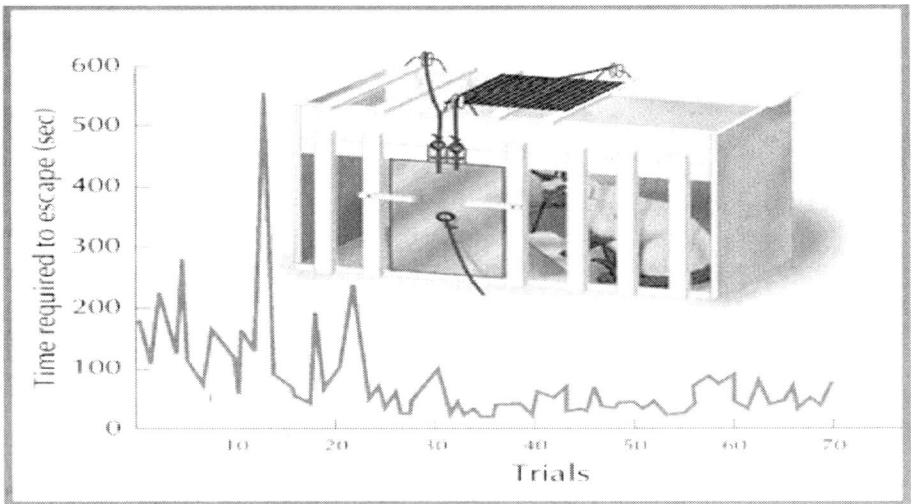

Initially, when the cats were put into the cages they would wander restlessly and meow, but they did not know how to escape. But after a while they would step on the switch on the floor by chance, and the door would open. To see if the cats could learn through observation, Thorndike made them watch other animals escaping from the box. He then compared the times of those who got to watch others escaping with those who did not. From this he discovered that there was no difference in their rate of learning.

Thorndike saw the same results with other animals, and he observed that there was no improvement even when he placed the animals' paws on the correct levers, buttons, or bar. These failures led him to fall back on a trial and error explanation of learning. Thorndike also discovered that if the animals accidentally stepped on the switch once, they would press the switch faster in each succeeding trial.

By recording the escape times, Thorndike was able to graph the times it took for the animals in each trial to escape, resulting in a learning curve. The animals had difficulty escaping at first, but eventually "caught on" and escaped faster and faster with each successive puzzle box trial.

The faster rate of escape resulted in the s-shape of the learning curve. The learning curve also suggested that different species learned in the same way but at different speeds. From this research, Thorndike was able to create his own theory of learning.

Thorndike wanted to distinguish clearly whether or not cats escaping from puzzle boxes were using insight. The instruments he used to answer this question were the learning curves revealed by plotting the time it took for an animal to escape the box each time it was in the box. He believed that if the animals were showing insight, then their time to escape would suddenly drop to a negligible period. This would also be demonstrated in the learning curve as a sudden drop; while animals using a more ordinary method of trial and error would show gradual curves. His finding was that cats consistently showed gradual learning. This was the first experimental apparatus designed to study operant behavior and was later followed by the invention of the Skinner box about which we talk later.

Thorndike was also noted for his theory of learning which can be summarized as follows:

1. The most basic form of learning is trial and error learning.

2. Learning is incremental not insightful.

3. Learning is not mediated by ideas.

4. All mammals learn in the same manner.

5. Law of readiness: Interference with goal directed behavior causes frustration and causing someone to do something they do not want to do is also frustrating.
A. When someone is ready to perform some act, to do so is satisfying;
B. When someone is ready to perform some act, not to do so is annoying.
C. When someone is not ready to perform some act and is forced to do so, it is annoying.

6. Law of Exercise: We learn by doing. We forget by not doing, although to a small extent only.
A. Connections between a stimulus and a response are strengthened as they are used.(law of use)
B. Connections between a stimulus and a response are weakened as they are not used.(law of disuse)

7. Law of effect: If the response in a connection is followed by a satisfying state of affairs, the strength of the connection is considerably increased whereas if followed by an annoying state of affairs, then the strength of the connection is marginally decreased.

8. Multiple Responses: A learner would keep trying multiple responses to solve a problem before it is actually solved.

9. Set or Attitude: Set or attitude is what the learner already possesses, like prior learning experiences, present state of the learner, etc., while it begins learning a new task.

10. Prepotency of Elements: Different responses to the same environment would be evoked by different perceptions of the environment which act as the stimulus to the responses. Different perceptions would be subject to the prepotency of different elements for different perceivers.

11. Response from analogy: New problems are solved by using solution techniques employed to solve analogous problems.

12. Associative Shifting: Let stimulus S be paired with response R. Now, if stimulus Q is presented simultaneously with stimulus S repeatedly, then stimulus Q is likely to get paired with response R.

13. Belongingness: If there is a natural relationship between the need state of an organism and the effect caused by a response, learning is more effective than if the relationship is unnatural.

Thorndike was one of the first pioneers of active learning, a theory that proposes letting children learn themselves, rather than receiving instruction from teachers. He was also a proponent of eugenics arguing that "selective breeding can alter man's capacity to learn, to keep sane, to cherish justice or to be happy. There is no more certain and economical a way to improve man's environment as to improve his nature."

Thorndike later made revisions. Thorndike had proposed three laws governing learning; the law of exercise, the law of readiness, and the law of effect. The **law of exercise** held that using a connection strengthened it and disuse weakened it. The **law of readiness** held that when a connection was available, its use would be satisfying to the organism.

Thorndike later abandoned these two. Most important was the **law of effect**. Initially, the law of effect stated that when a response to a stimulus led to pleasure, the S-R connection was strengthened, and when a response led to painful punishment, the connection was weakened. Thorndike later revised the law of effect, having found that punishment did not weaken S-R connections, but inhibited their expression, a view still held today.

Because Thorndike never proposed a comprehensive system of psychology, his ideas were subjected to detailed rather than systematic criticism. His law of effect and puzzle boxes received most criticism. Behaviorists objected to Thorndike's reference to "pleasure", a subjective conscious feeling, as the cause of learning. For pleasure, Edward R. Guthrie substituted "contiguity of stimulus and response" while Clark Hull called it "biological drive reduction."

Behaviorists like Skinner also defined reinforcers functionally as events that strengthen the responses that produced them. Later, as information-processing views of learning gained strength, psychologists like Edward C. Tolman, questioned Thorndike's law of effect in a new way. Thorndike assumed that rewards and punishments work via pleasure and pain, but they also provide information that a response was correct or incorrect. Experiments that separate the two, for example, making a painful stimulus indicate that a response was correct, have demonstrated that learning depends on the information value of reinforcers rather than on their subjective quality.

Wolfgang Köhler was fiercely critical of Thorndike's puzzle-box method. One of the driving issues in psychology of learning is whether learning occurs gradually or can occur suddenly via insight. Thorndike found no signs of insight in his puzzle-box studies. But Köhler found evidence of insight in his studies of problem solving by chimpanzees.

Köhler argued that Thorndike's method was faulty because it made insight impossible: Trapped in the puzzle box, the cat could not see the connection between the manipulandum and the door opening, and so was forced to resort to trial and error. But Köhler's showed that all the elements needed to solve a problem were available to the subject, who was able to assemble them insightfully into a solution. The force of Köhler's critique extends beyond issues of learning. Psychologists perform experiments in order to discover laws explaining behavior in real life. However, experiments are necessarily artificial. Accordingly, there is always the danger that they may lead psychologists to propose universal laws of behavior that are, in fact, laws induced by their experiments.

Despite these criticisms, Thorndike's influence was enormous. He initiated the S-R concept of learning elaborated by Clark Hull and others. This overshadowed the cognitive tradition of the Gestalt psychologists and Edward Tolman, which held that learning consisted of developing internal representations of the world. The law of effect provided the basis for Skinner's principles of reinforcement, though Skinner did not view operant learning as making connections. There is today a new "connectionist" (neural network) movement, and while not directly linkable to Thorndike one wonders if he had sown its seed.

CARL JUNG (1875-1961)

"Everything that irritates us about others can lead us to an understanding of ourselves"

Analytical Psychology
Dream analysis
The collective unconscious
Archetypes

In its 1955 cover story about Carl G. Jung entitled The Wise Old Man, *Time* Magazine concluded that Jung's "greatest achievement is that he has shown psychology a new direction".

They went on to say that "he has constructed a psychology for human beings who reach out toward the unknown, the intangible, the spiritual." By the time the story was printed Carl G. Jung was already an icon not only in his profession of psychology but also in popular culture. Between 1940-50,

Americans embraced his ideas on psychology, the arts and religion as well as his concepts of the "archetype" and the "collective unconscious". Jung described **archetypes** as patterns of behavior or symbolic imagery present in the minds of all individuals. These patterns inform cultural themes and images that express significant human concerns, such as birth, family, love, survival and death. They create a psychological registry of universal experience that Jung named the "collective unconscious." Such experiences form a treasury of powerful, shared images and symbols that are expressed in dreams, art, fairy tales, stories, myths, and religious motifs from across widely different times and cultures.

These Jungian concepts were inspirational to artists like Jackson Pollock, writers like Jorge Luis Borges, filmmakers like Federico Fellini and George Lucas, mythologists like Joseph Campbell and even chorographers like Martha Graham.

The **Myers-Briggs Type Indicator** (1962), based on Jung's description of introversion and extroversion and personality types, is even today commonly used in education, business, and industry. And Jung's explorations of non-Christian sources of spirituality, such as Gnosticism, alchemy, and Eastern contemplative traditions have influenced various "New Age" philosophies. So, who was Carl Jung?

Carl Gustav Jung otherwise C. G. Jung, was a Swiss psychiatrist and psychotherapist who founded analytical psychology. He was born in Kesswil, in the Swiss canton of Thurgau, on the 26 July 1875, the fourth but only surviving child of Paul Achilles Jung and Emilie Preiswerk. His father was an impoverished rural pastor in the Swiss Reformed Church while his mother had grown up in a wealthy Swiss family.

His mother suffered from depression and spent much of her time in bed. The young Carl bonded better with his father. When his mother was hospitalized for several months for an unknown physical ailment he was cared for by his aunt. But his mother's continued depression and absence from home adversely influenced her son's attitude towards women. Carl was a lonely, introverted child who believed he had two personalities.

When he was twelve he was pushed to the ground by a boy in his class and momentarily lost consciousness. He used this as an excuse not to go to school. But later when he realized how impoverished his family was he realized the need for academic excellence and began to study in earnest. In 1895, Jung entered the university of Basel to study medicine. By 1900 he was working at the Burghölzli psychiatric hospital in Zürich.

In 1903, Jung married Emma Rauschenbach, the daughter of a wealthy family in Switzerland. They had five children and while the marriage lasted until Emma's death in 1955, Jung was known to engage in open relationships with other women including patients and friends.

In 1906, he published *Studies in Word Association*, and later sent a copy of this book to Sigmund Freud. It was the beginning of a professional association and relationship between them. But their close friendship was fractured in 1912 after Jung published *Wandlungen und Symbole der Libido* (Psychology of the Unconscious), which emphasized the growing theoretical divergence between the two. Freud refused to consider Jung's ideas.

This rejection caused what Jung described as a "resounding censure." Everyone he knew dropped away except for two of his colleagues. Jung described his book as "... an attempt, only partially successful, to create a wider setting for medical psychology and to bring the whole of the psychic phenomena within its purview." When their relationship finally broke up in 1913 Jung suffered a difficult and pivotal psychological transformation. When the War began Jung was drafted in as an army doctor and soon made commandant of an internment camp.

Assumption	Jung	Freud
Nature and purpose of the libido.	A generalize source of psychic energy motivating a range of behaviors.	A source of psychic energy specific to sexual gratification.
Nature of the unconscious.	A storehouse of repressed memories specific to the individual and our ancestral past.	A storehouse for unacceptable repressed desires specific to the individual.
Cause of behavior.	Past experiences in addition to future aspiration.	Past experiences, particularly in childhood.

Jung's theories include:
The concept of introversion and extraversion;
The concept of the complex;

The concept of the collective unconscious, shared by all people. It includes the archetypes; and
Synchronicity as a mode of relationship that is not causal.

Although the terms **introversion and extraversion** were first popularized by Carl Jung, both the popular understanding and psychological age differ from his original intent. Extraversion tends to be manifested in outgoing, talkative, energetic behavior, whereas introversion is manifested in more reserved and solitary behavior. Virtually all comprehensive models of personality include these concepts in various forms.

Today, extraversion and introversion are typically viewed as a single continuum. So, to be high on one, it is necessary to be low on the other. But Carl Jung believed that everyone has both an extraverted side and an introverted side, with one being more dominant than the other. Rather than focusing on interpersonal behavior, however, Jung defined introversion as an "attitude-type characterized by orientation in life through subjective psychic contents" (focus on one's inner psychic activity); and extraversion as "an attitude type characterized by concentration of interest on the external object" (the outside world).

Jung developed the concept of the **complex** early on in his career. By complex he meant a personal unconscious, core pattern of emotions, memories, perceptions, and wishes organized around a common theme.

According to Jung's personality theory, complexes are building blocks of the psyche and the source of all human emotions. They are believed to operate "autonomously and interfere with the intentions of the will, disturbing the memory and conscious performance". He often used the term "complex" to describe a usually unconscious, repressed, yet highly influential symbolic material that is incompatible with the consciousness. Jung spoke of one specific type of complex which he called a **feeling-toned complex.**

For him this is the image of a certain psychic situation which is strongly accentuated emotionally and is, moreover, incompatible with the habitual attitude of consciousness. This image has a powerful inner coherence and a relatively high degree of autonomy, so that it is subject to the control of the conscious mind to only a limited extent. Jung said it behaved like "an animated foreign body in the sphere of consciousness."

Jung wrote about the **collective unconscious** as follows: "My thesis then, is as follows: in addition to our immediate consciousness, which is of a thoroughly personal nature and which we believe to be the only empirical psyche (even if we tack on the personal unconscious as an appendix), there exists a second psychic system of a collective, universal, and impersonal nature which is identical in all individuals. This collective unconscious does not develop individually but is inherited. It consists of pre-existent forms, the archetypes, which can only become conscious secondarily and which give definite form to certain psychic contents." He linked the collective unconscious to what Freud called "archaic remnants."

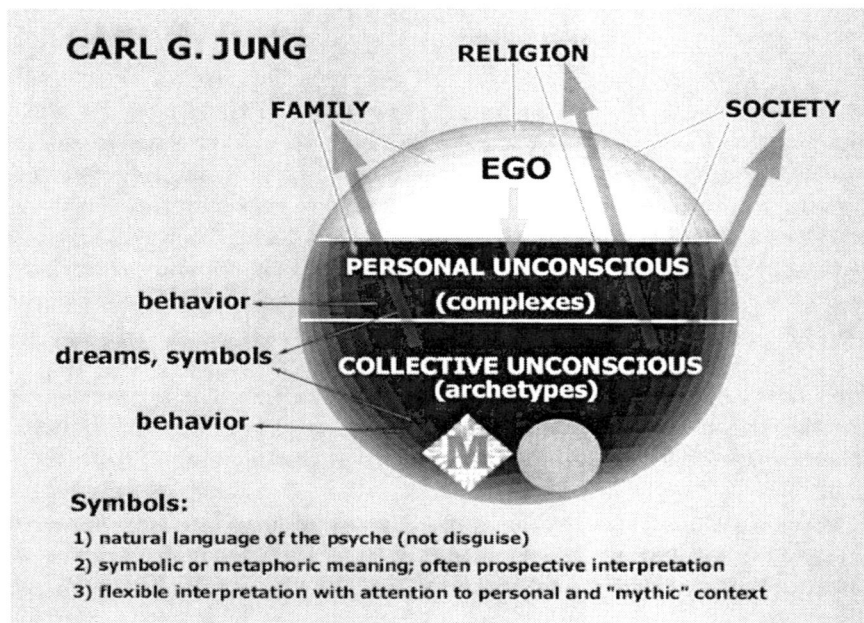

CARL G. JUNG

RELIGION

FAMILY

SOCIETY

EGO

behavior — PERSONAL UNCONSCIOUS (complexes)

dreams, symbols — COLLECTIVE UNCONSCIOUS (archetypes)

behavior —

Symbols:
1) natural language of the psyche (not disguise)
2) symbolic or metaphoric meaning; often prospective interpretation
3) flexible interpretation with attention to personal and "mythic" context

Archaic remnants are "mental forms whose presence cannot be explained by anything in the individual's own life and which seem to be aboriginal, innate, and inherited shapes of the human mind". Jung believed that **archetypes** are models of people, behaviors or personalities. He suggested that the psyche was composed of three components: the ego, the personal unconscious and the collective unconscious. For Jung, the ego represents the conscious mind while the personal unconscious contains memories, including those that have been suppressed. The collective unconscious is a unique component in that Jung believed that this part of the psyche served as a form of psychological inheritance containing as it does all of the knowledge and experiences we share as a species. Jung believed that these archetypes existed in the collective unconscious and that these models are innate, universal and hereditary. Archetypes are unlearned and function to organize how we experience certain things.

In his book *The Structure of the Psyche*, Jung wrote: "All the most powerful ideas in history go back to archetypes. This is particularly true of religious ideas, but the central concepts of science, philosophy, and ethics are no exception to this rule. In their present form they are variants of archetypal ideas created by consciously applying and adapting these ideas to reality.

For it is the function of consciousness, not only to recognize and assimilate the external world through the gateway of the senses, but to translate into visible reality the world within us." Although he identified four major archetypes, he also believed that there was no limit to the number that may exist.

The **four archetypes** he specifically identified were the Self; the Shadow; the Anima/Animus; and the the Persona.

The Self is an archetype that represents the unification of the unconsciousness and consciousness of an individual. The creation of the self occurs through a process known as individuation, in which the various aspects of personality are integrated. Jung often represented the self as a circle, square or mandala.

The Shadow which can appear in dreams as a snake, monster, demon or other wild or exotic creature is an archetype that consists of the sex and life instincts. The shadow is the darker side of the psyche and exists as part of the unconscious mind and is composed of repressed ideas, weaknesses, desires, instincts and shortcomings.

The Anima archetype is a feminine image in the male psyche and the Animus is a male image in the female psyche. The anima/animus represents the "true self" rather than the image we present to others and serves as the primary source of communication with the collective unconscious.

The Persona archetype is how we present ourselves to the world and represents all of the different social masks that we wear among different groups and situations. It acts to shield the ego from negative images.

The concept of **synchronicity** was first defined by Carl Jung, in the 1920s But during his life Jung prepared several slightly different definitions of synchronicity.

For example, in his book *Synchronicity: An Acausal Connecting Principle* (1960),

Jung wrote that: "How are we to recognize acausal combinations of events, since it is obviously impossible to examine all chance happenings for their causality? The answer to this is that acausal events may be expected most readily where, on closer reflection, a causal connection appears to be inconceivable."

Synchronicity is the occurrence of two or more events that appear to be meaningfully related but not causally related. Synchronicity holds that such events are "meaningful coincidences". And implies that, just as events may be connected by causality, they may also be connected by meaning.

Although he was a practicing clinician, Jung considered himself to be more of a scientist. He spent much of his life exploring such diverse matters as Eastern and Western philosophy, alchemy, astrology, and sociology, as well as literature and the arts.

In fact, his interest in philosophy and the occult led many critics to consider him as something of a mystic. And maybe he was, but his huge influence on popular psychology can never be denied. Today, therapists of every kind recognize a truth that Carl Jung was the first to articulate: "The most terrifying thing is to accept oneself completely."

JOHN B. WATSON (1878-1958)

"Give me a dozen healthy infants, well-formed, and my own specified world to bring them up in and I'll guarantee to take any one at random and train him to become any type of specialist I might select doctor, lawyer, artist, merchant-chief and, yes, even beggar-man and thief, regardless of his talents, penchants, tendencies, abilities, vocations, and race of his ancestors."

Behaviorism

John Broadus Watson was an American psychologist who is considered the father of the psychological school of behaviorism. By the time he began teaching at Johns Hopkins, the official discipline of psychology which originated in Europe in 1879 was barely thirty years old.

Watson was one of the first American psychologists to break the Freudian notion that our unconscious mind was behind most of our behavior. These ideas were quickly gaining acceptance among psychologists in Europe and later in the United States. In 1913, Watson made his most memorable declaration against Freud's theory in a paper he delivered at Columbia University entitled *Psychology as the Behaviorist Views It.* This lecture established him as a pioneer of a new school of thought that would later become known as Behaviorism. Watson stated that behaviorism was the science of observable behavior. He argued that only behavior that could be observed, recorded and measured was of any real value for the study of humans or animals.

His thinking was significantly influenced by the earlier classical conditioning experiments of Russian psychologist Ivan Pavlov. Watson was a radical thinker and a controversial figure who lived a scandalous life but left a lasting legacy to the field of psychology.

John Broadus Watson was born on the 9 January 1878 in Travelers Rest, South Carolina, America to Pickens Butler Watson and Emma K. Roe. His father was an alcoholic and his mother a religious fanatic who counselled vehemently against the sins of drinking, smoking and dancing. Her mother named John after a prominent Baptist minister in the hope he would follow his footsteps to preach the Bible but it was never going to happen. The harsh religious upbringing forever turned him against all forms of religion. When Watson was thirteen his father left the family to live with two Indian women. John never forgave him and neither did Emma Watson who sold the farm and moved to Greenville, South Carolina.

Socially maladjusted, John found it difficult to integrate into the new community of Greenville. He was a loner, a social outcast, a poor boy from a poor farm. When he eventually made it to college his academic performance was poor and his behavior delinquent. During high school he was arrested first for fighting with African Americans and then for discharging firearms within city limits. After high school he secured admission to Furman University in Greenville, South Carolina at the age of sixteen and left at twenty one with a master's. But he made few friends and was regarded as "unsocial." After he graduated he worked in a one room school in Greenville as principal, caretaker, janitor and handyman for the entire school. He called the school the "Batesburg Institute".

After petitioning the President of the University of Chicago, Watson entered the University of Chicago and began studying philosophy under John Dewey. Heavily influenced by Dewey, James Rowland Angell, Henry Herbert Donaldson and Jacques Loeb, Watson developed a highly descriptive, objective approach to the analysis of behavior that he would later call "behaviorism." Later, Watson became interested in the work of Ivan Pavlov and later included a highly simplified version of Pavlov's principles in his popular works. In 1903 he was awarded his Ph.D. from the University of Chicago.

In his dissertation, *Animal Education: An Experimental Study on the Psychical Development of the White Rat, Correlated with the Growth of its Nervous System*, he described the relationship between brain myelinization and learning ability in rats at different ages. He demonstrated that the degree of myelination was largely related to wand learning and discovered that the kinesthetic sense controlled the behavior of rats running in mazes. In 1908, Watson was offered and accepted a faculty position at Johns Hopkins University and was immediately promoted to the chair of the psychology department.

In 1913, Watson published the article *The Behaviorist Manifesto* in which he outlined the major features of his new philosophy of psychology. He described it in the following terms: "Psychology as the behaviorist views it is a purely objective experimental branch of natural science. Its theoretical goal is the prediction and control of behavior. Introspection forms no essential part of its methods, nor is the scientific value of its data dependent upon the readiness with which they lend themselves to interpretation in terms of consciousness. The behaviorist, in his efforts to get a unitary scheme of animal response, recognizes no dividing line between man and brute. The behavior of man, with all of its refinement and complexity, forms only a part of the behaviorist's total scheme of investigation."

Watson had already rejected Edward L. Thorndike's "Law of Effect" due to what Watson believed were unnecessary subjective elements. He viewed Ivan Pavlov's conditioned reflex as primarily a physiological mechanism controlling glandular secretions and it was not until 1916 that he accepted the more general significance of Pavlov's formulation. Watson believed the emphasis should be on the external behavior of people and their reactions on given situations, rather than the internal, mental state of those people.

In his opinion, the analysis of behaviors and reactions was the only objective method to get insight in the human actions. This idea, combined with the complementary ideas of determinism, evolutionary continuism, and empiricism has contributed to what is now called radical behaviorism. Watson believe that this new approach would lead psychology into a new era. He stated there was no psychology before Wundt and only confusion and anarchy afterwards.

Watson rejected the study of consciousness. He said it couldn't be studied, and that past attempts to do so have only been hindering the advancement of psychological theories. To him introspection was faulty and he urged that psychology be no longer considered the science of the "mind". Instead, he stated that all that mattered was the "behavior" of the individual, not their consciousness.

In the summer of 1920, John B. Watson made headline news but not for any of his theories. It was because of a well publicized affair he was conducting with his graduate student-assistant Rosalie Rayner. Watson's affair and subsequent divorce proceedings had become front-page news in the Baltimore newspapers. In October 1920, Johns Hopkins University asked Watson to leave his faculty position because of the affair. His wife Mary Ickes Watson, divorced him. Immediately following the divorce Watson married Rayner and they remained together until her death in 1935.

In 1928 Watson with the help of Rosalie Rayner published the book *Psychological Care of Infant and Child*. Here, Watson explained that behaviorists were starting to believe psychological care and analysis was required for infants and children. But Watson believed that children should be treated as young adults and warned against the dangers of over-protective mothers providing too much love and affection. Watson believed love is conditioned and said that society does not overly comfort children as they become young adults in the real world, so parents should not set up these unrealistic expectations. Watson disapproved of thumb sucking, masturbation, homosexuality, and encouraged parents to be more honest with their children about sex.

Although he wrote extensively on child-rearing in many popular magazines and in his book, *Psychological Care of Infant and Child* (1928), Watson later regretted having written in the area, saying that "he did not know enough" to do a good job. On that score he was probably right. Some critics like R. Dale Nance worried that Watson's personal indiscretions and difficult upbringings could have affected his views in his book.

Another critic, Suzanne Houk, shared similar concerns and believed that Watson only shifted his focus to child-rearing when he was fired from Johns Hopkins University due to his affair. Despite this, his book was extremely popular, selling over 100,000 copies after a few months, and many of his contemporaries come to accept his views.

Watson and Rayner came in for considerable criticism in relation to the infamous "Little Albert" experiment carried out in 1920. The Little Albert experiment was a case study showing empirical evidence of classical conditioning in humans. Watson was interested in finding support for his notion that the reaction of children, whenever they heard loud noises, was prompted by fear.

Furthermore, he reasoned that this fear was innate or due to an unconditioned response. He felt that following the principles of classical conditioning, he could condition a child to fear another distinctive stimulus which normally would not be feared by a child. Put another way, the aim of Watson and Rayner was to condition phobias into an emotionally stable child. "Albert", a nine month old boy was chosen from a hospital.

Initially, Albert was exposed, briefly and for the first time, to a white rabbit, a rat, a dog, a monkey, masks with and without hair, cotton, wool, burning newspapers, and other stimuli. At first, he showed no fear toward any of these items. He was then placed on a mattress on a table in the middle of a room. A white laboratory rat was placed near Albert and he was allowed to play with it. At this point, the child showed no fear of the rat. He began to reach out to the rat as it roamed around him.

In later trials, Watson and Rayner made a loud sound behind the child's back by striking a suspended steel bar with a hammer when the baby touched the rat. Little Albert responded to the noise by crying and showing fear.

After several such pairings of the two stimuli, Albert was again presented with only the rat. Now, however, he became very distressed as the rat appeared in the room. He cried, turned away from the rat, and tried to move away. It appeared that Albert now associated the white rat with the loud noise and was producing the fearful or emotional response of crying.

This experiment led to the following progression of results:

1. Firstly, the introduction of a loud sound (unconditioned stimulus) resulted in fear (unconditioned response), a natural response.

2. Secondly, the introduction of a rat (neutral stimulus) paired with the loud sound (unconditioned stimulus) eventually resulted in fear (unconditioned response).

3. Finally, the successive introductions of only a rat (conditioned stimulus) resulted in fear (conditioned response). Therefore, learning was demonstrated.

The experiment did not have a control subject. Watson had used the same kind of classical conditioning as Pavlov had used in his experiments with dogs. The experiment showed that the child seemed to generalize his response to furry objects so that when Watson sent a non-white rabbit into the room seventeen days after the original experiment, the child also became distressed. He showed similar reactions when presented with a furry dog, a seal-skin coat, and even when Watson appeared in front of him wearing a Santa Claus mask with white cotton balls as his beard. Albert, however, did not fear everything with hair; and there was some confusing results when pairing the noise with the rabbit and dog.

At the age of one year and 21 days when the experiment ended Albert exhibited an approach and avoidance conflict with the objects presented to him. Apparently, he was then removed from the hospital and no desensitizing ever took place. Critics latched on to this claiming that it is possible that Albert's fear responses continued post-experimentally. In fact, there was considerable criticism of the experiments to the point of outrage with allegations that Albert's mother knew nothing of the experiments or if she did she was coerced into allowing them continue.

In 2009, psychologists Hall P. Beck and Sharman Levinson published an article in which they identified "Little Albert" as Douglas Merritte, the son of Arvilla Merritte. More recent research disputes this. Psychologists Russ Powell and Nancy Digdon found that Little Albert was most likely William Albert Barger who died in 2007 at the age 87. The researchers stated that Albert had no known phobias other than a dislike of dogs and concluded he was unaware of his role as an infant test subject. Today, such an experiment would be considered unethical.

Later on in life, Watson changed careers and began working for the American advertising agency J. Walter Thompson where within two years he was made vice-president with an income several times higher than what he had earned as a psychologist.

He oversaw several high-profile advertising campaigns, for products like Ponds cold cream, Maxwell House coffee and Pebecco toothpaste. He retired from advertising at the age of 65 and lived on his farm until his death in 1956 at the age of 80. He was buried at Willowbrook Cemetery, Westport, Connecticut.

So what exactly is meant by the term Behaviorism? Essentially it refers to the school of psychology based on the belief that behaviors can be measured, trained, and changed. Behaviorism was first established in 1913 with the publication of Watson's paper "Psychology as the Behaviorist Views It." Between 1920-1950 Behaviorism grew to become the dominant force in psychology. Behaviorism, also known as behavioral psychology, is a theory of learning based upon the idea that all behaviors are acquired through conditioning. Conditioning occurs through interaction with the environment. Behaviorists believe that our responses to environmental stimuli shape our behaviors.

According to this approach, behavior can be studied in a systematic and observable manner with no consideration of internal mental states. It suggests that only observable behaviors should be studied, since internal states such as cognitions, emotions, and moods are too subjective.

As Watson's quote at the beginning of this article suggests, strict behaviorists believe that any person could potentially be trained to perform any task, regardless of factors such as genetic background, personality traits, and internal thoughts providing this is achievable within the limits of their physical capabilities. All it takes is the right conditioning.

Basically, there are two major types of conditioning, **classical conditioning** and **operant conditioning**.

Classical conditioning is a technique used in behavioral training in which a naturally occurring stimulus is paired with a response. Next, a previously neutral stimulus is paired with the naturally occurring stimulus. Eventually, the previously neutral stimulus comes to evoke the response without the necessity of the naturally occurring stimulus. The two elements are then known as the conditioned stimulus and the conditioned response.

Operant conditioning which is sometimes called instrumental conditioning, is a method of learning that occurs through reinforcements and punishments for behavior. Through operant conditioning, an association is made between a behavior and a consequence for that behavior. When a behavior is followed by a desirable consequence, the behavior becomes more likely to occur again in the future. But behaviors followed by negative outcomes, become less likely to happen again in the future.

The most important theorists in the field of Behaviorism are John B. Watson, Ivan Pavlov, B. F. Skinner, Edward Thorndike and Clark Hull. The theories began in 1863 when Ivan Sechenov published *Reflexes of the Brain*. Sechenov introduced the concept of inhibitory responses in the central nervous system. In 1900, Ivan Pavlov began studying the salivary response and other reflexes. In 1913, Watson published *Psychology as a Behaviorist Views* which outlined many of the main points of behaviorism. Thirty years later Clark Hull published *Principles of Behavior*. Then in 1948 B.F. Skinner published *Walden II* in which he described a utopian society founded upon behaviorist principles. In 1959, Noam Chomsky published his criticism of Skinner's behaviorism in his book *Review of Verbal Behavior*.

Many critics argue that behaviorism is a simply one-dimensional approach to understanding human behavior and that behavioral theories do not account for free will and internal influences such as moods, thoughts, and feelings. Nor does it account for other types of learning, especially learning that occurs without the use of reinforcement and punishment. They also claim that people and animals are able to adapt their behavior when new information is introduced, even if a previous behavior pattern has been established through reinforcement.

But the theory has many strengths. It is based upon observable behaviors, so it is easier to quantify and collect data and information when conducting research. Effective therapeutic techniques such as intensive behavioral intervention, behavior analysis, token economies, and discrete trial training are all rooted in behaviorism. These approaches are often very useful in changing maladaptive or harmful behaviors in both children and adults.

Another major benefit of behaviorism is that it allowed researchers to investigate observable behavior in a scientific and systematic manner. However, people like Freud, believed that behaviorisms failed by not accounting for the unconscious mind's thoughts, feelings, and desires that exert an influence on people's actions. Carl Rogers and other humanistic psychologists believed that behaviorism was too rigid and limited and that it failed to take into consideration things like free will. But while behaviorism is not as dominant today as it was during the middle of the twentieth century, it still remains an influential force in psychology.

MELANIE KLEIN (1882-1960)

"One of the many interesting and surprising experiences of the beginner in child analysis is to find in even very young children a capacity for insight which is often far greater than that of adults"

Object Relations Theory
Play Therapy

Apioneering and controversial Austrian psychoanalyst, Melanie Klein is regarded as one of the founding figures of psychoanalysis. In developing Freudian theories, she recognized the centrality of the infant's first relationships with its primary caregivers and elucidated the early mental processes that build up a person's inner emotional world.

Klein had an immense impact on child psychology and contemporary psychoanalysis and was a leading innovator in theorizing object relations theory.

Melanie Reizes Klein was born in Vienna on the 30 March 1882 into a middle-class Jewish family. Her father, Dr. Moriz Reisez, rebelled against his strict orthodox Jewish family, and went to medical school rather than becoming a rabbi. His first marriage, which was arranged by his parents, ended shortly after his dependent father died. He remarried, however, when he was over the age of forty. His new wife, Libusa Deutsch, was just 25 at the time. The couple had four children, including Melanie, the youngest.

Because Dr. Reisez's practice was quiet and money was needed, Libusa temporarily opened a shop of exotic plants and animals. By the time Melanie was five, however, the family had inherited enough money to buy a dental practice. The practice was successful and the family prospered. Because of her father's age and the favoritism that he showed to Melanie's sister, the two did not share a close relationship. His knowledge of literature and languages, however, impressed her greatly. Moriz died when Melanie was just eighteen.

Melanie was much closer to her mother, Libusa who up to her death in 1914 strived to ensure that her children had a happy childhood. Two of Melanie's siblings, Emmanuel and Sidonie, died at young ages. Sidonie, her second oldest sister, taught Melanie to read and write, hoping to pass all that she knew to her sister before dying. Emmanuel, her only brother, was also a great aid in her education. This knowledge helped her to pass entrance exams into various schools, which she hoped would lead her to university where she could study medicine. The deaths of these family members led to a depressive state that continued to be a part of Melanie's personality.

Initially, she was educated at the local gymnasium. Melanie became engaged at the age of nineteen to Arthur Stephen Klein, a friend of her brother's. During their two year engagement, Melanie studied art and history at Vienna University. Though she regretted it later in life, Melanie passed up medical school to follow her husband, an engineer who often moved to accommodate his business life. Consequently, she never received an academic degree. At twenty one she married Arthur Klein and settled in to raising a family. Eventually she had three children. Throughout her early married life she suffered from depression and "nerves," due in part to a difficult relationship with a domineering mother.

In 1910, the family moved to Budapest and she began a course of psychoanalysis with Sandor Ferenczi. Building on her intellectual interest in psychoanalysis Ferenczi encouraged Klein to psychoanalyze her own children. Until that time no one had tried analyzing children so without any guidance Klein set about developing a technique of child analysis that is still used today.

In 1918, Klein attended the International Psycho-Analytic Congress in Budapest, and was introduced to Sigmund Freud. She later recalled: "I remember vividly how impressed I was and how the wish to devote myself to psychoanalysis was strengthened by this impression."

A few years later she became a full member of the *Hungarian Psycho-Analytic Society*. By this time Klein's marriage had broken up so she left her husband and moved to Berlin with her three children. Here she joined the Berlin *Psycho-Analytic Society* and entered analysis with the eminent Karl Abraham. Abraham was developing Freud's concept of the death instinct in his own ideas about oral and anal sadistic impulses in infancy, ideas which Klein soon incorporated into her interpretations of children's play.

While Abraham encouraged her work, other Berlin analysts were less accepting. Not only was Klein a woman in a man's world she also had no academic qualifications, not even a bachelor's degree. When Abraham died in 1926, Klein moved to London to join the *British Psycho-Analytical Society*.

In London, Melanie Klein found that British psychoanalysts were more accepting of her and her intellect. They embraced her new ideas and were eager to learn more about her play technique. She spent the rest of her life there developing her theory of child development into a new school of psychoanalytic thought and training future analysts in her theory and technique.

Klein's first theoretical innovation was to incorporate the idea of the death instinct into her account of the development of an early superego, prior to the resolution of the Oedipus Complex. This challenge to Freud's theory of development coupled with her new play technique led to some controversy between the British analysts and the *Viennese Society* where Anna Freud was putting forward her own views on child analysis.

The 1927 Symposium on Child Analysis published in the *International Journal of Psychoanalysis* was the result. Klein followed this debate with some of her most important work over the next decade.

In 1932, Klein published *The Psychoanalysis of Children* in which she suggested that the infant has a primary object relation to the mother and experiences a psychic life dominated by sadistic fantasies deriving from an innate aggressive drive. In 1935, in a seminal paper entitled *A contribution to the psychogenesis of manic depressive states* (1935/1984), written a short time after the death of her son Hans, Klein explored the relationship between mourning and primitive defense mechanisms and introduced her idea of two fundamental phases of development:

the paranoid-schizoid position; and,

the depressive position.

Klein's ideas about schizoid defense mechanisms aroused fierce debate within the British Society, which held a series of controversial discussions during the war years to decide whether "Kleinianism," as it was now known, was really psychoanalysis or whether it diverged too far from Freud's original theory.

These "discussions" were really a protracted series of 'Scientific Meetings' of the *British Psychoanalytical Society* which took place between October 1942 and February 1944 between the Viennese school and the supporters of Melanie Klein. They led to a tripartite division of training in the Society after the war with the three groups of Kleinians, Anna Freudians and the Middle (or later Independent) Group.

The discussions explored the differences between 'classical' Freudian analysis and newer Kleinian theory. The Freudian side was led by Anna Freud and included Kate Friedlander, Ilse Hellman, and Willie Hoffer. They were vehemently resistant to the revisions of theory and method proposed by Klein. The Klein Group included Susan Isaacs, Joan Riviere, Paula Heimann and Roger Money-Kyrle.

The third group known as the "Middle Group", were the moderating influence between the other two groups and included Ella Freeman Sharpe, James Strachey, Sylvia Payne, Donald Winnicott, William Gillespie, Marjorie

Brierley, and later Michael Balint.

The final resolution was more political rather than theoretical, with a 'gentleman's agreement' being reached according to which both sides undertook never to attempt a take-over of the Society. The agreement stands to this day, with Freudian and Kleinian approaches co-existing side-by-side within the institution and upheld in separate training divisions. As a result, Klein was the first psychoanalyst to challenge Freud's account of psychic development and remain within the psychoanalytic movement.

By this time Klein was a powerful figure within the British Society: she was a member of the Training Committee, a training analyst, and leader of the Kleinian group, which included for a while John Bowlby and Donald Winnicott. However her victory came at a cost: her daughter the well-known psychoanalyst, Melitta Schmideberg, had opposed her during the Controversial Discussions and they remained estranged until the end of Klein's life. In the face of the loss of two of her children Klein found solace in her work. She continued to develop her ideas about schizoid defense mechanisms, including splitting, and the role they play in borderline conditions.

Her final work explored the themes of envy, gratitude, and reparation in the mother-infant relationship, themes which were so central to her own experiences as a daughter and a mother. Her last important book *Narrative of a Child Analysis* (1961), a detailed case history of the analysis of a young boy during the war, was published after her death from cancer in 1960.

Play Therapy: In her "play technique" the child's play activity is taken as symbolic of unconscious material and is interpreted in the same way that dreams and free associations are in adult analysis. Klein was the first psychologist to view children's play as a meaningful activity and her "play technique" later contributed to the development of play therapy.

Klein developed the technique of play therapy after World War I. As a substitute for Freud's free association, of which very young children are incapable, Klein developed the technique of play therapy to uncover children's unconscious motivations. She believed that children, through the use of play and drawings, projected their feelings in therapeutic sessions. She showed that the way children played with toys revealed earlier infantile fantasies and anxieties. Children's unconscious lives could be understood by analysts through their non-verbal behavior.

In her book *The Psychoanalysis of Children* (1932), she showed how these anxieties affected a child's developing ego, superego, and sexuality to bring about emotional disorders. Through her methods she attempted to relieve children of disabling guilt by having them direct toward the therapist the aggressive and Oedipal feelings they could not express to their parents. This was in major disagreement with Anna Freud who felt that children were unanalyzable.

Object Relations: Klein, along with Sigmund Freud and W.R.D. Fairbairn, contributed ideas to make up what we now know as object relations.

First Freud introduced the idea of object choice, which referred to a child's earliest relationships with his caretakers. Such people were objects of his needs and desires. The relationship with them became internalized mental representations.

Subsequently, Melanie Klein coined the term **part objects**, for example the mother's breast, which played an important role in early development and later in psychic disturbances, such as excessive preoccupation with certain body parts or aspects of a person as opposed to the whole person.

Finally, Fairbairn and others developed the so-called **object relations theory.** According to it, the child who did not receive good enough mothering increasingly retreated into an inner world of fantasy objects with whom he tried to satisfy his need for real objects, that was for relationships.

Internal Object: For Klein, the term internal object means a mental and emotional image of an external object that has been taken inside the self. The character of the internal object is colored by aspects of the self that have been projected into it. A complex interaction continues throughout life between the world of internalized figures and objects and in the real world (which are obviously also in the mind) via repeated cycles of projection and introjection.

The most important internal objects are those derived from the parents, in particular from the mother or breast into which the infant projects its loving (life instinct) or hating (death instinct) aspects. These objects, when taken into the self, are thought to be experienced by the infant concretely as physically present within the body, causing pleasure (good internal part-object breast) or pain (bad internal part-object breast).

The infant's view of the motivation of these objects is based partly on accurate perception by the infant of the external object and partly on the desires and feelings that the infant has projected into the external objects: a malevolent desire to cause pain in the bad object and a benevolent desire to give pleasure in the good object.

Internal objects are experienced as relating to each other within the self. They may be identified with and assimilated, they may be felt as separate from, but at the same time, as existing within the self.

Within Kleinian theory the state of the internal object is considered to be of prime importance to the development and mental health of the individual. The introjection of and identification with a stable good object is crucial to the ego's capacity to cohere and integrate experience.

Damaged or dead internal objects cause enormous anxiety and can lead to personality disintegration, whereas objects felt to be in a good state promote confidence and well-being.

Internal objects can exist on several levels. They can be more or less unconscious and more or less primitive.

Infantile internal objects are experienced initially concretely within the body and mind and constitute a primitive level of the adult psyche, adding emotional influence and force to later perceptions, feelings and thoughts.

Internal objects may be represented to the self in dreams, fantasies and in language. Internal objects are conceptually confusing in that they are described both from metaphsychological and phenomenological perspectives. Metapsychologically, the first internal objects are in part a creation of the life and death instincts, can affect the structure of the ego and are the basis of the superego. Phenomenologically they are the content of phantasy but of phantasy that has real effects.

The conceptualization of internal objects is inextricably linked to Klein's theory of the life and death instincts, her ideas about unconscious phantasy and her theories of the development from the paranoid-schizoid position to the depressive position within which there is a move from part-object to whole-object functioning. This means that no single definition can capture this concept.

Depressive position: According to Klein, this mental constellation is central to the child's development. It is normally first experienced towards the middle of the first year of life. It is repeatedly revisited and refined throughout early childhood, and intermittently throughout life. The main part of it is the realization of hateful feelings and phantasies about the loved object, usually the mother.

The term 'depressive position' is used in different but related ways. It can refer to the infantile experience of this developmental integration. More generally it refers to the experience, at any stage of life, of guilt and grief over hateful attacks and over the damaged state of external and internal objects, varying in level of felt catastrophe on a scale from normal mourning for loss to severe depression. The term is also loosely used to refer to 'depressive position functioning', meaning that the individual can take personal responsibility and perceive him-/herself and the other as separate.

Oedipus Complex: Freud's Oedipus complex, to the fore between ages 3 and 5 years, involves wish-fulfilling fantasies of the death of the same-sex parent, with usurpation of their place in the couple. Inverse forms are also central.

The boy's fear of castration by the vengeful father and the girl's fear of loss of love lead to the abandonment of these wishes and to installation of the superego. Freud describes all this at the phallic level. Klein, like Freud, sees the Oedipus complex as central, but modifies and extends his ideas in her new conceptions of an earlier Oedipus situation. She postulates infantile preconception with an exciting and terrifying parental couple, phantasied first as a 'combined figure': the maternal body containing the father's penis and rival babies.

This primitive version of a couple, phantasied as in continuous intercourse, exhibits sadistic oral, urethral and anal features due to projections of infantile sexuality and sadism. Phantasies about the maternal body link to Klein's new understandings of primary femininity and both the male and female Oedipus complexes. Primitive superego figures develop early, in relation to infantile sadism generally, not simply as a result of the oedipal situation. The splitting characteristic of paranoid-schizoid functioning facilitates clear and oscillating division of the part-object parents into ideal/loved ones and denigrated/hated ones.

Increasing awareness of whole objects, ambivalently regarded, and the onset of depressive guilt for attacks lead increasingly to the need to relinquish oedipal desires and to repair the internal parents, allowing them to come together. For Klein, the Oedipus complex and the depressive position are closely linked.

Klein continued to develop her ideas up to her death in 1960. She focused on the earliest months of life and also wrote her most controversial paper, in which she argued that envy is a destructive emotion which is an inevitable feature of human development and relationships.

She left behind a small loyal group of followers including Donald Winnicott, John Bowlby and Wilfred Bion. Klein's model of child psychoanalysis continues to be used. Her theories on anxieties and defenses and the theoretical concepts that she developed on their basis has had a profound influence on future developments in twentieth-century psychoanalytic techniques.

HELENE DEUTSCH (1884-1982)

"After all, the ultimate goal of all research is not objectivity, but truth"

The Mother of Psychoanalysis

Helene Rosenbach Deutsch was a radical Austrian born American psychoanalyst who was one of the most prominent female leaders in psychoanalysis.

She was the first woman to lead Sigmund Freud's *Vienna Psychoanalytic Society*. She contributed significantly to theory on the psychology of women that expanded the purview of Freud's male-dominant ideas about women from all accounts. She was also a social rebel in her time.

Deutsch was born in Przemysl, a non-Russian part of Poland to Jewish parents, Wilhelm and Regina Rosenbach, on the 9 October 1884. She was the youngest child in a family of three girls and one boy. She grew up hating her mother who beat her regularly because she was not a boy. Helene's brother was a weak willed man with many vices and was a major disappointment to his parents. Because of his son's unsuccessful nature, Wilhelm declared Helene his heir, making her his favorite child. Father's favorite still received regular beatings from her mother which caused her to believe that her father was weaker than her mother. Much of Helene's later theories seem to reflect on her early family dynamics. She left school at fourteen. While her mother had plans for her to marry and have children, Helene had her own plans.

Soon she began to write for the *Przemysl Voice*. Shortly afterwards, she ran away from home, refusing to return until her parents signed a consent form allowing her to attend University. At the age of sixteen, when she was studying for entrance to the University, she began an affair with the much older and already married Herman Lieberman. Some biographers claim she did this to spite her mother. The affair lasted on and off until 1912, when she married her husband, Felix Deutsch.

In 1910, Deutsch left Lieberman to study in Munich. Here she became pregnant by her lover and had the baby aborted. Prior to this she had been considered her father's heir and had planned to become a lawyer. However, after reading Freud's *Interpretation of Dreams* she became interested in psychoanalysis and her life was to change dramatically. Shortly after she married Felix, Deutsch graduated with a Doctorate in Medicine and began her work in Vienna University's Psychiatric Clinic under the direction of Wagner-Jauregg. It is here that she began to take on the "mother" role as a psychiatrist, a method that she would continue throughout her career.

In 1914 she left the Vienna clinic to study under Emil Kraepelin in Munich. Following several miscarriages she eventually gave birth to her son Martin in 1916. After this she began her work with Sigmund Freud and became a regular at his Wednesday night meetings. During this time she became interested in self-deception in women's mothering experiences. In 1918 she became one of the first women to join Freud's *Vienna Psychoanalytic Society*.

She began her career investigating narcissism in men and women basing one of her theories on her nephew who, after his brother's death, began to develop traits to attain the attention of his mother. Deutsch saw this and put it into her theory. She became interested in studying penis envy and castration anxiety after hearing Karl Abraham talk about them. In 1924, she began to look at women and sexuality closer and felt that problems are caused in women from a conflict between narcissism and mother's love, ideas which reflected on her own life. She was at the time experiencing difficulties managing her career and family and it was her husband who actually performed much of the "mothering" for their child.

From 1925 to 1933 she returned to the Vienna clinic to lead the women's section. In 1925, she published *The Psychology of Women's Sexual Functions* the first book by a psychoanalyst on the subject of women's psychology. Freud's influence on her was very evident in that she used many male Freudian terms for female body parts, rather than female ones. She believed that menstruation for a woman meant castration, as Freud would have said, and a lack of a baby. These ideas once again reflected on her own troubles with pregnancies earlier in her life. Deutsch felt that pregnancy, the ultimate goal of female sexuality, is anal and oral fixations are played out via morning sickness and miscarriage.

She was hugely disappointed when Freud refused to recognize her work as an expansion of his theory. She blamed his lack of credit on his daughter, Anna, who she claimed was jealous of her. It is possible that Deutsch saw herself rather than Anna Freud as the rightful heir of sorts to Freud. She was certainly considered one of his favorites.

In 1935, Deutsch left Vienna for America, followed by her husband the following year. They settled in Cambridge, Massachusetts. Deutsch lost all contact with her family after Germany invaded Poland. Her loss of contact, the death of her former lover Lieberman and her lack of patients due to her retirement caused her to suffer from depression. She immersed herself in writing a two-book project on women's psychology and became an Associate Psychiatrist at the Massachusetts General Hospital.

Her book, *The Psychology of Women* (1944), was heavily based on her own life. She believed that girls' problems were caused by a lack of detachment from their mothers and that girls are more internal and boys more external and those girls find it difficult to resist masculinity. She also claimed that women's sexuality depends wholly on the male and mothering. The entire goal of the women's sex drive is to have babies to mother. She also posited that infertility in women is caused either by the hatred of one's own mother's sexuality or if the woman felt she would be an incompetent mother.

After 1950, fearing that she would primarily be known for her work on women's psychology, she returned to her work on narcissism in men and women. Her husband died in 1964 which had a profound effect on her. She then for the first time realized how helpful he had been to her throughout her career and regretted that she didn't appreciate him more. She died on the 29 March 1982 at the age of 97.

OTTO RANK (1884-1939)

*"In the psychical sphere there are no facts,
but only interpretations of them"*

**Will Therapy
Trauma of Birth Theory**

Otto Rank was an Austrian psychologist who began as one of

Sigmund Freud's closest aides and ended as one of his fiercest critics. He is famous for his birth trauma and will therapy.

Rank's work diverged from Freud's when he became interested in the way the infant experiences separating from the mother at the time of birth. He developed the idea that freedom, namely independence from others, is essential to the development of our creativity. For Rank, how we deal with the independence from our mother that is thrust on us at birth, determines the type of personality we develop. His theory is still widely used in various therapies and counseling contexts, particularly in the areas of personal growth and self-actualization. Rank's insight that the balance between individuality and relationships with others, especially within the family, is key to healthy human development, is significant as we strive to understand and achieve our potential as true human beings.

He was born Otto Rosenfeld, on the 22 April, 1884 in Vienna, Austria. His parents comprised of a poor Jewish family of Simon Rosenfeld, an artisan jeweler, and Karoline Fleischner. His father is said to have had a drinking problem, and never cared much for his family.

Otto grew up indifferent toward religion, seeking solace in music and books. He read Henrik Ibsen, Arthur Schopenhauer, Friedrich Nietzsche and Sigmund Freud. After he finished trade school he began life as a locksmith. As the family only had enough money to educate one child that honor was give to Otto's older brother who chose to study law.

Otto became infatuated with Sigmund Freud, after reading *The Interpretation of Dreams*. In 1905 he presented Freud with his work *Der Kunstler* (The Artist), a small monograph subtitled *An Approach to a Sexual Psychology*.

Freud was so impressed with his work that he invited him to become secretary of the emerging *Vienna Psychoanalytic Society*. As a result he soon became Freud's "right-hand" man a position he held for almost twenty years. During this time Otto officially changed his name from Rosenfeld to Rank.

Freud believed that Rank was the most brilliant of his Viennese disciples. Freud also helped him to gain admission to the University of Vienna from which Rank obtained his Ph.D. in 1912. Rank proved to be an expert in philosophy, literature, mythology and psychoanalysis.

In fact, after Freud, Rank was the most prolific psychoanalytic writer, publishing several books and numerous papers. Between 1912 and 1924, he served as the editor of the *Internationale Zeitschrift für Psychoanalyse* (International Journal of Psychoanalysis).

During World War I, Rank served in the Austrian army in Poland. His experience of war was to dramatically change his views on life. Later, he began a friendship with Sandor Ferenczi, with whom he co-wrote several books.

In 1918, Rank married Beata Tola Mincer, with whom he had one child, Helene. The birth of his child enhanced Rank's interest in the Oedipus complex and the mother-child relationship. This resulted in Rank's career shift and ultimately his split with Freud in 1924.

In that year he published *Das Trauma der Geburt und seine Bedeutung für die Psychoanalyse* (The Trauma of Birth). The book caused a split with the Freudians. He was later expelled from the *Vienna Psychoanalytic Society*. In May 1926, he moved to Paris where he became a psychoanalyst for artists Henry Miller and Anaïs Nin, and lectured at the Sorbonne. For the next ten years, Rank continued to teach and practice in the United States and Europe.

In 1936 he settled in New York. By then, many psychoanalysts in the U.S. considered Rank the leader of psychoanalytic thought. His influence was particularly strong in Philadelphia, where some of his methods were adopted at the Pennsylvania School of Social Work. He travelled and lectured extensively on object-relational, experiential, and "here-and-now" psychotherapy, art, the creative will, and neurosis as a failure in creativity. In 1939, Rank divorced his first wife and married Estelle Buel. He was planning to become a U.S. citizen and move to California. However, just three months after his wedding he developed a kidney infection, which led to fatal septicemia. He died in New York City on the 31 October, 1939, just five weeks after Freud had passed away in London.

Rank is famous for his **trauma of birth theory.** He believed that we all suffer trauma by virtue of being born and of the inevitable, violent, physical and psychic separation we suffer at birth from our mother. For him the physical event of birth, where the infant moves from a state of perfect harmony and union with the mother into a painful state of separation resulting from the traumatic and violent circumstances of birth, constitutes the earliest anxiety that a human being experiences.

He says that that anxiety is the blueprint for all anxieties experienced later in life. In this theory he harkened back to Freud's early theory where he called birth the "first experience of anxiety and thus the source and prototype of anxiety" for the rest of the individual's life. He agreed with Freud's idea when he wrote that we are born into trauma and that trauma forms the "nucleus of the unconscious" and the essence of who we deeply are. The way the infant experiences this early separation from the mother, Rank wrote, becomes the foundation for all anxieties experienced later in the individual's life.

His theory and that of Freud is very similar to the one proposed by British psychoanalyst Wilfred Bion. Bion, too, believes that the infant is "born into trauma" and is born into an inner state of chaos and confusion. This is because their earliest 'feelings' are not feelings at all.

Bion calls them undifferentiated feeling 'states'. These are actually "un-thought thoughts" or "sense impressions" that are given to the mind before actual thinking comes into being. These "feeling states" or early sensations 'hit' the infant's mind in lightning bursts of sheer, inescapable experience–unmitigated events experienced in the fullness of their strength and reality. As such, these sensations are unbearable to the infant.

Rank has never really received the credit he deserves for his contributions to psychoanalysis and psychotherapy. Although he hated the Nazis, in 1939 the psychologist Erich Fromm labeled Rank's "will therapy" a Nazi-style philosophy. Rank's work was ignored for years, until the 1970s when it was resurrected by the psychologists Rollo May and Carl Rogers, among others, and by writers such as Anaïs Nin.

KAREN HORNEY (1885-1952)

"When one begins, as I did, to analyze men after a fairly long experience of analyzing women, one receives a most surprising impression of the intensity of this envy of pregnancy, childbirth, and motherhood, as well as of breasts and of the act of suckling"

Founder of Feminist Psychology

Karen Horney was a German born psychoanalyst famous for Feminine Psychology, her theory of neurotic needs and Neo-Freudian psychology.

She was born Karen Danielson in Blankenese, Schleswig-Holstein, Prussia, in the German Empire which is now near Hamburg, Germany on the 16 September, 1885. Her father, Berndt Wackels Danielson, was a ship's captain.

He was also a devoutly religious man. His children nick-named him the "bible thrower." He was authoritarian in nature. Her mother, Clotilde van Ronzelen, was the opposite. She was a well-educated liberal intellectual who encouraged Danielson in her studies. Her father was a widower with four teenage children.

Karen was the second child from his new marriage, the first being a more favored older brother called Berndt. Her father often made unflattering comments in relation to both her looks and her intelligence. Consequently Karen decided at the tender age of nine that if she couldn't be pretty, then she would be intelligent. Perhaps because of the lack of attention from her father whom she once described as a "cruel disciplinary figure" Karen suffered from depression from a very early age, something that she would contend with for the rest of her life.

At the age of thirteen, against her parent's wishes and without their support, she decided that she wanted to become a doctor. In 1904, when she was nineteen, her mother left her father and took the children with her. Karen entered medical school in 1906 and was therefore one of the first women to enter a German university. While there, she met economics major and aspiring law student, Oskar Horney. They married three years later.

Between 1910 and 1916 they were blessed with three children, all daughters, but it was not a particularly happy marriage. Her marriage proved consistent with the optional Freudian theory. Oscar was just as authoritarian and strict with his children as Karen's own father was with his. Within a single year she gave birth to her first daughter, Brigitte, and lost both of her parents. She entered psychoanalysis in an effort to cope with her depression. Karen studied at both the University of Göttingen and University of Berlin before graduating in 1913.

Her psychoanalyst was Freud disciple Karl Abraham. He later became her mentor at the *Berlin Psychoanalytic Society* where she became an analyst in private practice in addition to her hospital work. She was instrumental in helping to design the Society's training program which she subsequently directed. Her roles as woman doctor, wife, and mother inspired her research on female sexual development.

In 1923, her husband's firm became insolvent. Soon after he developed meningitis. The failure of his business left him bitter and argumentative and put a strain on the marriage. In the same year, her brother died of a pulmonary infection. Both events adversely affected her health and for the first time she thought about suicide.

In 1924, she published her work on the castration complex in women. She asserted that contrary to Freud's theory, the true source of penis envy was in the way female children were treated by their parents.

In 1926, she began to assert her independence and she and her three daughters moved out of her husband's house. It was the beginning of the end of the marriage. They were later to divorce.

Despite her increasing deviation from orthodox Freudian doctrine, she practiced and taught at the *Berlin Psychoanalytic Society* until 1932. However, Freud's increasing coolness toward her and her concern over the rise of Nazism in Germany motivated her to accept an invitation by Franz Alexander to become his assistant at the Chicago Institute of Psychoanalysis.

In 1932, she and her daughters emigrated to the United States. It was here she became friendly with fellow German psychologist Erich Fromm. They began an intimate relationship but it ended quickly and badly. She also befriended Irish-American Neo-Freudian psychiatrist and psychoanalyst Harry Stack Sullivan as well as Margaret Mead, Paul Tilch and Ruth Benedict. They helped influence her and reinforce her emerging belief in the importance of sociocultural factors in psychological development.

In 1937, she published the book *The Neurotic Personality of Our Time*. By 1941, she was Dean of the *American Institute of Psychoanalysis* and had set up her own organization, the *Association for the Advancement of Psychoanalysis*. She had set up this organization after becoming dissatisfied with the generally strict, orthodox nature of the psychoanalytic community.

It was her deviation from Freudian psychology that led to her resigning from her post. Thereafter, she soon took up teaching in the New York Medical College. She also founded a journal, named the *American Journal of Psychoanalysis*.

In 1952, friends and colleagues suggested opening a clinic in her name, which flattered Horney immensely. She died of cancer that same year (December 4, 1952) and, three years later, The Karen Horney Clinic opened as a research, training, and low-cost treatment center.

It was Karen Horney who originally coined the term feminist psychology. In her book, *Feminine Psychology*, a collection of articles she wrote on the subject from 1922–1937, she addresses previously held beliefs about women, relationships, and the effect of society on female psychology.

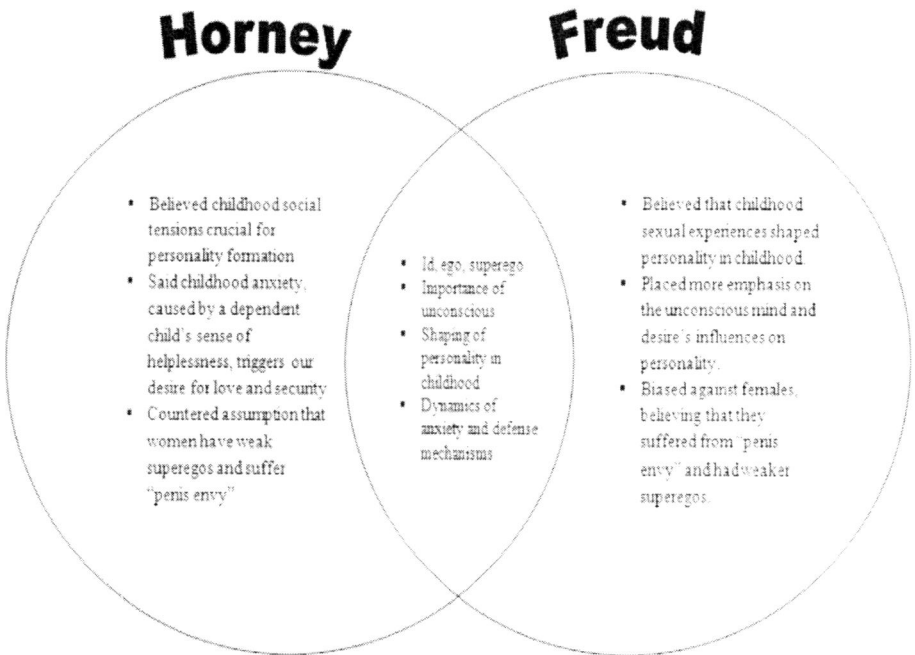

Horney   Freud

- Believed childhood social tensions crucial for personality formation
- Said childhood anxiety, caused by a dependent child's sense of helplessness, triggers our desire for love and security
- Countered assumption that women have weak superegos and suffer "penis envy"

- Id, ego, superego
- Importance of unconscious
- Shaping of personality in childhood
- Dynamics of anxiety and defense mechanisms

- Believed that childhood sexual experiences shaped personality in childhood
- Placed more emphasis on the unconscious mind and desire's influences on personality.
- Biased against females, believing that they suffered from "penis envy" and had weaker superegos.

Horney developed this form of psychology specifically in response to Sigmund Freud's theory of "penis envy." Some commentators consider her theory on neurosis to be a more important contribution to psychology.

Unlike her contemporaries, who believed that neurosis was a negative malfunction of the mind brought about by external stimuli like bereavement and divorce and such like, Horney believed neurosis to be a continuous process. She believed that neuroses commonly occur sporadically in one's lifetime.

Negative experiences during childhood and adolescence were important factors. Something like parental indifference towards the child, believing that a child's perception of events, as opposed to the parent's intentions, was the key to understanding a person's neurosis.

She considered that there were ten patterns of neurotic needs which are based upon things which she thought all humans require to succeed in life. While a person suffering from neurosis could theoretically exhibit all of these needs, in reality much fewer than the ten were needed to be present for a person to be considered a neurotic. Her ten needs can be identified as follows:

Moving Toward People

1. The need for affection and approval.

2. The need for a partner; to love and solve all their problems.

Moving Against People

3. The need for power and control.

4. The need to exploit and manipulate others.

5. The need for social recognition, prestige and limelight.

6. The need for personal admiration and to be valued.

7. The need for personal achievement.

Moving Away from People

8. The need for self- sufficiency and independence.

9. The need for perfection.

10. Lastly, the need to live as inconspicuous a life as possible

Karen Horney's contributions to psychology are considerable. She remains one of the only women to be included in personality theory texts. She was also the first woman to present a paper on feminine psychology at an international conference. Her critique of Freud highlighted the inferior position of women in society. She thought it wrong that women were defined in relation to men. She successfully argued that penis envy, if it ever did exist, was not rooted in a desire to actually possess a penis but, rather, in a desire for the status and recognition afforded to men by the culture in which we live.

She further argued that men's need to succeed and leave a name for themselves sprung from what she called **womb envy**. She introduced the concept of womb envy, suggesting that male envy of pregnancy, nursing, and motherhood led men to claim their superiority in other fields.

Horney was particularly moved to defend women against the charge that they were naturally masochistic. Women's dependence on men for love, money, security, and protection led women to overemphasize qualities like beauty and charm, Horney argued, but also to seek meaning through their relationships with husbands, children, and family. Karen Horney's legacy includes not only her influence on feminine psychology, humanistic and Gestalt psychology, but also on self-psychology, psychoanalysis, Albert Ellis' rational emotive therapy, feminism in general, and existentialism.

W. R. FAIRBAIRN (1889 – 1964)

Object Relations Theory

William R. Fairbairn was a Scottish psychiatrist and psychoanalyst who was one of the leading figures in the development of the object relations approach within psychoanalysis.

He was particularly interested in the difficulties that many of his clients had in making 'real' contact either with him, or with anyone else in their lives. He described the inner worlds of such clients as 'closed systems', in which their emotional energy was locked into relationships with internalized "objects". These "objects" were often imaginary representations of significant others, such as a person's mother or father.

He believed that the real aim of psychoanalytic treatment should be to effect breaches of the closed system which constitutes the client's inner world, and thus to make this world accessible to the influence of outer reality. This idea has become a cornerstone of much of the subsequent development of the object relations school of psychodynamic therapy.

William Ronald Dodds Fairbairn was born in Edinburgh in Scotland on the 11 August 1889 into a strict Protestant family. He was educated at Merchiston Castle School and later at Edinburgh University where he studied for three years in Divinity and Hellenic Greek studies. After a stint in the army he returned to college and undertook medical training. He later taught psychology and practiced psychoanalysis. He had a particular interest in war neuroses.

He earned his M.D. in 1927 and began teaching psychology at the Edinburgh University. In 1931, he was accepted as an associate member of the *British Psychoanalytical Society*, and by 1938, he was a full member.

He was a student of object relations and was active in the Independent Group of the *British Psychoanalytical Society*, a sector that focused on the relationships that exist between people, rather than on the relationships people hold with themselves.

Although he had a major influence on British object relations his influence would have been more effective if he hadn't decided to spend his entire career in Edinburgh where he was somewhat isolated from mainstream thinkers. He was one of the theory-builders for the Middle Group psychoanalysts. The Middle Group now called the Independent Group represent one of the three distinct sub-schools of the *British Psychoanalytic Society*.

They 'developed what is known as the British independent perspective, which argued that the primary motivation of the child is object-seeking rather than drive gratification'. They are strongly associated with the concept of countertransference. They are more concerned with the relationships between people than with the "drives" within them.

In his lifetime, Fairbairn published many articles and books, the most famous of which are *From Instinct to Self* and *Psychoanalytic Studies of the Personality* (1952). The latter represents the basis of Fairbairn's theories. The book is divided into theoretical and clinical sections with three distinct parts that embody Fairbairn's views on object relations.

In the first part, Fairbairn discusses his theories on psychosis, schizoid personalities, psychoneurosis, and the dynamic structure of object relationships. The second part of his book is a review of clinical studies, including themes of religion, grief, and physical impairment. In the third part of the book, Fairbairn discusses a range of topics, including politics, war, religion, and sexuality.

Fairbairn's most lasting contribution to psychology was the development of objects relations theory. While the term was originally created by Austrian psychoanalysis Otto Rank, Fairbairn further developed and popularized the concept.

In object relations theory, people tend to have relationships in adulthood that re-enact or build upon elements of early childhood. For example, a child who grew up in an abusive household might marry an abusive partner. A similar person might move to the other extreme and become so fearful of abuse that even the briefest expression of anger leads to terror.

Fairbairn emphasized that when a child's basic needs are not met, this may lead to introverted, standoffish behavior and the turning away from others. Instead, the child relies on a fantasy life to meet his or her needs, a process Fairbairn termed **internal object relations**.

Fairbairn also helped to develop the concept of **splitting,** which is now a key feature of mental health conditions such as borderline personality. According to Fairbairn, children who have neglectful parents separate the parents into two entities, the good parent, who sometimes responds to the child's needs, and the non-responsive parent, who neglects the child. This leads to splitting, which occurs when a child can't feel ambivalence or nuance. Instead, the child thinks in black and white terms, seeing the parent, and in many cases the self, as either all good or all bad.

Fairbairn's fundamental position is that libido is object seeking, not pleasure seeking as Freud thought. Fairbairn believed that what is central to the developing infant and the person going through life is the need for relationships, not the need for gratification.

For him, the vicissitudes of early intersubjective life are potentially traumatic and may give rise to defense mechanisms such as splitting and dissociation: "The child takes in what is too painful to bear, does not accept the object because it feels bad, splits it off from the good part of the object, and represses the unaccepted, bad part in the individual unconscious. The fate of the repressed bad objects, however, is to return from the inside."

Fairbairn wrote that the infant wants above all to love and be loved by another person (the "object"), but inevitably the mother or other caregiver can never quite be reassuring enough. The child conquers this worrying reality by dividing up the mother into separate representations. There is a central good object which is a loving and loveable person, idealized to a degree. There are also two bad objects: one is the exciting object, the caregiver insofar as he or she provokes longing, and the rejecting object, the caregiver insofar as he or she fails to meet this longing.

The two bad objects, and the self's uncomfortable relations with them, become dissociated from the central ego and its rose-tinted relation to the good object. The result associated with these split-off relationships return "from the inside" as various psychopathological symptoms. William Ronald Fairbairn died in his native Edinburgh at the age of 75.

JACOB MORENO (1899-1974)

"A meeting of two: eye to eye, face to face.
And when you are near I will tear your eyes out
and place them instead of mine,
and you will tear my eyes out
and will place them instead of yours,
then I will look at me with mine."

The Founder of Psychodrama

Jacob Moreno was an Austrian born American-based psychiatrist who was the initiator of sociometry, psychodrama, and group psychotherapy. His legacy has an essential thread: the primacy of relationships. His philosophy and strategies of research and therapy are as relevant today as they were then.

Jacob Levy Moreno was born Iacob Levy on the 18 May 1889 in Bucharest in the Kingdom of Romania. His father, Moreno Nissan Levy, was a Sephardi Jewish merchant from Bulgaria.

His mother, Paulina Wolf, was also a Sephardi Jew, born in Romania. When Jacob was six the family moved to Vienna. Jacob studied medicine, mathematics, and philosophy at the University of Vienna. In 1917 he received his M.D. and commenced a private practice as a psychiatrist in Vöslau, Austria, about 20 miles south of Vienna. He also served as a public health officer and within a year was appointed superintendent of the nearby Mittendorf State Hospital.

He had rejected Freudian theory while still a medical student, and became interested in the potential of group settings for therapeutic practice. He basically began where Freud left off, with his theory of interpersonal relations, and the development of his work in psychodrama, sociometry, group psychotherapy, sociodrama, and sociatry.

In his autobiography he describes his first meeting with Freud: "I attended one of Freud's lectures. He had just finished an analysis of a telepathic dream. As the students filed out, he singled me out from the crowd and asked me what I was doing. I responded, 'Well, Dr. Freud, I start where you leave off. You meet people in the artificial setting of your office. I meet them on the street and in their homes, in their natural surroundings. You analyze their dreams. I give them the courage to dream again. You analyze and tear them apart. I let them act out their conflicting roles and help them to put the parts back together again.'"

In 1918, he began a monthly magazine of philosophy and literature called *Daimon*. He continued to publish and edit it for several years and it boasted amongst its contributories such literary figures as Franz Werfel and Max Brod. But his real love was drama in general and the idea of theatrical improvisation in particular.

In 1921, he set up *Das Stegreiftheater*, the Spontaneity Theater. The next year he rented space in Vienna, where actors "put on spontaneous plays as suggested by the audience, did some 're-enactments' of daily news using a technique called 'the living newspaper,' or improvised on themes." One of these actors was an eighteen year old Peter Lorre.

In 1924 he invented and patented a device he called "radio film". It was a device for electromagnetic recording of sound on discs. In the meantime he continued with his improvisational presentations which enjoyed some critical and popular success.

In 1925, Moreno emigrated to America and settled in New York City. In 1926, he married Beatrice Beecher but the marriage would later end in divorce. He worked at Columbia University and the New School for Social Research. In 1927, he was licensed as a physician in New York State and practiced psychiatry in New York City from 1928.

His methods of psychotherapy emphasized several elements then considered innovative in their focus on group treatment and on improvisational re-enactment of experience. He developed a system he called **sociometry**, defined by Lucy Ozarin as "observational charting of how people interact in groups."

In 1932, he first introduced group psychotherapy to the American Psychiatric Association. For the next forty years he continued to develop his Theory of Interpersonal Relations and tools for social sciences he called sociodrama, psychodrama, sociometry, and sociatry.

In his paper *The Future of Man's World*, he explained that he developed these sciences to counteract "the economic materialism of Marx, the psychological materialism of Freud, and the technological materialism of our modern industrial age."

Applying the principles of sociometry and his ideas about the therapeutic value of spontaneous expression, he developed a technique he called psychodrama. This consisted of staging performances in which patients acted out their conflicts by playing roles in a social context. He identified psychodrama as a therapy based on Aristotle's idea of Greek tragedy as "catharsis."

Usually, a session took place on a stage with a therapist suggesting actions or scenes for the patient to perform, and sometimes included dramatic techniques that he called "deep actions," such as role reversal. The patient would assume the role of a person with whom he or she is in conflict, or interacting with other patients who served as foils. Patients found that in recapitulating and reworking their experience they were able to gain insights into their situations and relationships and discover methods of coping with interpersonal problems.

In 1935 he became an American citizen. In 1936 he founded the Beacon Hill Sanitarium, later renamed the Moreno Sanitarium and then the Moreno Institute, in Beacon, about 60 miles north of New York City, devoted to the therapeutic use of psychodrama. In 1938 he married Florence Bridge, with whom he had one child, Regina.

After they divorced he married for the third time in 1949, Zerka Toeman. They had one child, a boy called Jonathan. After a long illness he died in 1974 in New York City. At his request his epitaph reads "the man who brought laughter to psychiatry."

So, what exactly is psychodrama?

Psychodrama is a method of improvised acting in which clients use spontaneous dramatization, role playing and dramatic self-presentation to investigate and gain insight into their lives. It includes elements of theater and is usually conducted on a stage with props.

The idea is that by closely recreating real-life situations, and acting them out in the present, clients have the opportunity to evaluate their behavior and more deeply understand a particular situation in their lives. It is often used in a group scenario where each person in the group can become therapeutic agents for one another's scenes. But psychodrama is not group therapy or even a type of group therapy.

What should one expect is a **psychodrama session**? Usually one member of the group becomes the protagonist, and focuses on a particular situation to enact on stage. A variety of scenes are enacted. Usually they depict memories of particular events in the client's past, unfinished situations, inner dramas, fantasies, dreams, preparations for future risk-taking situations, or unrehearsed expressions of mental state in the here and now.

These scenes either approximate real-life situations or are externalizations of inner mental processes. Other members of the group may become auxiliaries, and support the protagonist by playing other significant roles in the scene.

One of the core elements of psychodrama is Moreno's theory of **spontaneity-creativity**, acting spontaneously through a readiness to improvise and respond in the moment. By encouraging clients to address a problem in a creative way, reacting in a spontaneous and impulsive manner, they may discover new solutions to their problems. The session focuses principally on a single participant, called the **protagonist**. Protagonists examine their relationships by interacting with the other actors and the leader, known as the director.

In psychodrama sessions, the participants explore internal conflicts by acting out their emotions and interpersonal interactions on stage. A session lasts between 90 and 120 minutes and is divided into three sections; the warm-up, the action and the post-discussion.

During the warm-up, the actors are encouraged to enter into a state of mind where they can be present in and aware of the current moment and are free to be creative usually effected through the use of different games and activities.

Next, the action section of the psychodrama session is the time in which the actual scenes themselves take place. Finally, in the post-discussion, the different actors are able to comment on the action and share their empathy and experiences with the protagonist of the scene.

A typical psychodrama session begins with a number of clients choosing the protagonist. The leader of the group, called the director, then requests the other clients to assist the protagonist in his "performance." This can involve portraying other characters in the drama, and/or by utilizing mirroring, doubling, role playing and reversal and soliloquy.

Mirroring is an important technique in psychodrama. In mirroring, the protagonist is first asked to act out an experience. After this, the client steps out of the scene and watches as another client/actor steps into their role and portrays the client. Later, the client is asked to comment on the action and/or re-enter the scene.

Doubling occurs where a client, the double, makes conscious any thoughts or feelings that another person is unable to express. This inability may arise because of inhibition, fear, shyness, anger, guilt or such like. Often the person is unaware of these thoughts or at least is unable to demonstrate their feelings.

Therefore the double attempts to make conscious and give form to the unconscious and/or under expressed material. The person who is being doubled is then entitled to disown any of the "double's" statements and to correct them as necessary. In this way, doubling itself can never be wrong.

Role playing is where the client portrays a person or object that is problematic to him or her while **role reversal** is a technique in which a client is asked to portray another person while a second actor portrays the client in the particular scene. This not only prompts the client to think as the other person, but also has some of the benefits of mirroring, as the client sees him- or herself as portrayed by the second actor.

In **soliloquy** the client speaks his or her thoughts aloud in order to build self-knowledge.

The clients act out a number of scenes in order to allow the protagonist to work through certain scenarios. While this is obviously beneficial for the protagonist is it helpful for the other clients who assist? Apparently so, as it allows them to assume the role of someone other than themselves and apply that experience to their own life. The focus is on the acting out the scenarios, rather than simply talking through them.

Often, all of the different elements of a stage production like stage, props, and lighting are used to heighten the reality of the scene.

The term **sociometry** first coined by Jacob Moreno is often used in relation to psychodrama. Sociometry is the study of social relations between individuals or interpersonal relationships. By extension it is a set of ideas and practices that are focused on promoting spontaneity in human relations. Classically, sociometry involves techniques for identifying, organizing, and giving feedback on specific interpersonal preferences an individual has and occurs in a psychodrama session where the group is allowed to choose the protagonist.

Moreno also coined the term **sociodrama.** Though similar to psychodrama is is different in that while psychodrama focuses on one patient within the group unit, sociodrama addresses the group as a whole. The aim is to explore social events, collective ideologies, and community patterns within a group in order to bring about positive change or transformation within the group dynamic.

It can be divided into three main categories: crisis, political and diversity sociodrama. Crisis sociodrama deals with group responses after a catastrophic event. Political sociodrama tries to address stratification and inequality issues within a society. Diversity sociodrama considers conflicts based on prejudice, racism or stigmatization in society.

Carl Hollander is another important practitioner in the field of psychodrama. Trained by Moreno, Hollander is best known for his creation of the **Hollander Psychodrama Curve**.

He uses the image of a curve to explain the three parts of a psychodrama session: the warm-up, the activity, and the integration. The warm-up exists to put patients into a place of spontaneity and creativity in order to be open in the act of psychodrama. The "activity" is the actual enactment of the psychodrama process. Finally, the "curve" moves to integration and serves as closure and a type of debriefing.

Although not widely practice today psychodrama has opened the doors to research possibilities for other psychological concepts such as group therapy and expansion of the work of Sigmund Freud. Group therapy organizations such as Alcoholics Anonymous often use psychodrama, and it is now being used in post-divorce counseling therapy for children.

Mainstream psychiatry was skeptical about Moreno in general and psychodrama in particular. The Science writer Martin Gardner referred to it as a type of cult and described it as one of "hundreds of new therapeutic gimmicks making their appearance in the more eccentric Freudian fringes". But it can be extremely effective in certain circumstances.

HARRY STACK SULLIVAN (1892-1949)

"I do not believe that I have had an interview with anybody in twenty-five years in which the person to whom I was talking was not annoyed during the early part of the interview by my asking stupid questions"

Interpersonal Psychoanalysis

Harry Stack Sullivan was an American psychiatrist who developed a theory of psychiatry based on interpersonal relationships called Interpersonal Psychoanalysis.

He believed that anxiety and other psychiatric symptoms arise in fundamental conflicts between the individual and his human environment and that personality development also takes place by a series of interactions with other people.

Sullivan made substantial contributions to clinical psychiatry, especially the psychotherapy of schizophrenia. He argued that the mental functions of schizophrenics, though impaired, are not damaged past repair and can be recovered through therapy. He was known to possess an extraordinary ability to communicate with schizophrenic patients, and described their behavior with clarity and insight unrivalled at that time.

He was born on the 21 February 1892 in Norwich, New York, into an Irish Catholic home. Little information is available about his early life. He was the only surviving child of a shy and retiring farmer and his partially invalide wife.

A lonely child, he had serious difficulties learning how to get along with other children at school. His only friends were the animals on the farm. He often spoke of the drastic reorganization of his personality during adolescence.

He attended the Chicago College of Medicine and Surgery and, after receiving his M.D. in 1917, worked as a civilian with the U.S. Army during World War I. In 1922 he became a liaison officer for the Veterans Administration at Saint Elizabeth's Hospital in Washington. It was here that he first encountered psychiatry as a specialty and developed his long-standing interest in schizophrenic patients.

Saint Elizabeth's Hospital was a major center of psychiatric activity. William Alanson White had introduced many new treatments there. In particular, he introduced the application of Freud's psychoanalytic principles to the diagnosis and treatment of hospital patients. While Sullivan's duties were only those of a consultant, he had diagnostic interviews with a large number of schizophrenic patients. Later, he moved to Sheppard and Enoch Pratt Hospital near Baltimore. It was here he first met Adolf Meyer and Clara Thompson.

He was assistant physician at Sheppard Pratt from 1923 to 1925 and then became director of clinical research, a position he held until 1930. This position gave him the opportunity for the detailed study of schizophrenic patients. Sullivan noted with approval Meyer's insistence that "mental illnesses" could be profitably considered "reaction types" to situations confronting the patient.

The concept of "illness" as a problem-solving effort became intrinsic to his whole work. In contrast to the usual view at that time, that nearly all such patients were damaged, if they recovered at all, he mentioned patients who were more competent after the episode than before and undertook a number of studies to try to identify the factors responsible.

One of Sullivan's characteristic conclusions was that the patient's own appraisal of his circumstances, his foreseeable future, as it were, was a major contributing factor to the outcome of a psychotic episode.

Sullivan did not, by any means, work in intellectual isolation. As these experiences with therapy led him to recognize the importance of interpersonal relations, he turned freely to social scientists for help including Lawrence K. Frank, W. I. Thomas, Ruth Benedict, Harold D. Lasswell, and Edward Sapir.

In 1930, Sullivan moved to New York where he turned his attention to the obsessive disorders. But financial pressures forced him to move back to Washington three years later and he devoted much of the rest of his time to teaching.

In 1933 he co-founded the William Alanson White Foundation, with branches in Washington and New York. Later he was involved in the establishment of the Washington School of Psychiatry and of the journal *Psychiatry*.

Sullivan never married. Although it was not publicly known at the time,

Sullivan was a homosexual who lived with his lover Jimmie. He was plagued almost throughout his adult life by poor health, suffering from heart disease, which twice was nearly fatal. The discovery of penicillin enabled him to live his last six, most productive years. His death was the result of a massive apoplexy. He died on the 14 January 1949 in Paris, France.

Sullivan is known primarily for his theory of interpersonal relations. Essentially, his theory holds that human experience primarily consists of interactions or transactions between people, whether the people are real, imaginary, or a blend of both the real and imaginary.

Thus, Sullivan's theory tends to merge with social psychology except that it emphasizes problems which are connected with psychotherapy. He rejected individual psychology partly because he thought that individuality cannot be scientifically understood, since no individual can be understood apart from his relationships with others.

While Sullivan did not emphasize **biological determinants**, he did assert that there are four generic factors which entered into, have a causative influence on any act. He identified these as biological potentiality, maturation, the "results" of previous experience, and foresight. However, it should be added that no one yet-knows how much weight should be given to biological determinants.

Sullivan believed that it is largely by means of the self that the limitations, facilitations, and opportunities of a society are mediated in personality. The self begins to develop in late infancy and grows through several stages, namely, infancy, childhood, the juvenile era, preadolescence, early adolescence, and late adolescence, normally culminating in maturity.

But, these **stages of development** are not instinctually determined. His formulations held that before one can enter into any stage (barring the first) in the normal course of development, one must have successfully "negotiated" the previous stage, for an arresting of development, due to environmental circumstances, can occur at any era and gravely handicap further growth. For such reasons, there are many "chronically juvenile" people who are chronologically adult.

Infancy: The first two stages are normally lived through in the home under the supervision of authoritative adults, on whom the powerless offspring depends not only for his physical survival but also for the necessities of psychological development.

Childhood: Childhood begins with the development of language and lasts for several years.

The Juvenile: According to Sullivan, this era is the time for becoming "social." For the first time, limitations and peculiarities of the home are open to remedy by the school and by the society of one's peers. Schooling is a wholly necessary experience for anyone growing up in a complex industrial society.

During this period, one begins to acquire supervisory patterns of the self, which pertain not only to moral conduct but to behavior generally. These supervisory patterns, developed in connection with authoritative figures in the home, school, and church, tend to make the juvenile more self-critical and they learn patterns of cooperation, competition, and compromise.

Preadolescence: Preadolescence extends roughly from 8½ to 12 years of age. During this era, the capacity to love matures: a relationship in which the satisfactions and security of another person, a "chum," a member of one's own sex, are as important to one as one's own satisfactions and security.

Adolescence and Late Adolescence: In Western society, adolescence is a notoriously difficult period for many people. New adjustments have to be accomplished; new relationships, for which there is no precedent in personal experience, have to be established; and one is expected to put away childish things once and for all. So, adolescence is a time of trial and of opportunity. There is a movement of interest toward members of the opposite sex.

Sullivan's life achievements are impressive. In 1933 he helped to found the William Alanson White Psychiatric Foundation. In 1936 he was instrumental in setting up the Washington (D.C.) School of Psychiatry. After World War II he helped establish the World Federation for Mental Health.

In 1938 he set up and served as editor of the journal *Psychiatry*. During the later years of his life he more fully articulated his ideas in books like *The Interpersonal Theory of Psychiatry* (1953), *The Fusion of Psychiatry and Social Science* (1964).

After his death Sullivan's theory of personality and his psychotherapeutic techniques continue to have a growing influence, particularly in American psychoanalytic circles.

FRITZ PERLS (1893-1970)

"I do my thing and you do your thing.
I am not in this world to live up to your expectations,
and you are not in this world to live up to mine.
You are you, and I am I,
and if by chance we find each other, it's beautiful.
If not, it can't be helped."

Gestalt Therapy

Fritz Perls was a German born psychiatrist and psychoanalyst who helped found Gestalt therapy which is an existential/experiential form of psychotherapy that emphasizes personal responsibility.

The therapy focuses on the individual's experience in the here and now, the therapist-client relationship, the environmental and social contexts of a person's life, and the self-regulating adjustments people make as a result of their overall situation. Gestalt Therapy is similar to Gestalt Psychology but is also different in that the central principle of gestalt psychology is that the mind forms a global whole with self-organizing tendencies. This principle maintains that when the human mind (perceptual system) forms a percept or gestalt, the whole has a reality of its own, independent of the parts. Gestalt Therapy is different to Gestalt theoretical psychotherapy which was was developed by the German Gestalt psychologist and psychotherapist Hans-Jürgen P. Walter and his colleagues in Germany and Austria.

Friedrich Salomon Perls was born on the 8 July 1893 in Berlin, Germany. His parents did not get along with each other. He had two sisters Else and Margariet. He was a bright student but he hated school and his teachers. At one stage it was thought that he would follow his uncle, Herman Staub, a famous lawyer, into the legal profession but Fritz had no interest in law.

When the First World War broke out he was deployed to the front line. War in the trenches seriously traumatized him. He qualified as a medical doctor after the war and became an assistant to Kurt Goldstein, who worked with brain injured soldiers.

He then became interested in psychoanalysis and in 1930 Wilhelm Reich became his supervising senior analyst in Berlin. In 1930 he married Lore

Posner, and they had two children together, Renate and Stephen. In 1933, the family fled first to the Netherlands, and then to South Africa, where Perls started a psychoanalytic training institute.

In 1942 he joined the South African army, and served as an army psychiatrist until 1946. While in South Africa, he was influenced by the "holism" of Jan Smuts. During this period Fritz Perls wrote his first book, *Ego, Hunger, and Aggression* (1942). The family left South Africa in 1946 and emigrated to New York. Here Perls worked briefly with Karen Horney, and Wilhelm Reich.

After living through a peripatetic episode, during which he lived in Montreal and served as a cruise ship psychiatrist, Perls finally settled in Manhattan. Together with Paul Goodman, Perls wrote his second book having been influenced by the work of Kurt Lewin and Otto Rank. Along with the experiential first part, written with Ralph Hefferline, the book was entitled *Gestalt Therapy* (1951).

Shortly afterwards, Fritz and Laura Perls founded the first Gestalt Institute in their Manhattan apartment. Perls traveled throughout the United States to conduct Gestalt workshops and training. In 1960 he left his wife behind in New York and moved to Los Angeles, where he practiced in conjunction with Jim Simkin. He became interested in Zen during this period, and incorporated the idea of mini-satori, a brief awakening, into his practice. He also traveled to Japan, where he stayed in a Zen monastery.

Eventually, he settled at the Esalen Institute in California where he collaborated with Ida Rolf, founder of Rolfing Structural Integration, to address the relationship between the mind and the body. In 1969 he left Esalen and started a Gestalt community at Lake Cowichan on Vancouver Island, Canada. On the 14 March 1970 he died of heart failure in Chicago.

So what is Gestalt Therapy?

The term *gestalt* refers to a whole that is greater than the sum of its parts. It is based on the idea of a whole being as connected with their environment, loved ones and memories. Therapy works toward creating full awareness of the here and now, both within the client and between client and therapist.

It derives many of its theories from gestalt psychology, although gestalt therapy does not completely mirror gestalt psychology. Gestalt psychology emphasizes that the brain is a self-organizing, holistic unit that is greater than the sum of its parts, while gestalt therapy emphasizes the present moment and personal responsibility. Gestalt therapy also incorporates aspects of Freudian and Reichian psychology.

Gestalt therapy is considered a humanistic, existential psychotherapy and emphasizes the present moment. The practice uses cognitive insight into current experiences. It stresses the importance of mindfulness.

It encourages clients to explore creativity to achieve satisfaction in areas of life that may have otherwise been blocked. While the basis of gestalt therapy is the client's own awareness of behavior, emotion, feelings, perception, and sensation, its focus is on relationships. These include relationships with the world, with other people, and with oneself.

Key components of the gestalt approach include:

1. A strong emphasis on the therapist-client relationship as a healing tool. The therapist doesn't tell the client what to do or act as the leader of therapy. Instead, gestalt therapists emphasize the teaching power of dialogue, with both the therapist and the client aiming for increasing authenticity.

2. Balancing data and subjective experience. Rather than prioritizing one source of information over another, gestalt therapists emphasize the helpfulness of all types of information, a practice sometimes called phenomenological awareness.

3. A person is more than the sum of his or her experiences. Like the gestalt theory for which it is named, gestalt therapy views a client as more than a collection of experiences or symptoms, treating the client as a dynamic organism in a constant state of change and evolution.

Gestalt therapists draw on existential theories in viewing clients as perpetually reacting to new circumstances and evolving their behavioral repertoire.

Does Gestalt Therapy work?

Gestalt therapists tend to see each individual as an integration of mind-body-emotion-spirit and believe that each of us possesses all the necessary ingredients for healthy living. We are born whole and full of possibilities. In the process of ongoing interaction with others and events in our lives we create adjustments as a way of coping with adversity.

Gestalt therapy works in two ways:

firstly, it helps clients gain a better understanding of identifying their feelings; and,

secondly, it shows them how those feelings are connected to their physical body.

Understanding the internal self is the key to understanding actions, reactions and behaviors. Gestalt therapy helps a client take the first step into this awareness so that they can acknowledge and accept these patterns. Clients undergo a journey of self-discovery. The therapy also empowers a client with the necessary skills to face stressful situations.

Gestalt therapists believe that the answers to our problems lie within us all. This wisdom helps each of us become more accepting of ourselves and others. This then carries over into our communication, decisions and relationships. Clients undergoing Gestalt therapy should feel more self-confident, calm and peaceful. The therapy is said to be an effective approach for managing tension, depression, anxiety, addiction, post-traumatic stress and other psychological challenges that prevent people from achieving a free and fulfilling life.

ANNA FREUD (1896-1982)

*"Creative minds always have been known to survive
any kind of bad training"*

Founder of Psychoanalytic Child Psychology

Anna Freud was the daughter of Sigmund Freud and the only child to enter the field of psychoanalysis. With Melanie Klein, many consider her to be the founder of psychoanalytic child psychology.

Anna was born on the 3 December 1895 in Vienna at a time when her father's radical theories of sex and the mind were starting to make him famous across Europe. She was regarded as a 'plain' child and she struggled at school, where she acquired the nickname of 'black devil'.

She endured a comparatively unhappy childhood and experienced difficulties getting along with her siblings, specifically Sophie Freud, who was the more attractive of the two. There is evidence that she may have suffered from depression and eating disorders. But she was a lively child with a reputation for mischief. She was also very close to her father.

After finishing her education at the Cottage Lyceum in Vienna in 1912 she went on to be a trainee and later qualified teacher there. She finally quit her teaching career because of tuberculosis. In 1918, her father started psychoanalysis on her and she became seriously involved with this new profession.

In 1922 she presented the paper "Beating Fantasies and Daydreams" to the *Vienna Psychoanalytic Society*. From 1925 to 1934, she was the *Secretary of the International Psychoanalytical Association*. In the meantime she continued child analysis and seminars and conferences on the subject.

In 1936, Anna Freud published her influential study of the "ways and means by which the ego wards off displeasure and anxiety", *The Ego and the Mechanisms of Defence*. It helped establish her professional reputation as a pioneering theoretician. This was the book that laid out for the first time the core idea that we instinctively try to protect our 'ego' that is, our acceptable picture of who we are, with a variety of defenses.

A defense mechanism takes immediate action to avoid pain. We instinctively try to stave off thoughts, memories and feelings that seem to endanger or threaten us, just as we instinctively try to protect ourselves physically. The problem is that in the act of defending ourselves in the immediate term, we harm our longer-term chances of dealing with reality and therefore of developing and maturing as a result.

Anna Freud highlighted ten key types of **defense mechanisms**.

Denial: We don't admit there is a problem. "I enjoy drinking every day and often suffer from hangovers but I'm not an alcoholic." Denial is the immediate survival mechanism.

We refuse to recognize there is a problem because to do so means we're going to have to do something about it which we really don't want to do. Denial isn't a lie. It's a defense mechanism like a smoke-screen that makes it very hard for us to see what's going on in our own lives.

Projection: This involves recognizing a negative feeling, but instead of seeing that it is one's own dark emotion, the feeling is given to, or projected onto, someone else.

Take a typical example at work. Your boss calls you and says he wants to see you right away in his office about something serious. Your first instinct is that he has found out you messed up on some project and he's going to sack you. You've got a picture in your head that he's going to be angry with you. But when you get to the office you discover he just wants to talk to you about an important new client. So all the emotions you felt, the fear, the anxiety and the anger are actually coming from you. You projected them onto your boss. You have given the negative feelings, that you don't want to recognize in yourself, to someone else.

Turning against the self: Defenses can be traced back to childhood. A child who was abandoned, or beaten by a parent might seek refuge in a thought which, though grim, is less awful than the alternatives.

The child might feel bad and worthless and believe that that is why its parent is behaving in this manner. So, the child thinks well I still have a good parent. Although it may be painful it can be less painful than the truth that one is actually in the hands of someone who doesn't care about them.

Sublimation: This defense mechanism involves redirecting unacceptable thoughts or emotions into 'higher' and ideally more constructive channels. For example many musicians have turned negative life experiences like drug or alcohol addiction into popular and resonating performances and songs, which have served to energize and inspire many people.

Regression: Here one becomes childish rather than taking a decision and accepting responsibility for their actions therefore trying to feel better to avoid the problem in the first place.

A core feature of regression is the conviction that troubles are always the fault of other people. It's a strategic return to the child's belief that the parents rule the world and can do anything, so if anything goes wrong they could and should put it right. And the one person who cannot possibly be blamed is, of course, the child.

Bad Taste: Instead of trying to seek a solution to a problem a child might try to solve it by throwing a tantrum. In effect, the tantrum means that they cannot be held responsible for this situation and must be helped because they are only a baby.

Rationalization: A key type of rationalization involves doing down the things one does not have but secretly would like. After being rejected for a job, the defensive rationalizer will say: "I didn't really want to work there anyway." They may have very much wanted the job but it is too painful and humiliating to admit they didn't get it. Accordingly, a more acceptable sense of oneself is preserved by creating the reasonable, rational fiction: I didn't really want it.

Intellectualization: This is similar to rationalization. It involves ignoring something very painful and important by starting a highly plausible conversation inside one's head about something entirely different.

Reaction formation: This involves doing the opposite of our initial, unacceptable feelings. Sometimes it is called 'over-compensating'. If we are embarrassed about being attracted to a workmate, we might be mean or aggressive towards them, instead of admitting our attraction.

Township children: Freud called this 'believing the opposite'. Our emotions cause us to feel anxious about their existence and so we negate them by doing the exact opposite.

Displacement: This is the redirection of a usually aggressive desire to a substitute recipient. A classic example is someone who may feel threatened by their boss and comes home and abuses their partner. A happier example might be kissing a stranger after hearing good news.

Fantasy: Fantasy avoids problems by imagining them away or disassociating oneself from reality. It can manifest itself in various ways from daydreaming to watching porn. We often use these moments to transport ourselves from the threatening world to find comfort elsewhere.

In 1938 the Freuds fled from Austria and emigrated to England. Here Anna continued her work and took care of her father, who finally died in the autumn of 1939. When she arrived in London, a conflict came to a head between her and Melanie Klein regarding developmental theories of children.

During the War, Freud took the opportunity to observe the effect of deprivation of parental care on children. She set up a center for young war victims, called The Hampstead War Nursery. Here the children got foster care although mothers were encouraged to visit as often as possible. The underlying idea was to give children the opportunity to form attachments by providing continuity of relationships.

Based on these observations Anna Freud published a series of studies with her long-time friend, Dorothy Tiffany-Burlingham, on the impact of stress on children. During the 1970s she was concerned with the problems of emotionally deprived and socially disadvantaged children, and she studied deviations and delays in development. She died in London on the 9 October 1982 and was cremated at Golders Green Crematorium.

Anna Freud established a group of prominent child developmental analysts including Erik Erikson, Edith Jacobson and Margaret Mahler who noticed that children's symptoms were ultimately analogue to personality disorders among adults and thus often related to developmental stages. But critics argue that she devoted much of her life to protecting her father's legacy and that she actually provided few original ideas to the theory of psychoanalysis. She once said she would make a very poor subject for a biography as there was little to say about her other than that she worked with children.

DONALD WINNICOTT(1896-1971)

True Self/False Self
Parenting

Donald Winnicott was an English pediatrician who became passionate about psychoanalysis and deserves his place in history because of the dramatic simplicity of his approach.

He proposed that the happiness and future satisfaction of the human race depended ultimately not so much on external political issues, but on something far closer to home: the way parents bring up their children.

He worked as a consultant in children's medicine at the Paddington Green Children's Hospital in London, and also played a crucial role in public education around child-rearing, delivering some six hundred talks on the BBC and publishing fifteen books including the bestselling *Home is Where We Start From*. He was was especially influential in the field of object relations theory. He was a leading member of the British Independent Group of the *British Psychoanalytical Society*, and was President twice.

Donald Woods Winnicott was born in Plymouth, Devon, in England on the 7 April 1896 to Sir John Frederick Winnicott and Elizabeth Martha Woods. His father was a wealthy merchant who was knighted in 1924 after serving twice as mayor of Plymouth. Although he enjoyed a prosperous upbringing and was ostensibly happy Donald felt he was oppressed by his mother, his nanny and two sisters.

His mother Elizabeth suffered from depression. He once referred to his childhood as a period in which he tried to make his living by keeping his mother alive. His father encouraged Donald's creativity.

He attended The Leys School, an expensive boarding school in Cambridge, before being admitted to Jesus College Cambridge to study medicine. With the onset of World War One his studies were interrupted and he was made a medical trainee at the temporary hospital in Cambridge. In 1917, he joined the Royal Navy as a medical officer on the destroyer HMS Lucifer before moving to St Bartholomew's Hospital Medical College in London.

He completed his medical studies in 1920. In 1923 he married Alice Taylor and secured a position as physician at the Paddington Green Children's Hospital in London. He worked there as a pediatrician and child psychoanalyst for 40 years. In 1923 he began a ten-year psychoanalysis with James Strachey. In 1927 he began training as an analytic candidate.

At the time, supporters of Anna Freud and Melanie Klein were engaged in an intellectual battle to secure the mantle of Sigmund Freud's true intellectual heirs. The result was the establishment of not two but three groups: the Freudians, the Kleinians, and the Middle later called the Independent Group of the *British Psychoanalytical Society*. Winnicott, although trained by Klein, attached himself to the Independent Group.

During World War Two, Winnicott served as consultant psychiatrist to the evacuee program. During this time he met and worked with Clare Britton, a psychiatric social worker who became his colleague in treating children displaced from their homes by wartime evacuation. In 1951 he divorced his first wife and married Clare. After the war he also saw patients in his private practice. Among contemporaries influenced by Winnicott was R.D. Laing, who wrote to Winnicott in 1958 acknowledging his help.

Winnicott died on the 28 January 1971 following the last of a series of heart attacks and was cremated in London. His wife Clare Winnicott oversaw the posthumous publication of several of his works.

Winnicott saw his world divided into two classes: "There are those who were never 'let down' as babies and who are to that extent candidates for the enjoyment of life and of living. There are also those who did suffer traumatic experiences of the kind that result from environmental letdown, and who must carry with them all their lives the memories of the state they were in at moments of disaster. These are candidates for lives of storm and stress and perhaps illness."

It was this second category that he wanted to save and spare in the next generation. So what would it take, in his eyes, to encourage the 'good enough' parent? Winnicott put forward a number of suggestions:

Remember that your child is very vulnerable:
Winnicott tried to impress upon his audience how psychologically fragile an infant is. A child doesn't understand itself, it doesn't know where it is, it is struggling to stay alive, it has no way of grasping when the next feed will come, it can't communicate with itself or others. A child isn't yet a person, the early months are accordingly an immense struggle.

Winnicott never loses sight of this, and repeatedly insists that it is those around the infant who have to 'adapt'. He believed that a child who has adapted to the world too early, or who has had inappropriate demands made upon it, will be a prime candidate for mental problems.

Let a child be angry:
Winnicott was aware that a healthy infant could experience violence and hate. If you forget to feed your child "it must feel to him as if the wild beasts will gobble him up." He believed it was vital for parents to allow rage to expend itself, and for them not in any way to be threatened or moralistic about 'bad' behavior: "If a baby cries in a state of rage and feels as if he has destroyed everyone and everything, and yet the people round him remain calm and unhurt, this experience greatly strengthens his ability to see that what he feels to be true is not necessarily real, that fantasy and fact, both important, are nevertheless different from each other."

He interpreted violent feelings against parents as a natural aspect of the maturational process. This is why he appreciated and spoke out for difficult adolescents: "A normal child, if he has confidence in mother and father, pulls out all the stops. In the course of time, he tries out his power to disrupt, to destroy, to frighten, to wear down, to waste, to wangle, and to appropriate. Everything that takes people to the courts (or to the asylums for that matter) has its normal equivalent in childhood… If the parents can stand up to all the child can do to disrupt the parents' world, things will settle down."

Make sure your child isn't too compliant:
Parents are delighted when infants and children follow their rules and refer

to them as "good children". But Winnicott was very scared of so-called 'good' children.

The point of the early years was to be able to express freely a lot of 'bad' feelings without consequences, and without fear of retribution. However, there might be parents who could not tolerate too much bad behavior and would demand compliance too early and too strictly.

For Winnicott this would lead to the emergence of what he called a '**False Self**'. This is a persona that would be outwardly compliant, outwardly good, but was suppressing its vital instincts; who was not able to properly balance up its social with its destructive sides and that couldn't be capable of real generosity or love, because it hadn't been allowed fully to explore selfishness and hate.

Only through proper, attentive nurture would a child be able to generate a '**True Self**'.

Winnicott believed that adults who can't be creative, who are somehow a little dead inside, are almost always the children of parents who have not been able to tolerate defiance, parents who have made their offspring 'good' way before their time. By doing so they had destroyed their capacity to be properly good, properly generous and kind.

Let your child be:
For Winnicott, if the parents are too chaotic, the child quickly tries to over-think the situation. Its rational faculties are over-stimulated. A parent suffering from depression might unwittingly force the child to be too cheerful thus giving it no time to process its own melancholy feelings.

Winnicott saw the dangers in a child who, in his words, has to 'look after mother's mood'. He also had a special hatred for 'people who are always jogging babies up and down on their knees trying to produce a giggle.' This was merely their way of warding off their own sadness, by demanding laughter from a baby who might have very different things on its mind.

Realize the gravity of the job you've taken on:
Winnicott tried to bolster worn out parents by reminding them of the utmost importance of the job they were doing: "'The foundation of the health of the human being is laid by you in the baby's first weeks and months. This thought should help when you feel strange at the temporary loss of your interest in world affairs. It is not surprising. You are engaged in founding the mental health of the next generation.'

He called parenting: 'the only real basis for a healthy society, and the only factory for the democratic tendency in a country's social system.'

Winnicott appreciated that sometimes things will go wrong but that is why we have psychoanalysis. In later years, the analyst acts as a substitute parent, a proxy 'good enough' figure who 'is in a position of the mother of an infant'. But even the analyst shouldn't force a cure down his or her throat, she should provide a safe place where bits of childhood that weren't completed or went awry can be recreated and rehearsed. Analysis is a chance to fill in the missing steps.

When talking about what parents should do for their children Winnicott was actually talking about love. For him love was about the surrender of the ego, a putting aside of one's own needs and assumptions, for the sake of close, attentive listening to another, whose mystery one respects, along with a commitment not to get offended, not to retaliate, when something 'bad' emerges, as it often does when one is close to someone, child or adult.

Since Winnicott's death, we've collectively grown a little better at parenting. But only a little. We may spend more time with our children but are we failing at adaptation?

MARGARET MAHLER (1897-1985)

Separation-Individuation Theory
In Child Development

Margaret Mahler was a Hungarian physician and psychiatrist. She was a also central figure in the world of psychoanalysis. Her main interest was in normal childhood development.

But she spent much of her time with psychiatric children and how they arrive at the "self." She is best known for originating the Separation-Individuation theory of child development.

Margaret Schönberger was born on the 10 May, 1897, into a Jewish family in Sopron, a small town in the Kingdom of Hungary. Her parents were Gustav Schonberger and Eugenia Weiner-Schonberger. Margaret was born six days after they married. Her father was a busy general practitioner. He had a very active social life being the Chief Public Health Official of their district and the President of the Sopron Jewish Community. Her mother was only nineteen when she was born and resented the fact that she had married and borne a child so young. Four years later a second daughter, Suzanne, was born. Suzanne was clearly her mother's favorite and one day Margaret overheard her telling her youngest child: "I have brought you into this world, I suckle you, I love you, I adore you, I live only for you, you are my whole life."

Margaret was shattered and later believed that the way her mother treated her was the reason she developed such an interest in pediatrics and psychoanalysis. One of the happiest moments of Margaret's childhood was when Suzanne who was two, put her cheek to a hot iron and ruined her face. Her mother was extremely strict and needless to say Margaret endured an unhappy childhood.

Margaret's father encouraged her to excel in mathematics and other sciences. One day after Margaret complained she had no boyfriends her father told her that she didn't need a man and that she was man enough for herself. From that day on Margaret believed if she ever did marry she would have to be the dominant party in the relationship.

After completing the High School for Daughters, she attended Vaci Utcai Gimnazium in Budapest. After she met the famous psychoanalyst Sándor Ferenczi she became fascinated by the concept of the unconscious. In September 1916, she began Art History studies at the University of Budapest, but a year later switched to Medical School. Three semesters later she began medical training at the University of Munich. In 1920 she transferred to the University of Jena.

Here she began to realize how important play and love were for infants in order for them to grow up mentally and physically healthy. She graduated in 1922 and left for Vienna to get her license to practice medicine. There she turned from pediatrics to psychiatry and, in 1926, started her training analysis with Helene Deutsch. It took her seven years to finally be accepted as an analyst.

She loved working with children; it was her passion. She loved the way the children gave her their attention and showed their joy in cooperating with her.

In 1936 at the age of 39 she married Paul Mahler, a chemist with a Ph.D., and a junior partner of Viennese Cordial Factory. The firm eventually went broke. Paul was an only son and very needy. Margaret felt he was inferior and knew that she dominated the relationship. They were a perfect match. They moved first to Britain and then to America. After receiving a New York medical license, she set up in private practice.

In 1939 she met Benjamin Spock and, after giving a child analysis seminar in 1940, she became senior teacher of child analysis. She joined the Institute of Human Development, the Educational Institute and the *New York Psychoanalytic Society*. In 1948 she worked on clinical studies on Benign and Malignant Cases of Childhood Psychosis. She died on the 2 October, 1985.

In her theory of **Separation-Individuation** Mahler speculates that after the first few weeks of infancy, in which the infant is either sleeping or barely conscious, the infant progresses first from the **Normal-Symbiotic Phase** in which it perceives itself as one with its mother within the larger environment, to an extended **Separation-Individuation Phase**. This stage consists of several stages or sub-phases in which the infant slowly comes to distinguish itself from its mother, and then, by degrees, discovers its own identity, will, and individuality.

According to Mahler, the Normal Symbiotic Phase extends from the first signs of conscious awareness at four to six weeks until about five months of age. In this phase the infant is now aware of its mother, but has no sense of individuality of its own. The infant and mother are as one, and there is a barrier between them and the rest of the world.

In the Separation-Individuation phase the infant breaks out of its "autistic shell" and begins to connect with its environment and with the people in it. Separation refers to the development of limits and to the differentiation in the infant's mind between the infant and the mother. Individuation refers to the development of the infant's ego, sense of identity, and cognitive abilities.

The Separation-Individuation phase is divided into three sub-phases, which occur in the following order, but which often overlap in time:

1. Hatching (5 to 9 months):
The infant becomes aware of the differentiation between itself and its mother. It becomes increasingly aware of its surroundings and interested in them, using its mother as a point of reference or orientation;

2. Practicing (9 to 16 months):
The infant can now get about on its own, first crawling and then walking freely. The infant begins to explore actively and becomes more independent

of its mother. The infant still experiences itself as one with its mother.

3. **Rapprochement** (15 months and beyond):
The young child once again becomes close to his mother, but begins to differentiate itself from his mother. The child realizes that his physical mobility demonstrates psychic separateness from his mother. The child may become tentative at this point, wanting his mother to be in sight so that, through eye contact and action, he can explore his world. Mahler further divided Rapprochement into three sub-stages:

A. The Beginning:
The young child is motivated by a desire to share discoveries with his mother.

B. The Crisis:
The child is torn between staying connected with his mother and venturing out from his mother and becoming more independent and adventurous.

C. The Solution:
The child resolves the above Crisis according to the dictates of his own newly forming individuality, to his fledgling use of language, and to his interaction with the temperament of his mother. Mahler believed that disruptions in the fundamental process of separation-individuation could result later in life in a disturbance in the ability to maintain a reliable sense of individual identity.

Mahler's achievements are all the more extraordinary by reason of the fact that she was persecuted because of her religion and prejudiced because of her gender. Many of the contributions she made to the area of child development are still used today by doctors and parents.

WILFRED BION (1897-1979)

"Restricting ourselves to verbal intercourse won't get us far with a silent patient. What kind of psychoanalysis is needed to interpret the silence? The analyst may think there is a pattern to the silence. If he cannot respect the silence, there is no chance of making any further progress. The analyst can be silent and listen; stop talking so that he can have a chance to hear what is going on... Some silences are nothing, they are 0, zero. But sometimes that silence becomes a pregnant one; it turns into 101; the preceding and succeeding sounds

turn it into a valuable communication, as with rests and pauses in music, holes and gaps in sculpture"

Group Processes
Psychosis and Thinking
Psychoanalytical Theory on Art and Creativity

Wilfred Ruprecht Bion was an influential British psychoanalyst with unique ideas on psychoanalysis and possibly the greatest psychoanalytic thinker after Sigmund Freud.

He was president of the *British Psychoanalytical Society* from 1962 to 1965. He is best known for his work on group processes. But he was also a major contributor on psychosis and on thinking, as well as developing psychoanalytic theory on art and creativity.

Bion was born on the 8 September 1897 in Mathura, North-Western Provinces, India, and educated at Bishop's Stortford College in England. At the age of seventeen he joined the British Army Tank Regiment to fight in the First World War and was awarded the D.S.O.

In 1918 he was demobilized and was admitted to Oxford University where he read Modern History and became intrigued by the writings of Kant, Plato, Hume, and Poincaré. This philosophical input was to exert a powerful influence on his later metapsychological formulations.

In 1924 he went to study medicine at the University College Hospital in London and qualified in 1929. His contact with the distinguished surgeon, Wilfred Trotter, was to inspire his interest in groups and herd instincts. His preoccupation with psychology flourished and was strengthened by his association with the John Rickman, a prominent member of the *British Psychoanalytic Society*, who introduced him to Melanie Klein and suggested that he be analyzed by her.

His training as an analyst was interrupted by the Second World War. Here he worked on the rehabilitation of officers suffering from shell-shock and other nervous problems.

His thoughts on groups are outlined in his *Experiences in Groups* (1961) and shows the development of his ideas, from his pre-psychoanalytic days to his later involvement with Freudian and Kleinian thinking. In his Introduction he emphasizes that the psychoanalytic approach through the individual, and his own approach via the group, are dealing with 'different facets of the same phenomena'.

Bion states that the **observations** fall into two categories: The Oedipal situation which relates to what he called the "pairing" group; and The Sphinx situation which centers on the myth of the Sphinx, relating to the withholding and subsequent revealing of knowledge.

Bion also stresses the significance of the Kleinian theory of projective identification and the interplay between the paranoid-schizoid and depressive positions.

Utilizing the theories of Freud and Klein, Bion goes on to tackle the nature of groups. His aim was to offer new ways of bringing psychoanalytic theory to bear on issues outside the consulting room, to illuminate the wider social, political and cultural domain.

Bion believes that no individual, even in isolation, can be considered as marginal to a group or lacking the active manifestations of group psychology. This is so even when the conditions that demonstrate this do not appear to be present.

Freud's theories and in particular his Oedipus Complex shows how important the family group is in the development of every human being. Klein's theories, particularly her hypotheses about early object relations, psychotic anxieties and primitive defenses, allow us to understand that the individual does not only belong to a family group from the start of life, but also that his first contact with his mother and other significant persons from his circle, exert a profound influence over his subsequent emotional development.

The psychotic anxieties aroused in relation to the first objects are reactivated in various adult situations. The individual must establish contact with the emotional life of the group which poses a dilemma of evolution and differentiation with having to face the fears associated with change.

Bion went on to work with small groups of patients at the Tavistock Clinic in an effort to help clarify group tensions. Bion stressed the importance of the emotional reactions of the observer who is often made to experience certain forms of projective identifications, from the members of the group who wish to cast him in the role of say, teacher, consultant, or parental figure. Bion deals with this by refusing to take on these roles assigned to him by the group.

He describes the group's resulting exasperation, confusion and anger, as he objectively and impassively witnessed their behavior, noticing that there often followed a re-instatement of some willing - and usually authoritative - person who would be prepared to carry out the roles designated to him or her, depending on the 'basic assumption' of the group.

Bion shows us that by participating in groups, a person has different ways of reacting. Two kinds of tendency appear. The first is directed toward the accomplishment of the task awhile the other seems to oppose it. Work is obstructed by a more primary, regressive activity, characteristic of the id-function.

Bion introduces specific terms that describe these common features observed in various experiences. The most important are his concepts of basic assumptions, group mentality, and the idea of the work group.

By **basic assumptions** he means the existence of a common, unanimous and anonymous opinion at any given moment.

Group mentality is the container of all the contributions made by the members of the group. The concept of basic assumptions tells us something about the content of this opinion. It also allows greater insight into the emotional phenomena expressed in groups.

Bion identified **three basic assumptions:**

1. Dependency,

2. Fight-flight, and

3. Pairing.

Once a group adopts any one of these basic assumptions, it interferes with the task the group is attempting to accomplish.

In **dependency**, the essential aim of the group is to attain security through, and have its members protected by, one individual who is essentially the leader. Resentment at being dependent may result in the group dethroning the leader, and then searching for a new leader to repeat the process.

In the basic assumption of **fight-flight**, the group behaves as though it has met to preserve itself at all costs. This can only be achieved by running away from someone or fighting someone or something. In fight, the group may be characterized by aggressiveness and hostility; in flight, the group may small talk, tell stories, arrive late or any other activities that serve to avoid addressing the task at hand.

The leader for this sort of group is one who can mobilize the group for attack, or lead it in flight. The final basic assumption group, pairing, exists on the assumption that the group has met for the purpose of reproduction.

Two people, regardless the sex of either, carry out the work of the group through their continued interaction. The remaining group members listen eagerly and attentively with a sense of relief and hopeful anticipation.

But although Bion is better known for his work on groups, the inroads he made into the understanding of psychosis and the study of thinking have probably been the most profound contributions that he made to psychoanalysis.

The theories of Melanie Klein prospered in the 1950s as her ideas about psychotic anxieties and defenses were tested with severely ill patients who were mainly diagnosed schizophrenics. A further Kleinian goal was to see how far psychotic patients could be analyzed without changing the essentials of the psychoanalytic method. This analysis saw the emergence of new material and significant pioneers included Hanna Segal and Herbert Rosenfeld.

Bion, Segal and Rosenfeld all agreed on the viability of the psychoanalytic method in treating psychotics finding empirical evidence of Klein's views that the fixation point for schizophrenia was in the paranoid-schizoid position.

They also agreed with her ideas on projective identification, the early and persecuting super-ego, the pain of depressive anxiety, and the retreat from it using the manic defenses and ones relating to the paranoid-schizoid position.

Bion brought Klein's theories further and began to develop ideas about the differences between the normal and pathological experience of the paranoid-schizoid position.

This led him to a distinction between projective identification used to evacuate and fragment mental contents, and projective identification as a form of communication that could influence the recipient and could in turn be influenced by him.

His analysis of psychotic thinking and the role of the paranoid-schizoid position allowed him to create a theory of thinking and creativity that many consider is one of the most original we have today. Bion's theories eventually revealed radical departures from both Kleinian and Freudian theory. At one stage, he endeavored to understand thoughts and thinking from a mathematical and scientific point of view. He thought that there was too little precision in the existing vocabulary, and produced his own process called "The Grid". But this was later abandoned in favor of a more intuitive approach, epitomized in his work the *Memoir of the Future*. Although he left a reputation which has steadily grown, many commentators consider that his writings are often gnomic and irritating. But few disagree that they are always stimulating.

S.H.FOULKES (1898-1976)

Group Analysis
Group Analytic Society

Sigmund H. Foulkes was a German-British psychiatrist who developed a group theory for small groups alternate to the Wilfred Bion's ones which is the foundation of the Foulkesian group psychotherapy movement.

He was the founder of group analysis which is a particular type of group therapy. He also set up the *Group Analytic Society*, and the Institute of Group Analysis (IGA), London.

He was born Sigmund Heinrich Fuchs in Karlsruhe, Germany on the 3 September 1898. He was the youngest of five; four brothers and a sister. He himself was seven years younger than the one before him. His family were well to do Jews who had settled in Karlsruhe since 1870.

His father, Gustav Fuchs, was a timber merchant and importer and his mother, Sarah (Claire) Durlacher, a woman of great beauty, from a family of wine merchants. He lived in a huge house with his father's extended family. His grandmother had 18 children, 15 living and 13 of which were males. Foulkes was always surrounded by a large and loving family.

He studied medicine in Heidelberg and Frankfurt where he graduated in 1923. He then worked for two years and studied with the neurologist Kurt

Goldstein.

Between 1928-1930 he trained as a psychoanalyst in Vienna under Helene Deutsch. Later, he returned to Frankfurt and became director of the clinic of the newly formed *Institute of Psychoanalysis*. In 1933 he emigrated to England as a refugee with his wife Emma and three children.

Here he continued to work as a psychoanalyst and became a training analyst after obtaining a medical qualification. He changed his name to S.F. Foulkes and with the assistance of Ernest Jones became a member of the *British Psycho-Analytical Society*.

In 1939 he moved to Exeter where he became a psychotherapist in a large psychiatric practice. Here he conducted his first group-analytic psychotherapy. He then joined the army and was posted to the Military Neurosis Centre at Northfield in 1942 where he took part in developing a range of innovative treatments many of which were group based.

After the War, he resumed his psychoanalytic practice and he quickly started to conduct group analytic groups in his private practice. Later he worked at St Bartholomew's Hospital in London where he remained until his retirement in 1963. He continued his dual practice in individual psychoanalysis and group analysis until his retirement. However, he continued to work in private practice after his retirement

So, what is group analysis?

In a group, everyone and no-one is a therapist. In a group, analytic understanding the group is the therapist, which means that group analysis is a form of psychotherapy "by the group, of the group, including its conductor" (S. H. Foulkes).

While the primary psychological unit is the group, the primary biological unit is the individual. Foulkes described it in the following terms in his book group *Analytic Psychotherapy: Method an Principles*: "Group analytic psychotherapy is a method of group psychotherapy initiated by myself from 1940 onwards in private psychiatric practice and out-patient clinics…it is not a psychoanalysis of individuals within a group. Nor is it a psychological treatment of a group by a psychoanalyst. It is a form of psychotherapy by the group of the group including its conductor. The principles can be applied to all forms of human groups."

In a group analytic understanding, the individual is seen as a nodal point in a network of group relations. Psychopathology can be understood through an analysis of the conflictual group relations. Analyzing is the task of the group. Through analyzing, the group creates meaning. Under the specific conditions of a group analytic setting which follows well-defined rules, the group analytic attitude, slowly adopted by all group members, promotes the development of an intermediate space with clear boundaries.

Within these boundaries the group members, including the conductor, develop the ability to communicate and listen to each other. This is conducted in a non-judgmental, free-floating, non-directive and non-manipulative way providing for maximum freedom of expression.

Conflicts which develop in this dynamic network of group relations can then be understood as figures on the background of the unconscious transference and counter-transference processes. Transference and counter-transference form the link to the outside world.

Each patient brings his or her world into the group. Communication becomes the aim in such a free-floating process. As Foulkes says: "In learning to communicate, the group can be compared with a child learning to speak."

With this group analytic attitude the group conductor deviates from the regressive need of the group for a leader. Foulkes says that "The group shows a need for a leader in the image of an omnipotent, godlike father figure" so the main task of a group analytic conductor is in this context "to wean the group from this need for authoritative guidance..." The conductor has to become "free from (the) temptation to play this godlike role, to exploit it for his own needs." This is the basic group analytic attitude.

So, in what way is such a group process therapeutic?

Foulkes defined the healing effect of groups as follows: "The deepest reason why patients can reinforce each other's normal reactions and wear down and correct each other's neurotic reactions, is that collectively they constitute the very norm from which, individually, they deviate." Groups are brought together by the need to belong.

In order to make this cohesion very strong all differences within the group have to be denied at first. Another possibility is the fusion with an omnipotent leader and his or her ideology. Individuality is denied. The need to belong to a unified group, makes differences within the group unconscious, the so-called social unconscious of the group. Through the process of a free-floating association within the group an exchange between different views and experiences can start. This differentiation process goes along with a very painful and slow process of accepting the otherness of the other.

How does it work?

Usually there is a small circle of chairs and a table is placed in the center. The therapist is part of the circle, a "magic circle" at a distance at which the group will work best. There may be several types of communication nets within the circle, even if they are not formalized. These could be group centered, leader centered, isolation or links in a chain. The optimal size of a group is seven but there should be at least five including the therapist.

S. H. Foulkes died suddenly from a coronary thrombosis in 1976 at the age of 77, whilst conducting a seminar.

ERICH FROMM (1900-1980)

"Immature love says: 'I love you because I need you.'
Mature love says 'I need you because I love you.'"

Neo- Freudian Psychoanalysis
Escape from Freedom (1941) & The Art of Loving (1956)

Erich Fromm was a German psychoanalyst and sociologist who studied the effect of society on the human psyche in such works as *To Have or to Be* and *Escape from Freedom*.

He is widely regarded as one of the most important psychoanalysts of the twentieth century. Although influenced by Freud, Fromm later became part of a group known as the neo-Freudians which included Karen Horney and Carl Jung. He became critical of many of Freud's ideas including the Oedipus complex, the life and death instincts and the libido theory. Fromm believed that society and culture also played a significant role in individual human development.

Fromm also had a major influence on humanistic psychology. Fromm believed that life was a contradiction because we are all both part of nature and separate from it. He believed that certain basic existential needs arise from this conflict and identified those as relatedness, creativity, rootedness, identity and a frame of orientation.

Erich Seligmann Fromm was born on the 23 March, 1900, in Frankfurt am Main in Germany. He was the only child of Orthodox Jewish parents. His father was a wine merchant. He once described his own childhood as "highly neurotic." The fact that his mother suffered from depression and his father was characteristically temperamental prejudiced a happy childhood for Erich.

When World War One broke out in 1914, the young Fromm developed a strong interest in the behavior of groups and began searching for answers to his questions in the writings of Sigmund Freud and Karl Marx.

In 1918 he entered the University of Frankfurt am Main to study jurisprudence. As a young student Fromm became a rebel, forsaking his religion to become an atheist. He completely debunked religion as the basis of strife, discord and inequality and maintained that it spewed hatred.

He then attended the University of Heidelberg to study sociology under Alfred Weber, Karl Jaspers, and Heinrich Rickert. In 1922 he received his Ph.D. in sociology from Heidelberg and went on to train as a psychoanalyst in Frieda Reichmann's psychoanalytic sanatorium in Heidelberg.

In 1926, he married Freida who was ten years his senior. The marriage dissolved after four years. In 1927 he set up his own clinical practice and three years later joined the Frankfurt Institute for Social Research and completed his psychoanalytical training.

As the Nazi regime rose to power Fromm moved first to Switzerland and then to America where he attended Columbia University in New York. Here he met and became influenced by Karen Horney and Harry Stack Sullivan. They became part of a Neo-Freudian school of psychoanalytical thought.

In 1943 he helped form the New York branch of the Washington School of Psychiatry. The following year he married Henny Gurlandin and became a U.S. citizen. In 1946 co-founded the William Alanson White Institute of Psychiatry, Psychoanalysis, and Psychology.

In 1949 he emigrated to Mexico City in the hope of alleviating his second wife's illness. He established a psychoanalytical section in the medical school at the National Autonomous University of Mexico (UNAM). His second wife Henna died in 1952 and he re-married in 1953, this time to

Annis Freeman.

He also taught as a professor of psychology at Michigan State University from 1957 to 1961. After 1962 he was an adjunct professor of psychology at the graduate division of Arts and Sciences at New York University. He taught at UNAM until his retirement, in 1965, and at the Mexican Society of Psychoanalysis (SMP) until 1974. In 1974 he emigrated to Switzerland.

Much of Fromm's work was influenced by Sigmund Freud. But by the time he first arrived in America his principles began to clash with those of the American Freudians.

Fromm credited a person's psyche as the consequence of biology and as well as society. His predominant emphasis was on the consequences of consumerism on the consciousness of one's own individuality.

Fromm studied Freud in great detail and concluded that an inconsistency existed between Freud's initial theories before and after the First World War. Pre War Freud explains human urges as a struggle between needs and suppression. Post War Freud explains the same human urges as a tussle between Eros (Life instinct) and Thanatos (Death instinct).

According to Freud both these impulses merge and clash inside the individual. Eros signifies all the life affirming qualities like love, sexuality, imagination, pride, and progeneration. Thanatos on the other hand refers to the life denying negative impulses of violence, brutality, annihilation and death. Fromm identified this inconsistency and accused Freud and his supporters of failing to admit the inconsistencies in the two hypotheses.

He further evaluated Freud's twofold thinking. Fromm believed that the Freudian explanation of the human consciousness as conflicts of two extremes was confined and restricting.

He later denounced Freud as a misogynist who was bound by his inability to reason beyond the patriarchal norms of his time. Nevertheless Fromm held Freud and his achievements in great reverence because despite the numerous loopholes in his theories Fromm maintained that Freud together with people like Einstein and Marx were among the intellectual forerunners of the modern era.

Fromm's writings were noteworthy as much for their social and political commentary as for their philosophical and psychological underpinnings. His first seminal work *Escape from Freedom* (1941) is regarded as one of the founding works of political psychology. His second important work was *Man for Himself: An Inquiry into the Psychology of Ethics* (1947).

These books outlined Fromm's theory of human character. However, his most popular book was *The Art of Loving* (1956) which became an international bestseller, recapitulated and complemented the theoretical principles of human nature found in his earlier books but this time to a far greater audience.

The biblical story of **Adam and Eve** and their exile from the Garden of Eden is essentially the cornerstone of Fromm's humanistic philosophy. Fromm posited that being able to distinguish between good and evil is generally considered to be a virtue, and that biblical scholars consider Adam and Eve to have sinned by disobeying God and eating from the Tree of Knowledge.

Fromm departed from traditional religious orthodoxy on this point and instead extolled the virtues of humans taking independent action and using reason to establish moral values rather than adhering to authoritarian moral values.

He used the Adam and Eve story as an allegorical explanation for human biological evolution and existential angst. He argued that when Adam and Eve ate from the Tree of Knowledge, they became aware of themselves as being separate from nature while still being part of it. This is the reason why they felt "naked" and "ashamed". They had evolved into human beings, conscious of themselves, their own mortality, and their powerlessness before the forces of nature and society. They were no longer united with the universe as they were in their instinctive, pre-human existence as animals.

According to Fromm's theory, the awareness of a disunited human existence is a source of guilt and shame. Fromm believed that the solution to this existential dichotomy is found in the development of one's uniquely human powers of love and reason.

As regards **love**, Fromm considered it to be an interpersonal creative capacity rather than an emotion. He distinguished this creative capacity from what he considered to be various forms of narcissistic neuroses and sado-masochistic tendencies that are commonly held out as evidence of what we call "true love".

Fromm believed that the experience of "falling in love" was evidence of one's own inability to understand the true nature of love.

He held that true love involved respect, care, responsibility, and knowledge. He believed that qualities of care and responsibility are generally absent from most human relationships. He also asserted that few people in modern society had respect for the autonomy of their fellow human beings, much less the objective knowledge of what other people truly wanted and needed.

Fromm believed that embracing our **freedom of will** was healthy, whereas escaping freedom through the use of escape mechanisms was the root of psychological conflicts. He identified three common **escape mechanisms**.

Automaton Conformity:
This involves changing one's ideal self to conform to a perception of society's preferred type of personality. By doing this we tend to lose our true self in the process. This type of escape mechanism displaces the burden of choice from self to society.

Authoritarianism:
This happens when we give control of ourselves to another. By submitting our freedom to someone else, we remove the freedom of choice almost entirely

Destructiveness:
He identifies this as any process which attempts to eliminate others or the world as a whole, all to escape freedom. For him "the destruction of the world is the last, almost desperate attempt to save myself from being crushed by it".

Fromm often used the term **biophilia** which literally means "love of life or living systems." Fromm used it to describe a psychological orientation of being attracted to all that is alive and vital. The term was later popularized by Edward O. Wilson in his 1984 book of the same name. Wilson uses the term in the same sense when he suggests that biophilia describes "the connections that human beings subconsciously seek with the rest of life".

Fromm uses it as a description of a productive psychological orientation and "state of being" once writing "I believe that the man choosing progress can find a new unity through the development of all his human forces, which are produced in three orientations. These can be presented separately or together: biophilia, love for humanity and nature, and independence and freedom."

Fromm claimed that we all have **eight basic needs**: Relatedness; Transcendence; Rootedness; Sense of Identity; Frame of Orientation; Excitation and Stimulation; Unity; and Effectiveness.

1. Relatedness – Relationships with others, care, respect, knowledge.

2. Transcendence – Creativity, develop a loving and interesting life.

3. Rootedness – Feeling of belonging.

4. Sense of Identity – This is where we see ourselves as a unique person and part of a social group.

5. Frame of orientation – Understand the world and our place in it.

6. Excitation and Stimulation – Actively strive for a goal rather than simply respond.

7. Unity – A sense of oneness between one person and the "natural and human world outside."

8. Effectiveness – The need to feel accomplished.

Fromm's two most notable critics were Herbert Marcuse and Noam Chomsky. Marcuse claimed that in the beginning Fromm was a radical theorist, but in the end he was a conformist. He also claimed that Fromm in removing Freud's libido theory and other radical concepts reduced psychoanalysis to a set of idealist ethics, which only embrace the status quo. While Fromm accepted that Freud deserves substantial credit for recognizing the central importance of the unconscious, he argued that Freud tended to reify his own concepts that depicted the self as the passive outcome of instinct and social control, with minimal volition or variability.

Fromm argued that we should not accept these concepts as dogma and that social psychology requires a more dynamic theoretical and empirical approach. Meanwhile, Noam Chomsky while he liked Fromm' attitudes, thought his work was sometimes superficial. Fromm was undoubtedly one of the most creative yet controversial figures in the history of the psychoanalytic movement. He is one of the most intriguing and yet one of the least understood. His legacy is strewn with ironies.

In the 1940s and 1950s he was one of the most popular psychoanalytic writers. His landmark book *Escape from Freedom* helped raise the consciousness of many readers about the nature and origin of authoritarianism and submissiveness. Yet today Fromm's work is almost completely ignored.

Fromm was also one of the first analysts to expose the weakness of Freud's libido theory. As an alternative to Freud's instinctivist and physicalistic metapsychology, Fromm developed a view of human beings as primarily driven by their need to be related to the world and to others. He critiqued Freud's structural theory - id, ego, and superego - and moved toward a self psychology deeply rooted in the humanistic tradition. Going beyond Freud's dualistic drive theory he postulated a theory of existential needs that recognized the multimotivational nature of human experience.

Today, all these issues, which were once considered heretical are now at the center of some of the most promising developments in psychoanalysis. And yet, except for Greenberg and Mitchell (1983) Fromm almost never gets credited as the pioneer he was. Fromm believed that the concept of neutrality and the couch were often used by the analyst defensively. He advocated an empathic immersion in the patient's experience as a basis for real change. Nevertheless, he was at times considered by some who were in analysis with him as intimidating and overbearing. Fromm was not free from the dogmatic tendencies that he so effectively criticized.

Erich Seligmann Fromm died at his home in Muralto in Switzerland on the 18 March 1980.

MILTON ERICKSON (1901-1980)

"A goal without a date is just a dream"

Family Therapy
Medical Hypnosis

Milton Erickson was an American psychiatrist and psychologist who specialized in medical hypnosis and family therapy. He was founding president of the *American Society for Clinical Hypnosis*.

Erickson was also a fellow of the American Psychiatric Association, the

American Psychological Association, and the American Psychopathological Association. He has been described as an "unorthodox psychiatrist, congenial family doctor, ingenious strategic psychotherapist and master hypnotherapist." His influence has revolutionized Western psychotherapy. Thanks largely to Erickson the subject of hypnosis became respectable and is now widely recognized as one of the most powerful tools for change.

Milton Erickson was born on the 5 December 1901 into a poor farming community in Aurum, Nevada, America. He had seven sisters and one brother. He didn't speak until he was four. Only later did he find out he suffered from severe dyslexia. He was also tone deaf and color blind. At the age of seventeen, he was paralyzed for a year by a bout of polio which was so acute his doctor warned his parents he might die.

One night when his condition was at its worst he claimed he had an "autohypnotic lash of light experience" which changed his life. During his recovery at a time when he could hardly move and was unable to speak Erickson became aware of the power of non-verbal communication and how body language, tone of voice and the way that these non-verbal expressions often directly contradicted the verbal ones.

The young boy began to recall "body memories" of the muscular activity of his own body. By concentrating on these memories, he slowly began to regain control of parts of his body until he was eventually able to talk and use his arms. While still unable to walk, he decided to undertake on his own a thousand mile canoe trip following which he could walk assisted by a cane.

This experience influenced Erickson's technique of using "ordeals" in a therapeutic context. Realizing he would be no use on a farm he decided to become a doctor. He loved it so much he acquired a separate psychology degree while he was still studying medicine.

Later, while in his fifties, he contracted post-polio syndrome, leaving him even more paralyzed. But by this time he himself had developed a strategy for recovery. After this second recovery, he was confined to a wheelchair and suffered chronic pain which he controlled with self-hypnosis.

In the early 1950s, anthropologist Gregory Bateson involved Erickson as a consultant as part of his research on communication. It was through Bateson that Erickson met Richard Bandler, Jay Haley and John Grinder all of whom were so influenced by him that they wrote several books about Erickson.

In 1973, Jay Haley published *Uncommon Therapy*. This was the first time that Erickson's approaches and theories were introduced to those outside the clinical hypnosis community.

Six years later he and Ernest L. Rossi published *Hypnotherapy: An Exploratory Casebook, by Milton H. Erickson and Ernest L. Rossi.* Erickson developed an extensive use of therapeutic metaphor and story as well as hypnosis and coined the term **brief therapy** for his method of addressing therapeutic change in relatively few sessions. He was famous for his ability to "utilize" anything about a patient to help them change, including their beliefs, favorite words, cultural background, personal history, or even their neurotic habits. His techniques greatly influenced Virginia Satir.

Erickson believed the unconscious mind to be creative, solution-generating, and often positive, that it was always listening and that, whether or not the client was in a trance, suggestions could be made which would have a hypnotic influence. This was so long as those suggestions found resonance at the unconscious level.

Erickson would see if the client responded to one or another kind of indirect suggestion and allow the unconscious mind to participate actively in the therapeutic process. By doing this, what seemed like a normal conversation, might induce a hypnotic trance, or a therapeutic change in the subject.

Erickson even believed that it was appropriate for the therapist to go into trance. He maintained that going into a trance is a common, everyday occurrence and most of us do not consciously recognize these episodes as hypnotic phenomena. And because he expected trance states to occur naturally and frequently, he was prepared to exploit them therapeutically. He also discovered many verbal and non-verbal techniques for increasing the likelihood that a trance state would occur.

He acknowledged that there were many types of trance like deep or light which would suggest a one-dimensional continuum of trance depth, but Erickson would often work with multiple trances in the same client. He posited that there are multiple states that may be utilized.

Erickson's approach to hypnosis was unique in that it was permissive, accommodating and indirect. For example, where a classical hypnotist might say "You are now entering a deep trance", an Ericksonian hypnotist would be more likely to say "you can comfortably learn how to go into a trance".

In this way, he provides an opportunity for the subject to accept the suggestions they are most comfortable with, at their own pace, and with an awareness of the benefits. The subject knows they are not being pressurized. They are in control and willingly take part in their transformation. Ericksonian hypnosis is often known as **Covert Hypnosis** or **Conversational Hypnosis** because the induction takes place during the course of a normal conversation.

Erickson believed that it was not possible consciously to instruct the unconscious mind which he maintained responds to openings, opportunities, metaphors, symbols, and contradictions. Effective hypnotic suggestion, then, should be "artfully vague", leaving space for the subject to fill in the gaps with their own unconscious understandings.

A trained hypnotherapist would construct these gaps of meaning in a way most suited to the individual subject. Rather than saying "You will stop smoking" they might say "You can become a non-smoker". The first is a direct command, to be obeyed or ignored while the second is an opening, an invitation to possible lasting change, without pressure, and is less likely to raise resistance.

Richard Bandler and John Grinder said that type of "artful vagueness" was a central characteristic of their 'Milton Model', a systematic attempt to codify Erickson's hypnotic language patterns.

Erickson wrote extensively about **confusion**. A confused person has their conscious mind busy and occupied and is in a trance of their own making. Accordingly, they are more likely to enter trance without resistance. Confusion might also be created. This can be achieved by the use of ambiguous words, complex or endless sentences, pattern interruption or a myriad of other techniques.

Although James Braid, the Scottish surgeon who coined the term "hypnotism", claimed that focused attention was essential for creating hypnotic trances it can sometimes be difficult for clients suffering from acute pain, fear or suspicion to focus on anything at all.

Accordingly Erickson suggested other techniques for inducing trance: "... long and frequent use of the confusion technique has many times effected exceedingly rapid hypnotic inductions under unfavorable conditions such as acute pain of terminal malignant disease and in persons interested but hostile, aggressive, and resistant..."

Among Erickson's most famous innovations is the **hypnotic handshake induction**. This is a type of confusion technique. The hypnotist begins to shake hands with the subject, but then interrupts the flow of the handshake in some way. Sometimes this is done by grabbing the subject's wrist instead. If the handshake continues to develop in a way which is out-of-keeping with expectations, a simple, non-verbal trance is created. This may then be reinforced or utilized by the hypnotist. All these responses happen naturally and automatically without telling the subject to consciously focus on an idea.

This induction works because shaking hands is one of the actions learned and operated as a single "chunk" of behavior. If the behavior is diverted or frozen midway, the subject literally has no mental space for this. He is stopped in the middle of unconsciously executing a behavior that hasn't got a "middle" part.

The mind responds to this by suspending itself in trance until either something happens to give a new direction, or it "snaps out". A trained hypnotist is able to use that momentary confusion and suspension of normal processes to induce trance quickly and easily. Richard Bandler was a keen proponent of the handshake induction, and developed his own variant, which is commonly taught in NLP workshops.

Erickson was aware that many of us are intimidated by hypnosis and the therapeutic process. So he allowed for the resistance of the individual patient. In the therapeutic process he said that "you always give the patient every opportunity to resist". Here are some more relevant quotes pertaining to resistance. Erickson believed that often the apparently active resistance encountered in subjects is no more than an unconscious measure of testing the hypnotist's willingness to meet them halfway instead of trying to force them to act entirely in accord with his ideas.

Although Erickson is most famous as a hypnotherapist he also developed effective **therapeutic techniques**, many of which are not explicitly hypnotic, but are extensions of hypnotic strategies and language patterns. Erickson recognized that resistance to trance resembles resistance to change, and developed his therapeutic approach with that awareness. Jay Haley identified several strategies.

Encouraging Resistance:
Erickson believed that the classic therapeutic request to "tell me everything

about..." was both aggressive and disrespectful. Instead, Erickson would actually ask the resistant patient to withhold information and only to tell what they were really ready to reveal.

He recorded his approach as follows: "There are a number of things that you don't want me to know about, that you don't want to tell me. There are a lot of things about yourself that you don't want to discuss, therefore let's discuss those that you are willing to discuss." This puts no pressure on the subject and as they have come to discuss things they will mention everything when they are ready to.

Communicating by Metaphor:

A prime example is provided by David Gordon in his book *Phoenix* (1981): "I was returning from high school one day and a runaway horse with a bridle on sped past a group of us into a farmer's yard looking for a drink of water. The horse was perspiring heavily. And the farmer didn't recognize it so we cornered it. I hopped on the horse's back. Since it had a bridle on, I took hold of the tick rein and said, "Giddy-up."

Headed for the highway, I knew the horse would turn in the right direction. I didn't know what the right direction was. And the horse trotted and galloped along. Now and then he would forget he was on the highway and start into a field. So I would pull on him a bit and call his attention to the fact the highway was where he was supposed to be. And finally, about four miles from where I had boarded him, he turned into a farm yard and the farmer said, "So that's how that critter came back. Where did you find him?" I said, "About four miles from here." "How did you know you should come here?" I said, "I didn't know. The horse knew. All I did was keep his attention on the road."

Encouraging a Relapse:

Sometimes Erickson would arrange for his patients to fail in their attempts to improve, for example by overreaching. Although failure is part of life, in that fragile time where the patient is learning to live, think and behave differently, a random failure can be catastrophic. But Erickson believed that by deliberately causing a relapse he could control the variables of that failure, and to cast it in a positive therapeutic light for the patient.

Encouraging a Response by Frustrating It:

This paradoxical approach is designed to act directly on the patient's own resistance to change. An obese patient might be asked to gain weight. A stubbornly silent family member in a family therapy might be deliberately ignored until the frustration obliges them to blurt out some desperate truth.

Once again, this approach has its roots in Erickson's hypnotic language patterns of the form "I don't want you to go into a trance yet".

Utilizing Space and Position:
The physical position or even the posture of the patient can play a significant part of the subjective experience. Manipulating these factors can contribute to a therapeutic transformation.

As Erickson put it: "If I send someone out of the room - for example, the mother and child, I carefully move the father from his chair and put him into mother's chair. Or if I send the child out, I might put mother in the child's chair, at least temporarily. Sometimes I comment on this by saying, "As you sit where your son was sitting, you can think more clearly about him." Or, "If you sit where your husband sat, maybe it will give you somewhat of his view about me".

Over a series of interviews with an entire family, I shuffle them about, so that what was originally mother's chair is now where father is sitting." This is something similar to Fritz Perls' use of an "empty chair" where the client was often invited to occupy the chair and thus take on the role of the person imagined to be sitting there.

Emphasizing the Positive:
Erickson claimed that his sensory "disabilities" of dyslexia, color blindness, and being tone-deaf helped him to focus on aspects of communication and behavior which most other people overlooked. He would often compliment the patient for a symptom, and would even encourage it, in very specific ways. "Emphasizing the positive" is similar to the concept of "positive reformulation" in Gestalt Therapy.

Prescribing the Symptom and Amplifying a Deviation:
Erickson would often instruct his patients to actively and consciously perform the symptom that was bothering them usually with some minor deviation. In many cases, the deviation could be extenuated and used as a "wedge" to transform the entire behavior.

Seeding Ideas:
Sometimes Erickson would see to it that his patients are exposed to an idea, often in a metaphorical form before using it for a therapeutic purpose. He referred to this as "seeding ideas".

In the example: "Have you ever been in a trance before?" he seeds the idea that a trance is imminent. The presupposition inherent in the word before is "not now, but later".

Avoiding Self-Exploration:
As with most brief therapy practitioners, Erickson was entirely uninterested in analyzing the patient's early psychological development. Sometimes he would discuss the patient's background, but only as much as it pertained to the resources available to the patient in the present.

An example of Erickson's innovative and masterly style can be seen in the following exchange from which we can all learn a lot:

INTERVIEWER: You don't feel that exploring the past is particularly relevant? I'm always trying to get clear in my mind how much of the past I need to consider when doing brief therapy.

ERICKSON: You know, I had one patient this last July who had four or five years of psychoanalysis and got nowhere with it. And someone who knows her said, "How much attention did you give to the past?" I said, "You know, I completely forgot about that."

That patient is, I think, a reasonably cured person. It was a severe washing compulsion, as much as twenty hours a day. I didn't go in to the cause or the etiology; the only searching question I asked was "When you get in the shower to scrub yourself for hours, tell me, do you start at the top of your head, or the soles of your feet, or in the middle? Do you wash from the neck down, or do you start with your feet and wash up? Or do you start with your head and wash down?"

INTERVIEWER: Why did you ask that?

ERICKSON: So that she knew I was really interested.

INTERVIEWER: So that you could join her in this?

ERICKSON: No, so that she knew I was really interested.

Like most controversial, innovative geniuses, Erickson was not without his critics. Some of his central presuppositions have been questioned by other researchers and the vagueness of his explanations have led to a variety of competing interpretations of his approach.

André Weitzenhoffer, publicly criticized Erickson's approach in favor of what he calls the semi-traditional, scientific, approach. Jeffrey Masson questioned the accuracy of Erickson's case reports and was concerned that in some cases Erickson had sometimes acted in a sexually inappropriate manner while engaged in counselling.

Milton Erickson died on the 25 March 1980, leaving four sons, four daughters, and love him or hate him, a lasting legacy to the worlds of hypnotherapy, psychology, psychiatry, psychotherapy, and communications. He is a huge influence in the world of psychology.

CARL ROGERS (1902-1987)

"When I look at the world I'm pessimistic,
but when I look at people I am optimistic."

Client Centered Therapy

Carl Rogers was an American psychologist who was one of founders of the client-centered approach to psychology. He is is regarded by many as the most influential psychologist of the twentieth century.

He is also considered to be one of the founding fathers of psychotherapy research and his person-centered approach is widely used in psychotherapy and counseling (client-centered therapy) and in education (student-centered learning).

Rogers is known for practicing "unconditional positive regard," which is defined as accepting a person without negative judgment of a person's basic worth. In this approach, the therapist's goal is to offer unconditional positive regard to the client. The goal is that the individual will be able to grow emotionally and psychologically and eventually become a fully-functioning person. He was born on the 8 January, 1902, in Oak Park, Chicago, Illinois to Walter A. Rogers and Julia M. Cushing. He was the fourth of six children. His father was a civil engineer and his mother a homemaker and devout Pentecostal Christian.

An intelligent child Carl could read well before he even entered kindergarten. As a child he was strictly religious, independent and insular. He attended the University of Wisconsin–Madison, where he studied agriculture, history and religion. Following a trip to China when he was twenty he began to doubt his religious convictions.

In 1924, he graduated from University of Wisconsin and enrolled at Union Theological Seminary. After two years he left to attend Teachers College, Columbia University in New York. He qualified from Teachers with an M.A. in 1938 and a Ph.D. in 1931.

From 1935-1940 he lectured at the University of Rochester. In 1939 he published *The Clinical Treatment of the Problem Child*, based on his experience in working with troubled children. He was strongly influenced in constructing his client-centered approach by the post-Freudian psychotherapeutic practice of Otto Rank.

In 1940 he became professor of clinical psychology at Ohio State University. In 1942 he published his second book, *Counseling and Psychotherapy*, in which he suggested that the client has the power to resolve their own difficulties and gain the insight necessary to restructure their life providing they have established a sound relationship with an accepting therapist. In 1945, he set up a counseling center at the University of Chicago and two years later was elected President of the American Psychological Association.

In 1956, he became the first President of the American Academy of Psychotherapists. Between 1957-1963 he taught psychology at the University of Wisconsin, Madison.

In 1961, he published his best selling book, *On Becoming a Person*. In the same year he was elected a Fellow of the American Academy of Arts and Sciences. In 1963 he became a resident at the new Western Behavioral Sciences Institute (WBSI) in La Jolla. In 1968 he left the WBSI to help found the Center for Studies of the Person. He remained a resident of La Jolla for the rest of his life until his sudden death in 1987.

Rogers was a humanistic psychologist. While he agreed with the main assumptions in the theories put forward by Abraham Maslow, Rogers went further and added that for a person to "grow", they need an environment that provides them with genuineness, acceptance and empathy.

By genuineness he meant openness and self-disclosure; by acceptance he meant being seen with unconditional positive regard; and by empathy he meant being listened to and understood. These three factors are essential in order that relationships and healthy personalities will develop as they should. Rogers believed that every person can achieve their goals, wishes and desires in life. When, or rather if they did so, self actualization took place. For a person to reach their potential a number of factors must be satisfied.

Rogers' humanistic theory of the self is based directly on the "phenomenal field" personality theory of Combs and Snygg (1949). But Rogers extensively elaborated his own theory in his sixteen books. As of 1951 **Roger's theory involved nineteen propositions** which he set out as follows:

1. All individuals or organisms exist in a continually changing world of experience i.e. the phenomenal field, of which they are the center.

2. The organism reacts to the field as it is experienced and perceived. This perceptual field constitutes "reality" for the individual.

3. The organism reacts as an organized whole to this phenomenal field.

4. A part of the total perceptual field gradually becomes differentiated as the self.

5. Because of interaction with the environment and as a result of evaluational interaction with others, the structure of the self is formed. That "self" is an organized, fluid but consistent conceptual pattern of perceptions of characteristics and relationships of the "I" or the "me", together with values attached to these concepts.

6. The organism has one basic tendency and striving which is to actualize, maintain and enhance the experiencing organism.

7. The best vantage point for understanding behavior is from the internal frame of reference of the individual.

8. Behavior is basically the goal-directed attempt of the organism to satisfy its needs as experienced, in the field as perceived.

9. Emotion accompanies, and in general facilitates, such goal directed behavior, the kind of emotion being related to the perceived significance of the behavior for the maintenance and enhancement of the organism.

10. The values attached to experiences, and the values that are a part of the self-structure, in some instances, are values experienced directly by the organism. Sometimes the values are introjected or taken over from others, but perceived in distorted fashion, as if they had been experienced directly.

11. The experiences that occur in our life are either,
(a) symbolized, perceived and organized into some relation to the self;
(b) ignored because there is no perceived relationship to the self structure; or,
(c) denied symbolization or given distorted symbolization because the experience is inconsistent with the structure of the self.

12. Most of the ways of behaving that are adopted by the organism are those that are consistent with the concept of self.

13. Sometimes behavior may occur because of organic experiences and needs which have not been symbolized. This kind of behavior may be inconsistent with the structure of the self but where it is the behavior is not "owned" by the individual.

14. Psychological adjustment exists when the concept of the self is such that all the sensory and visceral experiences of the organism are, or may be, assimilated on a symbolic level into a consistent relationship with the concept of self.

15. Psychological maladjustment will occur where the organism denies awareness of significant sensory and visceral experiences, which consequently are not symbolized and organized into the gestalt of the self structure. Basic or potential psychological tension will result when this happens.

16. Any experience which is inconsistent with the organization of the structure of the self may be perceived as a threat, and the more of these perceptions there are, the more rigidly the self structure is organized to maintain itself.

17. Under certain conditions, involving primarily complete absence of threat to the self structure, experiences which are inconsistent with it may be perceived and examined, and the structure of self revised to assimilate and include such experiences.

18. When the individual perceives and accepts into one consistent and integrated system all his sensory and visceral experiences, then he is necessarily more understanding of others and is more accepting of others as separate individuals.

19. As the individual perceives and accepts into his self structure more of

his organic experiences, he finds that he is replacing his present value system which is based extensively on introjections which have been distortedly symbolized, with a continuing organismic valuing process.

Rogers believed that every person can achieve their goals wishes, and desires in life. When they did so self-actualization took place. For Rogers those of us who are able be self-actualize are called **fully functioning persons.**

This means that the person is in touch with the here and now. They are aware of their subjective experiences and feelings. They are continually growing and changing. Rogers said it was wrong to think of this as an end or completion of life's journey. Rather he saw it a process of always becoming and changing. Rogers identified various characteristics of the fully functioning person:

1. A growing opening to experience:
Both positive and negative emotions are accepted. Negative feelings are not denied, but worked through (rather than resort to ego defense mechanisms). They move away from defensiveness and have no need for subception. He called subception a perceptual defense that involves unconsciously applying strategies to prevent a troubling stimulus from entering consciousness.

2. An existential lifestyle:
Living each moment fully and being in touch with different experiences as they occur in life, avoiding prejudging and preconceptions. Being able to live and fully appreciate the present, not always looking back to the past or forward to the future. This will bring excitement, daring, adaptability, tolerance, spontaneity, and a lack of rigidity and suggests a foundation of trust.

3. Fully functioning people trust their own judgment and their ability to choose behavior that is appropriate for each moment:
They do not rely on existing codes and social norms but trust that as they are open to experiences they will be able to trust their own sense of right and wrong.

4. Creativity:
They will feel more free to be creative. They will also be more creative in the way they adapt to their own circumstances without feeling a need to conform. They do not play safe all the time. This involves the ability to adjust and change and seek new experiences.

5. Freedom of choice:
They are not restrained by the restrictions that influence an incongruent individual. They can make a wider range of choices more fluently. They believe that they play a role in determining their own behavior and so feel responsible for their own behavior.

6. Reliability and constructiveness:
They can be trusted to act constructively. An individual who is open to all their needs will be able to maintain a balance between them.

7. Rich and full life:
A fully functioning person enjoys a rich, full and exciting life. Rogers suggests that they experience joy and pain, love and heartbreak, fear and courage more intensely.

Rogers believed that a fully functioning person is one who is in touch with his or her deepest and innermost feelings and desires. They understand their own emotions and place a deep trust in their own instincts and urges.

Unconditional positive regard plays an essential role in becoming a fully functioning person. He suggests that people have an actualizing tendency, or a need to achieve their full potential which he refers to as **self-actualization.**

A fully-functioning person is continually working toward becoming self-actualized. This individual has received unconditional positive regard from others, does not place conditions on his or her own worth, is capable of expressing feelings, and is fully open to life's many experiences.

For Rogers, humans have one basic motive which is the tendency to self-actualize by which he meant to fulfill one's potential and achieve the highest level of 'human-beingness' we can. He compared it to a flower that will grow to its full potential but only if the conditions are right. But unlike the flower the potential of the individual human is unique, and we are meant to develop in different ways according to our personality.

Rogers believed that people are inherently good and creative. They only become destructive when a poor self-concept or external constraints override the valuing process. He believed that in order for a person to achieve self-actualization they must be in a **state of congruence**.

Self-actualization occurs when a person's "ideal self" that is the person they would like to be, is congruent with their actual behavior (i.e. their self-image). The notion of "self" or "self-concept", which Rogers describes as "the organized, consistent set of perceptions and beliefs about oneself" is central to Rogers' personality theory.

The "self" is the humanistic term for who we really are as a person. It is our inner personality, something like our soul, or what Freud would call the psyche. The self is influenced by the experiences a person has in their life, and our interpretations of those experiences. Two primary sources that influence our self-concept are childhood experiences and evaluation by others. Rogers says that we want to feel, experience and behave in ways which are consistent with our self-image and which reflect what we would like to be like, our ideal-self. The closer our self-image and ideal-self are to each other, the more consistent or congruent we are and the higher our sense of self-worth.

A person is said to be in a state of incongruence if some of the totality of their experience is unacceptable to them and is denied or distorted in the self-image.

The self-concept includes three components:

1. Self worth which is the same as self-esteem: what we think about ourselves. Rogers believed feelings of self-worth developed in early childhood and were formed from the interaction of the child with the mother and father.

2. Self-image: How we see ourselves, which is important to good psychological health. Self-image includes the influence of our body image on inner personality. Self-image has an affect on how a person thinks feels and behaves in the world.

3. Ideal self: This is the person who we would like to be. It consists of our goals and ambitions in life. It is always changing as, for example, the ideal self as a teenager is unlikely to be the ideal self as an adult.

Self-worth may be seen as a continuum from very high to very low. A person who has high self-worth is one who faces challenges in life, accepts failure and unhappiness at times, and is open with people. A person with low self-worth may avoid challenges in life, not accept that life can be painful and unhappy at times, and will be defensive and guarded with other people.

Rogers believes that it is important for us to be regarded positively by others. We need to feel valued, respected, treated with affection and loved. Positive regard is to do with how other people evaluate and judge us in social interaction. Rogers made a distinction between **unconditional positive regard** and **conditional positive regard.**

Unconditional positive regard:

This is where parents, significant others and the humanist therapist accepts and loves the person for what he or she is. Positive regard is not withdrawn if the person does something wrong or makes a mistake.

The consequences of unconditional positive regard are that the person feels free to try things out and make mistakes, even though this may lead to getting it worse at times. Those who are able to self-actualize are more likely to have received unconditional positive regard from others, especially their parents in childhood.

Conditional positive regard:

This is where positive regard, praise and approval, depend upon us behaving in ways that others think correct. Hence we are not loved for the person we are, but only on condition that we behave in ways approved by others.

At the extreme, a person who constantly seeks approval from other people is likely only to have experienced conditional positive regard as a child. This is where Rogers introduces the concept of congruence.

Where a person's ideal self and actual experience are consistent or very similar, then a state of congruence exists. But a total state of congruence is rare. Usually we experience a certain amount of incongruence which occurs when our ideal self and actual experience are different. The closer our self-image and ideal-self are to each other, the more consistent or congruent we are and the higher our sense of self-worth.

Rogers also developed learner-centered teaching. He described his approach to education in Client-Centered Therapy and wrote *Freedom to Learn* devoted exclusively to the subject in 1969. Revised twice the new Learner-Centered Model is similar in many regards to this classical person-centered approach to education. Rogers developed the following five hypotheses regarding learner-centered education:

1. He believed that a person cannot teach another person directly; a person can only facilitate another's learning. This is because we all exist in a

constantly changing world of experience in which we are the center. Each person reacts and responds based on perception and experience. The belief is that what the student does is more important than what the teacher does.

The focus is on the student. Therefore, the background and experiences of the learner are essential to how and what is learned. Each student will process what he or she learns differently depending on what he or she brings to the classroom.

2. Rogers thought that a person learns significantly only those things that are perceived as being involved in the maintenance of or enhancement of the structure of self. Therefore, relevancy to the student is essential for learning. The students' experiences become the core of the course.

3. In 1951 Rogers wrote "Experience which, if assimilated, would involve a change in the organization of self, tends to be resisted through denial or distortion of symbolism".

If the content or presentation of a course is inconsistent with preconceived information, the student will learn if he or she is open to varying concepts. Being open to consider concepts that vary from one's own is vital to learning. Therefore, gently encouraging open-mindedness is helpful in engaging the student in learning. Also, it is important, for this reason, that new information be relevant and related to existing experience.

4. "The structure and organization of self appears to become more rigid under threats and to relax its boundaries when completely free from threat". If students believe that concepts are being forced upon them, they might become uncomfortable and fearful. Threats contain barriers.

Accordingly, an open, friendly environment in which trust is developed is essential in the classroom. Fear of retribution for not agreeing with a concept should be eliminated. A class taught with support will help alleviate fear which in turn will encourage students to learn.

5. "The educational situation which most effectively promotes significant learning is one in which (a) threat to the self of the learner is reduced to a minimum and (b) differentiated perception of the field is facilitated"

The teacher should be open to learning from the students and also working to connect the students to the subject matter. Frequent interaction with the students will help achieve this goal. The teacher should be a mentor who guides rather than the expert who tells. This is instrumental to student-centered, nonthreatening, and unforced learning.

How does client-centered therapy work?

Rogers originally called his system of therapy "non-directive therapy" but later replaced the term "non-directive" with the term "client-centered". Later he changed the term client-centered to person-centered because even before the publication of his system of therapy in 1951 Rogers believed that the principles of his therapy could be applied in a variety of contexts and not just in the therapy situation.

As a result he started to use the term person-centered approach to describe his overall theory. Person-centered therapy is the application of the person-centered approach to the therapy situation. Other applications include a theory of personality, interpersonal relations, education, nursing, cross-cultural relations and other "helping" professions and situations.

Rogers' therapy was an extension of his theory of personality development. It was known as client-centered therapy because the basis of the therapy was designed around the client. According to Rogers each of us has within us the inherent tendency to continue to grow and develop. As a result of this our self-esteem and self-actualization continues to be influenced throughout our lives.

But, this development can only be achieved through what he calls "unconditional positive regard." In order for a client to experience total self-actualization the therapist must express complete acceptance of the patient. He found that this was best achieved through the method of "reflection". This is where the therapist continually restates what the client has said.

The purpose of this is to show complete acceptance and to allow the patient to recognize any negative feelings that they may be experiencing. While the therapist may make small interruptive remarks in order to help identify certain factors, generally the client is allowed to direct the course of the session.

Rogers began to use the expression "client" instead of "patient" because while those he was counselling needed help there were not medically ill. Today in the field of psychology it is universally accepted that those being counselled should be called clients and not patients.

As time passed Rogers' theory began to be known as "people-centered" due to its expansion beyond psychotherapy to such areas as education, marriage, leadership, parent-child relationships, and the development of professional standards.

There are several basic elements that apply to each of these which could be stated in the following terms:

1. The client comes for help. This is the most significant step within the steps of therapy. They have taken it upon themselves to take the first step for help even if they don't recognize this as the reason they're there.

2. The helping situation is defined. The client is made aware that with assistance the client can work out their own solutions to their problems.

3. The therapist encourages free expression of feelings providing the client with a friendly, interested, and receptive attitude which helps to bring about free expression.

4. The therapist accepts, recognizes, and clarifies any negative feelings. Whatever the negative feelings are the therapist must say and do things which helps the client recognize the negative feelings at hand.

5. When the therapist's negative feelings have been expressed they are followed by expressions of positive impulses which make for growth.

6. The therapist accepts and recognizes the positive feelings in the same manner as the negative feelings.

7. There is insight, understanding of the self, and acceptance of the self along with possible courses of actions. This is the next important aspect because it allows for new levels.

8. Then comes the step of positive action along with decreasing the need for help.

Rogers' enduring legacy is that today the vast majority of all therapists are "Rogerian" in style, irrespective of their clinical or theoretical orientation. This is because most therapists subscribe, at least in part, to the holy trinity of Rogers's psychotherapeutic method:

1. "Unconditional positive regard" or full acceptance by the therapist of clients as they are;

2. A complete empathic understanding of clients which is clearly communicated to them; and

3. "Congruence," or being authentic, genuine, and transparently "real" with their clients.

Of course, strictly speaking this holy trinity was not invented by Rogers but he was probably the first psychologist to put them all together in a single package.

Rogers rejected the determinism of Freudian psychoanalysis and Skinnerian behaviorism believing that the "self-actualized" or "fully functioning" person was by definition a subjectively free being.

He democratized psychotherapy itself. He accomplished this by deflating the delusions of grandeur held by some practitioners by merging the distinction between psychotherapist which was then usually applied only to psychiatrists and psychoanalysts, and counselor, a catch-all term including just about anybody who gave helpful advice.

Furthermore, he also democratized the relationship between therapist-counselor and client. He believed that clients themselves, not their therapists, knew best what was hurting them and what needed fixing. Their own inner knowledge just had to be gently coaxed out of them. They didn't need to have their words "interpreted" back to them.

Rogers believed that what clients needed was the undemanding presence of a compassionate, deeply attuned listener. They needed a therapist who didn't diagnose them or explain their problems to them or ask many specific questions. They needed someone who wasn't going to tell them what to do. Rogers's famous nondirective approach was "reflective listening."

Although he was not without his critics, his continuing influence has more than silenced them. Over the last twenty years, psychotherapy research has repeatedly demonstrated that the success of counseling and therapy depends less on any particular method than on the common factors shared by virtually all therapists which included support, empathic understanding, positive regard, genuineness, and the ability to establish a strong emotional bond with clients.

Furthermore, recent neuroscience research has established that the sense of attuned connection that the therapist forges with a client works in therapy because people are neurobiologically wired to respond positively to positive emotional signals from others.

The caring, responsive, attentive human presence endorsed by Rogers is the most powerful force for emotional healing that exists or ever will exist. That's why Carl Rogers is regarded as the world's most influential psychologist of the twentieth century.

B.F. SKINNER (1904-1990)

"A failure is not always a mistake, it may simply be the best one can do under the circumstances. The real mistake is to stop trying"

Behaviorism
The Skinner Box

Burrhus Frederic Skinner was an American psychologist, behaviorist, and social philosopher who invented the operant conditioning chamber, also known as the Skinner Box.

Skinner believed that human free will is actually an illusion and any human action is the result of the consequences of that same action. Developing the principle of reinforcement he said that if the consequences were bad, there was a high chance that the action would not be repeated; however if the consequences were good, the actions that led to it would be reinforced. He also developed his own philosophy of science called radical behaviorism and coined the term operant conditioning. Along with John B. Watson and Ivan Pavlov he is considered a pioneer of modern behaviorism.

He was born on the 20 March 1904 in Susquehanna, Pennsylvania, America to William and Grace Skinner. His father was a lawyer. His younger brother Edward, died at sixteen from a cerebral hemorrhage. Initially, he wanted to become a writer and attended Hamilton College in New York. He later attended Harvard University after receiving his B.A. in English literature in 1926. It was at Harvard that he invented his prototype for the Skinner Box.

Following his graduation he unsuccessfully tried to write a great novel while he lived with his parents, which he later called the Dark Years. But it was his encounter with John B. Watson's Behaviorism which led him into graduate study in psychology and to the development of his own operant behaviorism.

In 1931 he received a Ph.D. from Harvard and remained there as a researcher until 1936. He then taught at the University of Minnesota at Minneapolis and later at Indiana University, before returning to Harvard as a tenured professor in 1948. He remained at Harvard for the rest of his life. In 1936, Skinner married Yvonne Blue. The couple had two daughters, Julie and Deborah. He died of leukemia on the 18 August, 1990.

Skinner believed that while we do have such a thing as a mind, it is simply more productive to study observable behavior rather than internal mental events. He believed that the best way to understand behavior is to look at the causes of an action and the consequences of that action, an approach he called operant conditioning. Operant conditioning was based on the work of Edward Thorndike who studied learning in animals using a puzzle box to propose the theory known as the "Law of Effect".

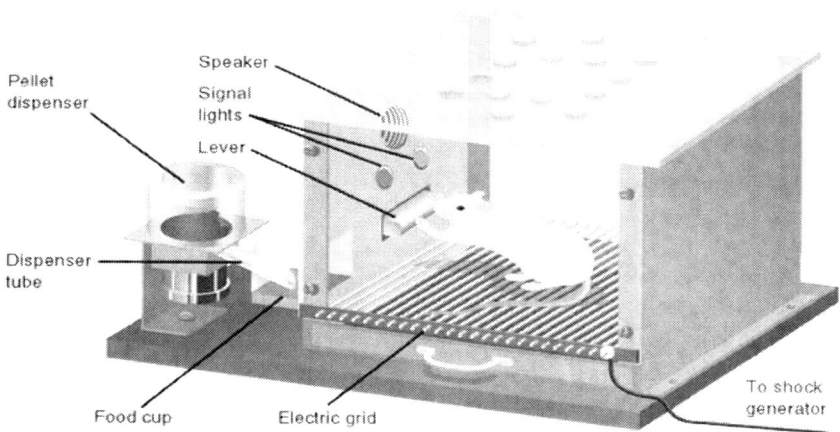

Although he is regarded as the father of Operant Conditioning, Skinner borrowed extensively from Thorndike's law of effect.

Skinner introduced a new term into the Law of Effect which he called **Reinforcement**. Behavior which is reinforced tends to be repeated, that is, strengthened; behavior which is not reinforced tends to die out-or be extinguished, that is weakened. Skinner studied operant conditioning by conducting experiments using animals which he placed in a **Skinner Box** a construction which was very like Thorndike's puzzle box

What does the term **operant conditioning** actually mean?

It can be translated as changing behavior by the use of reinforcement which is given after the desired response. Skinner identified three types of responses or operant that can follow behavior.

1. Neutral operants:
These are responses from the environment that neither increase nor decrease the probability of a behavior being repeated.

2. Reinforcers:
These are responses from the environment that increase the probability of a behavior being repeated. Reinforcers can be either positive or negative. Skinner showed how positive reinforcement worked by placing a hungry rat in his Skinner box.

The box contained a lever in the side and as the rat moved about the box it would accidentally knock the lever. Immediately it did so a food pellet would drop into a container next to the lever. The rats soon learned to head straight to the lever after a few times of being put in the box.

The consequence of receiving food if they pressed the lever ensured that they would repeat the action again and again. Positive reinforcement strengthens a behavior by providing a consequence an individual finds rewarding.

For example, if your mother gives you $20 as a reward each time you clean your room you are more likely to repeat this behavior in the future, thus strengthening the behavior of cleaning the room.

The removal of an unpleasant reinforcer can also strengthen behavior. This is known as negative reinforcement because it is the removal of an adverse stimulus which is 'rewarding' to the animal.

Negative reinforcement strengthens behavior because it stops or removes an unpleasant experience. For example, if you do not clean your room and $20 is deducted from your weekly allowance the chances are you will clean it so as to avoid paying the fine, thus strengthening the behavior of cleaning your room.

Skinner showed how negative reinforcement worked by placing a rat in the box and subjecting it to a mild electric shock which caused it some discomfort. As the rat moved about the box it would accidentally knock the lever. Immediately it did so the electric shock would be switched off. The rat quickly learned to go straight to the lever after a few times of being put in the box. The consequence of escaping the electric shock ensured that it would repeat the action again and again.

Skinner even went as far as to teach the rats to avoid the electric shock by turning on a light just before the electric current came on. The rats soon learned to press the lever when the light came on because they knew that this would stop the electric current being switched on.

3. Punishers:
These are responses from the environment that decrease the likelihood of a behavior being repeated. Punishment weakens behavior. Punishment can be defined as the opposite of reinforcement since it is designed to weaken or eliminate a response rather than increase it.

Like reinforcement, punishment can work either by directly applying an unpleasant stimulus like a shock after a response or by removing a potentially rewarding stimulus, for instance, deducting someone's allowance to punish undesirable behavior. But it should be noted that it is not always easy to distinguish between punishment and negative reinforcement.

So, what are the major assumptions of the behaviorist approach?

Firstly, psychology should be seen as a science, to be studied in a scientific manner. Skinner's study of behavior in rats was conducted under carefully controlled laboratory conditions.

Secondly, behaviorism is primarily concerned with observable behavior, as opposed to internal events like thinking and emotion. In this regard it should be pointed out that Skinner did not posit that the rats learned to press a lever because they wanted food. All he did was concentrate on describing the easily observed behavior that the rats acquired.

Thirdly, the major influence on human behavior is learning from our environment. In the Skinner study, because food followed a particular behavior the rats learned to repeat that behavior.

Finally, there is not a lot of difference between the learning that takes place in humans and that in other animals. Accordingly, research like, for example, classical conditioning can be carried out on animals like Ivan Pavlov's dogs as well as on humans like Watson's Little Albert.

Skinner proposed that the way humans learn behavior is much the same as the way the rats learned to press a lever. So, the emphasis of behavioral psychology is on how we learn to behave in certain ways.

We are all constantly learning new behaviors and how to modify our existing behavior. Behavioral psychology is the psychological approach that focuses on how this learning takes place.

One of Skinner's best known critics was Noam Chomsky. Chomsky had four main criticisms of Skinner's work. He claimed his laboratory work could not be extended to humans. When it was extended to humans it represented "scientistic" behavior attempting to emulate science but which was not scientific.

He said that Skinner was not a scientist because he rejected the hypothetico-deductive model of theory testing; and he claimed that Skinner had no science of behavior.

Other criticisms levied against his theories include one that operant conditioning fails to taken into account the role of inherited and cognitive factors in learning. Accordingly, it is an incomplete explanation of the learning process in humans and animals.

Kohler (1924) found that primates often seem to solve problems in a flash of insight rather than by trial and error learning. Also (Bandura, 1977) posits that social learning theory suggests that humans can learn automatically through observation rather than through personal experience.

The use of animal research in operant conditioning studies also raises the issue of extrapolation. Some psychologists argue we cannot generalize from studies on animals to humans as their anatomy and physiology is different from humans, and they cannot think about their experiences and invoke reason, patience, memory or self-comfort.

Despite these criticism in one 2002 survey of psychologists, Skinner was identified as the most influential psychologist of the twentieth century.

While behaviorism is no longer a dominant school of thought, Skinner's work in operant conditioning remains vital today. Mental health professionals often utilize operant techniques when working with clients, teachers frequently use reinforcement and punishment to shape behavior in the classroom, and animal trainers rely heavily on these techniques to train dogs and other animals.

There is little doubt that Skinner's remarkable legacy has left both a lasting mark on psychology and numerous other fields ranging from philosophy to education.

ABRAHAM MASLOW (1908-1970)

"If you plan on being anything less than you are capable of being, you will probably be unhappy all the days of your life"

Hierarchy of Needs

Abraham Maslow was an American psychologist best known for creating Maslow's hierarchy of needs, a theory of psychological health predicated on fulfilling innate human needs in priority, culminating in self-actualization.

Abraham Harold Maslow was born in Brooklyn, New York on the 1 April 1908. His parents were impoverished first generation Russian immigrants. Maslow was the oldest of seven children. As a child he was classed as "mentally unstable" by a psychologist.

Although they were poor his parents valued education and sought to give him the best they could afford. Growing up in Brooklyn was difficult and he was often subject to anti-Semitic attacks. He rarely got along with his mother, and eventually developed a strong revulsion to her. He grew up with few friends and spent much of his youth reading books in libraries. He attended the Boys High School in Brooklyn and later the City College of New York.

In 1926 he began taking night time legal classes in addition to his undergraduate studies but it proved too much and he almost dropped out. After City College he went to the University of Wisconsin to study psychology. In 1928, he married his first cousin Bertha.

Maslow's psychology training at UW was decidedly experimental-behaviorist. Here he conducted research into primate dominance behavior and sexuality. His early experience with behaviorism would leave him with a strong positivist mindset. His attitude to research was peculiar in that he regarded it as a waste of time.

He was so ashamed of his master's thesis that he removed it from the psychology library. He still obtained his degree and his master's was later published. He continued his research at Columbia University on similar themes. It was here that he met his mentor Alfred Adler.

After World War II, Maslow began to question the way psychologists had come to their conclusions. He developed his own ideas on how to understand the human mind, calling his new discipline humanistic psychology.

Working with anthropologist Ruth Benedict and Gestalt psychologist Max Wertheimer, Maslow began taking notes about them and their behavior which would be the basis of his lifelong research and thinking about mental health and human potential.

He wrote extensively on the subject, borrowing ideas from other psychologists but adding significantly to them, especially the concepts of a hierarchy of needs, metaneeds, metamotivation, self-actualizing persons, and peak experiences.

In 1967, he suffered his first heart attack which almost killed him. Three years later he again suffered a heart attack while jogging in Meno Park in California. This time the attack was fatal. He died on the 8 June 1970 at the age of 62.

His legacy to psychology is enormous. Maslow wanted to understand what motivates people. He believed that people possess a set of motivation systems unrelated to rewards or unconscious desires. In 1943 he wrote that people are motivated to achieve certain needs. When one need is fulfilled a person seeks to fulfil the next one, and so on.

The earliest and most widespread version of Maslow's *hierarchy of needs* includes five motivational needs, often depicted as hierarchical levels within a pyramid. This five stage model can be divided into basic (or deficiency) needs (e.g. physiological, safety, love, and esteem) and growth needs (self-actualization).

The basic needs are said to motivate people when they are unmet. The need to fulfil such needs will become stronger the longer the duration they are denied. For example, the longer a person goes without food the more hungry they will become. One needs to satisfy lower level basic needs before progressing on to meet higher level growth needs. Once these needs have been reasonably satisfied, one may be able to reach the highest level called self-actualization.

Every person is capable and has the desire to move up the hierarchy toward a level of self-actualization. But our progress is often disrupted by our failure to meet lower level needs. Life experiences like losing one's job or divorce may cause an individual to fluctuate between levels of the hierarchy. In Maslow's opinion only one in a hundred people become fully self-actualized. This is because our society rewards motivation primarily based on esteem, love and other social needs.

The original hierarchy of needs five-stage model includes:

1. Biological and Physiological Needs:
Air, food, drink, shelter, warmth, sex, sleep.

2. Safety Needs:
Protection from elements, security, order, law, stability, freedom from fear.

3. Love and Belongingness Needs:
Friendship, intimacy, affection and love, from work group, family, friends, romantic relationships.

4. Esteem Needs:
Achievement, mastery, independence, status, dominance, prestige, self-respect, respect from others.

5. Self-Actualization Needs:
Realizing personal potential, self-fulfillment, seeking personal growth and peak experiences. Maslow posited that human needs are arranged in a hierarchy: "It is quite true that man lives by bread alone, when there is no bread. But what happens to man's desires when there is plenty of bread and when his belly is chronically filled?

At once other (and "higher") needs emerge and these, rather than physiological hungers, dominate the organism. And when these in turn are satisfied, again new (and still "higher") needs emerge and so on. This is what we mean by saying that the basic human needs are organized into a hierarchy of relative prepotency."

It is important to note that Maslow's five stage model was expanded in 1970s to include cognitive and aesthetic needs and later transcendence needs. The original five stage model became a seven stage and finally an eight stage model.

1. Biological and Physiological Needs:

Air, food, drink, shelter, warmth, sex, sleep, etc.

2. Safety Needs:
Protection from elements, security, order, law, stability, etc.

3. Love and Belongingness Needs:
Friendship, intimacy, affection and love, - from work group, family, friends, romantic relationships.

4. Esteem Needs:
Self-esteem, achievement, mastery, independence, status, dominance, prestige, managerial responsibility, etc.

5. Cognitive Needs:
Knowledge, meaning, etc.

6. Aesthetic Needs:
Appreciation and search for beauty, balance, form, etc.

7. Self-Actualization Needs:
Realizing personal potential, self-fulfillment, seeking personal growth and peak experiences.

8. Transcendence Needs:
Helping others to achieve self actualization.

Instead of focusing on what goes wrong with people, Maslow wanted to focus on what goes right. He was interested in human potential, and how we fulfill that potential. He believed that human motivation is based on people seeking fulfillment and change through personal growth. Self-actualized people are those who were fulfilled and doing all they were capable of.

He investigated the individual's need for personal growth and discovery that is present throughout a person's life. He believed that a person is always 'becoming' and never remains static in these terms. In self-actualization a person comes to find a meaning to life that is important to them.

Because each person is unique the motivation for self-actualization leads people in different directions. For some, self-actualization might be achieved through writing or creating works of art, for others through sport, or in a corporate setting.

Maslow believed self-actualization could be measured through the concept of **peak experiences.** Peak experiences occur when we experience the world totally for what it is, and there are feelings of euphoria, joy and wonder.

It is important to remember that self-actualization is a continual process of becoming rather than a perfect state one reaches of a 'happy ever after'.

Maslow described self-actualization in the following terms: "It refers to the person's desire for self-fulfillment, namely, to the tendency for him to become actualized in what he is potentially. The specific form that these needs will take will of course vary greatly from person to person. In one individual it may take the form of the desire to be an ideal mother, in another it may be expressed athletically, and in still another it may be expressed in painting pictures or in inventions."

How do we know if we are self-actualized?

According to Maslow this can be identified through various characteristics. And, although we are all, theoretically, capable of self-actualizing, most of us will not do so, or only to a limited degree. In his estimation only two percent of people will reach the state of self actualization. By studying eighteen people, including Abraham Lincoln and Albert Einstein Maslow identified fifteen characteristics of a self-actualized person:

1. They perceive reality efficiently and can tolerate uncertainty;

2. They accept themselves and others for what they are;

3. They are spontaneous in thought and action;

4. They are problem-centered (not self-centered);

5. They have an unusual sense of humor;

6. They are able to look at life objectively;

7. They are highly creative;

8. They are resistant to enculturation, but not purposely unconventional;

9. They are concerned for the welfare of humanity;

10. They are capable of deep appreciation of basic life-experience;

11. They establish deep satisfying interpersonal relationships with a few people;

12. They achieve peak experiences;

13. They have a need for privacy;

14. They enjoy democratic attitudes;

15. They have strong moral and ethical standards.

Maslow considered that the following types of behavior lead to self-actualization.

(a) Experiencing life like a child, with full absorption and concentration;

(b) Trying new things instead of sticking to safe paths;

(c) Listening to your own feelings in evaluating experiences instead of the voice of tradition, authority or the majority;

(d) Avoiding pretense (game playing) and being honest;

(e) Being prepared to be unpopular if your views do not coincide with those of the majority;

(f) Taking responsibility and working hard;

(g) Trying to identify your defenses and having the courage to give them up.

While people achieve self-actualization in their own unique way, they tend to share certain characteristics. But it is a matter of degree. As Maslow points out "There are no perfect human beings."

Of course, it is not necessary to have all fifteen characteristics to become self-actualized. Furthermore, it is not just self-actualized people who will display them. For Maslow, self-actualization did not equate with perfection. Self-actualization merely involves achieving ones potential. A person who has achieved self-actualization may still be vain, impolite and silly.

Maslow's hierarchy of needs theory has made major contributions in the field of education. Rather than reducing behavior to a response in the environment, Maslow adopts a holistic approach to education and learning, regarding the entire physical, emotional, social, and intellectual qualities of an individual and how they impact on learning.

Before a student's cognitive needs can be met they must first fulfil their basic physiological needs. A hungry student will find it difficult to focus on learning. Students need to feel emotionally and physically safe and accepted within the classroom to progress and reach their full potential.

Maslow believes that it is important that students know they are valued and respected in the classroom and to this end the teacher should create a supportive environment. For example students with low self-esteem will not progress to their academic potential until their self-esteem is strengthened.

The biggest problem with Maslow's theory is with his methodology. He formulated the characteristics of self-actualized individuals from undertaking a qualitative method called biographical analysis. He looked at the biographies and writings of just eighteen people. These were people that he himself simply considered to be self-actualized.

Then from these sources he developed a list of qualities that seemed characteristic of this specific group of people, as opposed to humanity in general. This type of approach presents numerous problems from a scientific perspective.

One such problem is that it could be reasonably argued that a biographical analysis as a method is extremely subjective as it is based entirely on the opinion of the researcher. Personal opinion is prone to bias. Bias reduces the validity of any data extracted in this manner. Accordingly, Maslow's operational definition of self-actualization cannot be blindly accepted as scientific fact because it isn't.

Secondly, Maslow's biographical analysis focused on a biased sample of self-actualized individuals. It was limited to highly educated white males like Thomas Jefferson, Abraham Lincoln, Albert Einstein, William James, Aldous Huxley, Gandhi, and Beethoven.

And while he later conducted a study involving self-actualized females, including Eleanor Roosevelt and Mother Teresa, they comprised a small proportion of his sample. This makes it difficult to generalize his theory to females and individuals from lower social classes or different ethnicity and prejudices the validity of his findings.

Thirdly, it is nearly impossible to empirically test Maslow's concept of self-actualization in a way that causal relationships can be established.

Fourthly, Maslow's assumption that the lower needs must be satisfied before a person can achieve their potential and self-actualize is difficult to accept and is not always the case. Therefore Maslow's hierarchy of needs in some aspects has been falsified.

Fifthly, through examining cultures in which large numbers of people live in poverty, for example in India, it is clear that people are still capable of higher order needs such as love and belongingness.

But according to Maslow, people who have difficulty achieving very basic physiological needs such as food and shelter, are not capable of meeting higher growth needs. Furthermore, many creative people, like Vincent Van Gogh, experienced poverty throughout their lifetime, yet it could be argued that they achieved self-actualization.

In 2011, researchers Tay and Diener, tested Maslow's theory by analyzing the data of 60,865 participants from 123 countries, representing every major region of the world. Respondents answered questions about six needs that closely resemble those in Maslow's model: basic needs (food, shelter); safety; social needs (love, support); respect; mastery; and autonomy.

They also rated their well-being across three discrete measures: life evaluation (a person's view of his or her life as a whole), positive feelings (day-to-day instances of joy or pleasure), and negative feelings (everyday experiences of sorrow, anger, or stress). The results of the study support the view that universal human needs appear to exist regardless of cultural differences. However, the ordering of the needs within the hierarchy was not correct.

As Diener states: "Although the most basic needs might get the most attention when you don't have them, you don't need to fulfill them in order to get benefits [from the others]." Even when we are hungry, for instance, we can be happy with our friends. They're like vitamins. We need them all."

While Maslow's work fell out of favor with many academic psychologists, his theories are enjoying a resurgence due to the rising interesting in positive psychology.

ROLLO MAY (1909-1994)

"Depression is the inability to construct a future"

The father of Existential Psychotherapy
Humanistic Psychology
Love and Will (1969)

Rollo May was an American psychologist, often referred to as "the father of existential psychotherapy" who differs from other humanistic psychologists in showing a sharper awareness of the tragic dimensions of human existence.

His type of humanistic psychology focused on the individual, as opposed to the behaviorist psychology and Freudian psychoanalysis that was prevalent in the 1940s and 1950s.

May's writings were both practical and spiritual and they promoted the power and worth of the individual. As such, they contributed to the development of the human potential movement.

He is the author of the influential book *Love and Will* which looks at the deep, internal dilemmas humans face through their relationships.

Rollo Reece May was born on the 21 April 1909 in Ada, Ohio in America to Earl Tittle May and Matie Boughton. He was the first son of a family with six children. His father, a field secretary for the Young Men's Christian Association, moved the family to Michigan when May was still a child

He experienced a difficult childhood. His parents divorced. His sister was diagnosed with schizophrenia. His mother often neglected the children and he was obliged to care for them on his own.

He attended Michigan State University, but after his involvement with a radical student magazine magazine, which was critical of the state legislature, he was expelled. He transferred to Oberlin College and received a bachelor's degree in English.

He later spent three years teaching in Greece at Anatolia College. During this time he studied with doctor and psychotherapist Alfred Adler, whose his later work also shares theoretical similarities. He became ordained as a minister shortly after coming back to America.

He later left the ministry to pursue a degree in psychology. He was plagued with ill health and in 1942 spent eighteen months in a sanitarium suffering from tuberculosis. He later attended Union Theological Seminary for a B.D. during 1938, and finally to Teachers College, Columbia University for a Ph.D. in clinical psychology in 1949.

May and his first wife were divorced in 1969 and in 1971 he married Ingrid Schöll. That marriage ended in 1978. In 1989, May married Georgia Lee Miller Johnson.

He is the founder of Saybrook Graduate School and Research Center in San Francisco. He spent the final years of his life in Tiburon on San Francisco Bay. A victim of declining health, he died from congestive heart failure in 1994.

May along with Ernest Angel and Henri F. Ellenberger, was co-editor of the first American book on existential psychology called *Existence* (1958). The book which was a collection of essays was a huge influence on the emergence of American humanistic psychology. It introduced American readers to translations of work by existential-phenomenological psychologists such as Eugene Minkowski, Ludwig Binswanger, Erwin Straus and Roland Kuhn. May's essays, *The Origins and Significance of the Existential Movement in Psychology* and *Contributions of Existential Psychotherapy* proved that, for his time, May enjoyed a deep understanding of the possibilities and benefits of an existential psychology.

In the former, May writes that in order for a psychologist to serve his client well he must participate in the world of that client. He argues that existential psychology is best equipped to help the clinician to do so without doing violence to the client. He claims that the existential approach refuses to force a client to conform to a pre-articulated theoretical system.

Furthermore, it does default to using "techniques" as a defense against fully engaging with the client. He also warns that existential psychotherapy is not simply another splinter of the Freudian tradition. It grew spontaneously without the influence of a single leader, and rather than seeking to construct a new theoretical school of therapy, it seeks, instead, "to analyze the structure of human existence, an enterprise which, if successful, should yield an understanding of the reality underlying all situations of human beings in crises". May notes that, out of mainstream psychotherapy, there are several resistances to the existential approach.

Essentially, what May is saying is that traditional psychological theory had more often concealed what is really going on with the patient rather than revealing such happenings in a constructive and therapeutic way. His strongest argument is his assertion that "every scientific method rests upon philosophical presuppositions."

May was influenced by American humanism. He was interested in reconciling existential psychology with other philosophies. He considered Otto Rank to be the most important precursor of existential therapy.

Abraham Maslow is a humanist psychologist. May digs deeper into the awareness of the serious dimensions of a human's life than Maslow did. Erich Fromm agreed with many of May's ideas. Fromm studied the ways people avoid anxiety by conforming to societal norms rather than doing what they please. Fromm also focused on self-expression and free will.

Just like Sigmund Freud, May defined certain **stages of development** in life. These stages are not as strict as Freud's psychosexual stages, rather they signify a sequence of major issues in each individual's life:

Innocence:

The pre-egoic, pre-self-conscious stage of the infant. An innocent is only doing what he or she must do. However, an innocent does have a degree of will in the sense of a drive to fulfill needs.

Rebellion:
The rebellious person wants freedom, but does not yet have a good understanding of the responsibility that goes with it.

Ordinary:
The normal adult ego learned responsibility, but finds it too demanding, and so seeks refuge in conformity and traditional values.

Creative:
The authentic adult, the existential stage, self-actualizing and transcending simple egocentrism.

May defined "anxiety" in his book *The Meaning of Anxiety* as "the apprehension cued off by a threat to some value which the individual holds essential to his existence as a self."

He also quotes Danish philosopher Søren Kierkegaard: "Anxiety is the dizziness of freedom". It is from from his own time in the sanatorium when he had tuberculosis that May's interest in isolation and anxiety developed. His feelings of depersonalization and isolation gave him important insight into the subject.

He believed that anxiety is actually essential to a person's growth and, in fact, contributes to what it means to be human. Anxiety and feelings of threat and powerlessness are important because it gives humans the freedom to act courageously as opposed to conforming to be comfortable.

One way in which he proposes to fight anxiety is by displacing anxiety by fear as he believes that "anxiety seeks to become fear". He believes that by changing anxiety to a fear, a person can discover incentives to either avoid the feared object or find the means to remove this fear of it.

In his book *Love and Will*, he focuses on love and sex in human behavior. He also outlines five different types of love. He believes that love and sex should not be separate, but that society has separated them two different ideologies.

His five types of love are as follows:

Sex: Lust, tension release;

Eros: Procreative love, savoring, experiential;

Philia: Brotherly love, liking;

Agape: Unselfish love, devotion to the welfare of others;

Authentic love: Incorporates all other types of love.

May was a major critic of the 1960s sexual revolution believing that "free sex" was replacing the ideology of free love. He explains that love is intentionally willed by an individual. Sexual desire is the complete opposite.

To give into these impulses does not actually make one free, but to resist these impulses is the meaning of being free. May believed that the Hippie subculture and sexual mores of the 1960s, as well as commercialization of sex and pornography, influenced society to such an extent that people believed that love and sex are no longer associated directly.

According to May, emotion has become separated from reason, making it acceptable socially to seek sexual relationships and avoid the natural drive to relate to another person and create new life. He believed that sexual freedom can cause society to neglect more important psychological developments. May suggests that we should rediscover the importance of caring for another.

May also highlighted a crisis within psychotherapy caused by psychotherapists who had broken away from the Jungian, Freudian and others by creating their own "gimmicks." These gimmicks gave too much emphasis to the self instead of focusing more on "man in the world".

Despite certain criticisms, the contribution that Rollo May made to psychology is huge. He expanded the theory of existentialism in ways that continues to beguile and inspire new research. Although his approach to psychology may have been unscientific he broadened many views and by doing so, he impacted the field with an untouchable vigor.

He also uncovered what he believed to be the basic components of authentic love, how the importance of values in one's life can impede or develop one's personality and the nature of anxiety.

ERIC BERNE (1910-1970)

*"A loser doesn't know what he'll do if he loses but talks about
what he'll do if he wins and a winner doesn't talk about what
he'll do if he wins but knows what he'll do if he loses"*

Transactional Analysis
Games People Play

Eric Berne was a Canadian psychiatrist who is best known as
the founder of transactional analysis and for his seminal work
Games People Play.

He was born Eric Lennard Bernstein on the 10 May 1910 in Montreal,
Quebec, Canada to a Jewish family. His parents were physician David
Bernstein, and writer, Sara Gordon. He had a sister called Grace who was
five years younger. After the death of his father in 1921 his mother never
remarried and brought up the two children on her own.

Bernstein went to McGill University and received his bachelors in 1931 and
his doctorate degree in medicine and surgery in 1935. After he graduated he
began a residency in psychiatry at Yale University. Here he studied
psychoanalysis under Paul Federn, an Austrian-American psychologist who
is largely remembered for his theories involving ego psychology and
therapeutic treatment of psychosis.

He married his first wife Elinor McRae in 1942. They had two children.
They divorced acrimoniously in 1945. In 1943, after becoming an American
citizen, Bernstein changed his legal name to Eric Berne. During the Second
World War he worked in the United States Army Medical Corps, reaching
the rank of Major.

He was discharged in 1945. Afterwards, he resumed his studies under Erik
Erikson at the San Francisco Psychoanalytic Institute and practiced at Mt.
Zion Hospital. Erikson was a German-born American developmental
psychologist and psychoanalyst known for his theory on psychosocial
development of human beings.

In addition to technical papers on psychoanalysis, Berne published *The Mind in Action* in 1947. He became a group therapist attached to several hospitals in San Francisco. He also began to develop the Ego-State Model introduced by Paul Federn.

In 1948 Berne's work began to diverge from the mainstream of psychoanalytic thought. He published his work in several technical journals, but met with largely negative reactions. His break became formal in 1949 when he was rejected for membership in the San Francisco Psychoanalytic Institute. In the same year he married Dorothy DeMass Way, with whom he also had two children before their divorce in 1964.

He wrote a series of papers and articles on intuition. In one such article he described how he had developed an almost uncanny ability to guess the civilian occupation of soldiers from just a few moments' conversation with them. His interest in the faculty of intuition led to his groundbreaking work on transactional analysis.

It was for his work in **Transactional Analysis** for which he is most famous. Berne mapped interpersonal relationships to three ego-states of the individuals involved: the Parent, Adult, and Child state. He then investigated communications between individuals based on the current state of each. He called these interpersonal interactions transactions and used the label games to refer to certain patterns of transactions which popped up repeatedly in everyday life.

Transactional analysis integrates the theories of psychology and psychotherapy containing as it does elements of psychoanalytic, humanist and cognitive ideas. According to the International Transactional Analysis Association, Transactional Analysis "is a theory of personality and a systematic psychotherapy for personal growth and personal change".

The theory describes how people are structured psychologically. It uses what is perhaps its best known model, the ego-state (Parent-Adult-Child) model, to do this. The same model helps explain how people function and express their personality in their behavior.

Berne maintained that there are **four life positions** that a person can hold. Holding a particular psychological position has profound implications for how an individual operationalizes his or her life. These are the four positions:

1. I'm OK and you are OK:
This is the healthiest position about life and it means that I feel good about

myself and that I feel good about others and their competence.

2. I'm OK and you are not OK:

Here I feel good about myself but I see others as damaged or less than and it is usually not healthy,

3. I'm not OK and you are OK:

Here the person sees him/herself as the weak partner in relationships as the others in life are definitely better than the self. The person who holds this position will unconsciously accept abuse as normal.

4. I'm not OK and you are not OK:

This is the worst position possible as it means that I believe that I am in a terrible state and the rest of the world is as bad. Consequently there is no hope for any ultimate supports.

I'm OK You're OK

	I am not OK You are OK One down position Get away from, Helpless	I am OK You are OK Healthy Position Get on with, Happy
OTHERS	I am not OK You are not OK Helpless position Get away with, Helpless	

Others axis: You are ok with me / You are not ok with me

Self axis: I am not OK with Me / I am OK with Me

SELF

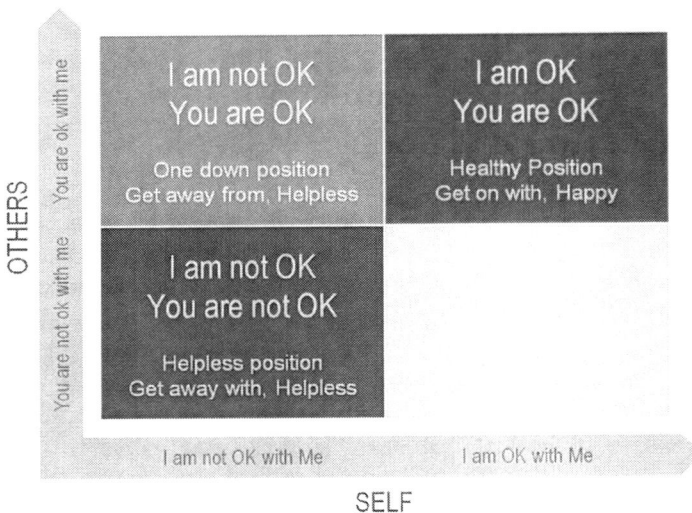

Transactional Analysis offers a theory for child development by explaining how our adult patterns of life originated in childhood. It is based on the idea of a "Life (or Childhood) Script".

This is the assumption that we continue to re-play childhood strategies, even when this results in pain or defeat. Thus it claims to offer a theory of psychopathology. In practical application, Transactional Analysis can be utilized in the diagnosis and treatment of many types of psychological disorders.

It has also been used in education by assisting teachers to remain in clear communication at an appropriate level. But its use expands to counselling and consultancy, as well as management and communications training.

Berne's first full book on Transactional Analysis was published in 1961 and called *Transactional Analysis in Psychotherapy*. Two years later he published *Structures and Dynamics of Organizations and Groups* which examined the same analysis in a broader context than one-on-one interaction.

But it was his 1964 best-selling book **Games People Play** which catapulted Berne into the top echelons of psychotherapy. Although written for professional therapists it became popular with anyone with an interest in psychotherapy. The book presented everyday examples of the ways in which people are caught up in the games they play. Berne gave these games memorable and popular titles such as "Now I've Got You, You Son of a Bitch", "Wooden Leg", "Why Don't You... / Yes, But...", and "Let's You and Him Fight".

In Berne's explanation of transactions as games, when the transaction is a zero-sum game, that is one which must be won at the other's expense, the person who benefits from a transaction and wins the game is referred to as White, and the victim as Black. It thus mirrors the pieces in a chess game.

Some of Beck's terminology became a part of popular American vocabulary. After his worldwide success, Eric got married for a third time in 1967 to Torre Peterson. They resided in Carmel, California. He continued to write but undertook some clinical work in San Francisco. This marriage also ended in divorce in 1970. He died in Carmel in California on the 15 July 1970.

MURRAY BOWEN (1913-1990)

*"That which is created in a relationship
can be fixed in a relationship"*

**Family Therapy
Bowen Theory**

Murray Bowen was an American psychiatrist who was a pioneer of family therapy and one of the founders of systemic therapy. Beginning in the 1950s, he developed a systems theory of the family known as Bowen Theory.

Murray Bowen was born on the 31 January 1913 in Waverly, Tennessee, America. His family had lived in Tennessee since the Revolution. He was the oldest of five children. His father died in 1974 at the age of 87 and his mother died in 1982 at the age of 95. He was married with four children.

He attended the University of Tennessee, Knoxville, where he obtained his B.Sc. in 1934. He then transferred to the Medical School, in Memphis, where he became a medical doctor in 1937. He served his internship at Bellevue Hospital, New York City and worked at Grasslands Hospital, Valhalla, New York, until 1941.

He saw five years active duty with the US Army between 1941-46, rising to the rank of Major. Although accepted into the Mayo clinic as a surgeon his interest in medicine switched to psychiatry.

Between 1946-1954 he worked at the Menninger Foundation, Topeka, in Kansas. His background interest in science led to the development of a new theory, which uses evolution and systems ideas to replace Freud. The theory showed enough promise for him to seek full-time research in a neutral center.

Between 1954-1958 he worked at the National Institute of Mental Health, Bethesda, in Maryland, where he conducted research with families who had a member diagnosed with schizophrenia.

During this five year project, families lived in the research ward for durations of one to three years. Bowen based his working hypothesis for the research on the theoretical assumption that the psychosis in the patient was a symptom of a larger family problem. He departed from the usual theoretical position which considers the psychosis a disease located only in the patient.

In the process of the research, Bowen found that the relationship patterns in the live-in families were also present in less disturbed and normal families to varying degrees. His theory, which he developed over two decades, became known as the Bowen Theory.

In the late 1950s, the Chair of the Department of Psychiatry at Georgetown

University became convinced of the importance of Bowen's discoveries about families in general, and invited him to join the department. He taught there from 1959 until his death in 1990.

At Georgetown, Bowen focused on the development of the theory, and on less severe emotional problems. He began multi-generational research on families, including his own. By 1965, he had developed the fist six interlocking concepts of his theory. He regarded his own work on differentiating himself within his family of origin as "the most important turning point in [his] entire professional life".

In 1972, the Environmental Protection Agency invited Bowen to present a paper on "predictable human response to crisis situations". His paper provided the impetus for a new addition to his interlocking concepts. The theory was now extended to society at large. This concept, societal emotional process, along with sibling position, based on Toman's (1976) work, completed the theory as it is today.

Bowen believed that the majority of clients can change themselves if given a chance. Most therapists are trying so hard to be therapeutic, they cannot "think" theory. He said that good therapy is determined by the way a theorist thinks about human problems. When the therapist cannot think theory, the theoretical gap is closed by some fixed version of Freud, the therapy is less efficient than it could be.

Bowen summarized his theory using **eight interlocking concepts**:

1. Differentiation of Self
2. Nuclear Family Emotional System
3. Triangles
4. Family Projection Process
5. Multigenerational Transmission Process
6. Emotional Cutoff
7. Sibling Position
8. Societal Emotional Process

Differentiation of Self:
This is his most important concept. Differentiation of self is one's ability to separate one's own intellectual and emotional functioning from that of the family. It describes how people cope with life's demands and pursue their goals on a continuum from most adaptive to least.

Variations in this adaptiveness depend on several connected factors, including the amount of solid self, the part of self that is not negotiable in relationships. For example, a person who has well thought out principles enhances solid self because they will not be swayed by public opinion. A person with less solid self will feel more pressure to think, feel, and act like others.

This fusion between two people generates more chronic anxiety as one becomes more sensitive to what the other thinks, feels, and does. Acute anxiety also plays a role. A fairly well differentiated person can develop symptoms under acute anxiety, but will probably return to adaptive functioning soon after. A less differentiated person may live in a stress free environment and therefore function quite well for long periods of time.

Level of differentiation refers to the degree to which a person can think and act for self while in contact with emotionally charged issues. It also refers to the degree to which a person can discern between thoughts and feelings. At higher levels of differentiation, people maintain separate, solid selves under considerable stress and anxiety.

They manage their own reactivity and choose thoughtful actions. At lower levels of differentiation, people depend on others to function, and they develop significant symptoms under stress. They often act destructively, based on anxious reactions to the environment. Reason fuses with emotion. Even highly intelligent people can be poorly differentiated.

To have a well-differentiated "self" is an ideal that no one realizes perfectly because like with Abraham Maslow's concept of "self-actualization", it's a quale, a concept or idea without literal physical or material example. Even if total self-differentiation is achieved in a given moment it is temporary and ephemeral. Those with generally higher levels of "self differentiation" recognize that they need others, but they depend less on others' acceptance and approval.

Triangles:
These are the basic molecule of human relationship systems. In family systems theory, whenever two people have problems with each other, one or both may "triangle in" a third member. Bowen emphasized the idea that people respond to anxiety in a relationship by forming a triangle. They shift the focus to a third person. In a triangle, two are on the inside and one is on the outside.

For example, rather than talk with her husband about something that frustrates her a new mother might preoccupy herself with her new child.

Here the wife diminishes her anxiety by ignoring its source which is the relationship between her and her husband. The husband is on the outside and the wife and child are on the inside.

Similarly, in the same situation, instead of talking with his wife about their marriage and dealing with his frustration with her, the husband might spend more time at work. He would then be making work as the inside relationship excluding his wife. In both examples anxiety is reduced, but neither husband nor wife resolves the source of their anxiety.

Triangles usually have two individuals or entities in conflict, and another entity or individual uninvolved with the conflict is brought in. When tension is not high, the relationship between the first two individuals is desirable. The two original people in the relationship or conflict are the inside positions of the triangle. The insiders bond when they prefer each other, but in the case of conflict, another entity or individual called the outsider is brought in.

This is an effort by one of the two insiders to either defuse and avoid the situation, or to team up against the other insider. The insiders may actively exclude the outsider when tensions are not low between the insiders. Being excluded may provoke intense feelings of rejection and the outsider works to get closer to one of the insiders.

The positions of these relationships are not fixed. If mild to moderate tension develops between the insiders, the most uncomfortable insider will move closer to an outsider. The remaining original insider then switches places with the outsider. The excluded insider becomes the new outsider and the original outsider is now an insider. Predictably the new outsider may move to restore closeness with one of the current insiders.

At a high level of tension, the outside position becomes the most desirable. If the insiders conflict severely, one insider may opt for the outside position by getting the current outsider to take their place in the conflict with the other insider. If the maneuvering insider succeeds, they gain the more comfortable position of being on the outside of the conflict that the other two are now involved in. When the tension and conflict subside, the outsider may try to regain an inside position.

Bowen researchers consider triangles a natural function of living systems. Triangles can have either negative or positive outcomes depending on how their members manage anxiety and reactivity. Bowen postulated that if one member of the triangle remains calm and in emotional contact with the other two, the system automatically calms down. On the other hand, with enough stress and reactivity, members lock into a triangular position, and develop symptoms.

Nuclear Family Emotional Process:
The nuclear family manages differentiation and anxiety with conflict, distance, over and under functioning reciprocity, which at extremes can lead to dysfunction in a spouse, and child focus. People engaged in conflict fight, argue, blame and criticize each other. Partners who distance tend to be emotionally unavailable and to avoid potentially uncomfortable, though important, topics. Reciprocity in relationships occurs when one person takes on responsibilities for the twosome. The two people slide into overadequate and underadequate roles. This can become so extreme that one partner becomes incapacitated either with an illness of a general lack of direction. Child focus is discussed more under the next concept.

Family Projection Process:
The fixed triangle is evident in the family projection process, where parents in a nuclear family focus anxiety on a child and the child develops problems. Parents then usually attempt to get the child to change or they ask an expert to "fix" the child. Experienced Bowen family systems consultants report that when parents can instead manage their own anxiety and resolve their own relationship issues, the functioning of the child automatically improves.

Emotional Cutoff:
This is the mechanism people use to reduce anxiety from their unresolved emotional issues with parents, siblings, and other members from the family of origin. To avoid sensitive issues, they either move away from their families and rarely go home; or, if they remain in physical contact with their families, to avoid sensitive issues, they use silence or divert the conversation.

Though cutoff may diminish their immediate anxiety, these unresolved problems contaminate other relationships, especially when those relationships are stressed. The opposite of an emotional cut-off is an open relationship. It is a very effective way to reduce a family's over-all anxiety. Continued low anxiety permits motivated family members to begin the slow steps to better differentiation. Bowen wrote, "It might be difficult for such a family [that has severe cut-offs] to begin more emotional contact with the extended family, but any effort toward reducing the cut-off with the extended family will soften the intensity of the family problem, reduce the symptoms, and make any kind of therapy far more productive."

Multigenerational Transmission Process:
Differentiation of Self is transmitted through the multigenerational transmission process. This concept describes patterns of emotional process through multiple generations.

It offers a way of thinking about family patterns that goes beyond a dichotomy of genes versus environment. One of the ways family patterns are transmitted across generations is through relationship triangles.

Sibling Position:
This is a concept which Bowen adopted from the research of Walter Toman. It affects variation in basic and functional levels of differentiation as well. Oldest, youngest, and middle children tend toward certain functional roles in families, influenced also by the particular mix of sibling positions in it and the sibling positions of parents and other relatives.

Societal Emotional Process:
This is the last concept that Bowen developed. It refers to the tendency of people within a society to be more anxious and unstable at certain times than others. Environmental stressors like overpopulation, scarcity of natural resources, epidemics, economic forces, and lack of skills for living in a diverse world are all potential stressors that contribute to a regression in society.

Murray Bowen developed theories and invented terms now used, or at least known, by every family therapist practicing in America. His eight interlocking concepts are firmly assimilated into the fabric of the field. As Braulio Montalvo says: "Bowen was the intellectual beacon for everyone who was first trying to understand the family. Almost every major concept in family therapy can be traced back to him. He taught everybody."

His student Robert Aylmer, summed up his work when he said: "Bowen was the first to realize you can't translate the individual psychoanalytic concepts into the language of families, and the first to see the family as a structure in itself, which had its own wiring."

HEINZ KOHUT (1913-1981)

"If you want to hurt somebody and you want to know where his vulnerable spot is you have to know him, before you can put in the right dig, that's very important"

Self Psychology

Heinz Kohut was an Austrian born, American psychoanalyst who was the first person to conceptualize a psychology of the self. Self psychology is an influential school of thought within psychodynamic theory which helped transform the modern practice of analytic and dynamic treatment approaches.

His new psychoanalytic ideas were revolutionary. During the late 1960s and early 1970s, when Kohut produced his seminal work, psychoanalysis had become stalled in the development of its theories. This inertia was largely due to a blind adherence to the theories of Sigmund Freud.

At that time, any new psychoanalytic idea, or extension of a previous idea, was considered primarily on the basis of whether or not it fit properly with Freud's thinking. It was a brave analyst who submitted a truly new psychoanalytic idea that went beyond Freud's conceptualizations. Kohut not only produced new innovative ideas but also modeled a brave commitment to science through his ability to veer away from psychoanalytic dogma and take a fresh look at it.

Unfortunately, he paid the price by being ostracized by the psychoanalytic establishment. In spite of this, Kohut, with the essential support of a small group of colleagues, continued his explorations until his untimely death in 1981 at the age of 67.

Kohut was born on 3 May 1913, in Vienna, Austria-Hungary, to Felix Kohut and Else Lampl. He was their only child. His parents were assimilated Jews living in Alsergrund who had married two years previously.

His father was an aspiring concert pianist, but he abandoned his dreams having been traumatized by his experiences in World War I. He then went into business with a man named Paul Bellak. His mother opened her own shop sometime after the war which was almost unheard of at the time.

Else's relationship with her son can be described as "narcissistic enmeshment". He didn't go to school until the fifth grade. Before that he was taught by several tutors, a line of "Fräuleins and mademoiselles".

Special care was taken that he learned French. From 1924 on he attended the Döblinger Gymnasium in Grinzing where the Kohuts had built a house. During his time at the school he had one more tutor, but the role of this person was to engage him in educational discussions, to take him to museums, galleries, and the opera.

This educator, a man, was the first friend he ever had. His mother had ensured he was socially isolated from his peers.

In 1929, Kohut spent two months in Saint-Quay-Portrieux in Brittany to study French. At school he wrote his thesis on Euripides' play *The Cyclops*. His Latin teacher, who had anti-Semitic sentiments and later participated in the Austrian Nazi movement, accused him of having plagiarized this work. The thesis was only accepted after Kohut's father intervened and threatened legal action.

In 1932 Kohut entered the medical faculty of the University of Vienna. It took him six years to qualify. During this time he spent six months in internships in Paris, first at the Hôtel-Dieu and then at the Hôpital Saint-Louis. The latter hospital specialized in the treatment of syphilis, which provided shocking experiences for Kohut.

In Paris he became friends with a Jewish medical student from Istanbul called Jacques Palaci. In 1937, Kohut's father died of leukemia. Sometime later Kohut entered psychotherapy with Walter Marseilles. Later in 1938 he began psychoanalysis with August Aichhorn, a close friend of Sigmund Freud.

The annexation of Austria to Germany by Hitler in March 1938 presented difficulties for Kohut, as he still had to take his final exams at the medical faculty. He was eventually allowed to take them, after all the Jewish professors had been removed from the university. Kohut eventually left Austria, landing first in a refugee camp in Kent, England.

In February 1940 he was allowed to travel in a British convoy to Boston, from where he travelled to Chicago by bus. Musicologist Sigmund Levarie, who had earlier emigrated to live with an uncle in Chicago arranged a visa for him and invited him to join him there.

As regards his theories, Kohut referred to empathy as **vicarious introspection.** He believed that the failure of parents to empathize with their children and the responses of their children to these failures was "at the root of almost all psychopathology."

For the child to move from grandiose to cohesive self and beyond, meant a slow process of disillusionment with phantasies of omnipotence, mediated by the parents: "This process of gradual and titrated disenchantment requires that the infant's caretakers be empathetically attuned to the infant's needs."

Correspondingly, in dealing with earlier failures in the disenchantment process in therapy, Kohut "highlights empathy as the tool par excellence, which allows the creation of a relationship between patient and analyst that can offer some hope of mitigating early self pathology."

Utilizing vicarious introspection allows the therapist to reach conclusions earlier with less dialogue and interpretation. It also creates a stronger bond between the client and therapist. In fact, Kohut believed that the implicit bond of empathy itself has a curative effect. But he warned that "the psychoanalyst must also be able to relinquish the empathic attitude" to maintain intellectual integrity.

Empathy had been utilized by psychologists long before Kohut but he was the first to acknowledge it as a powerful therapeutic tool, extending beyond "hunches" and vague "assumptions," and enabling empathy to be described, taught, and used more actively.

Kohut also wrote extensively about **self objects**, the external objects that function as part of the "self machinery". Self objects are objects which are not experienced as separate and independent from the self. They are persons, objects or activities that "complete" the self, and which are necessary for normal functioning.

Kohut believed that observing the client's self object connections to be a fundamental part of self-psychology. Self objects include everything from the transference phenomenon in therapy, relatives, and items. They are like Winnicott's transitional objects. The self object-function, what it does or the self, is often taken for granted and seems to take place in a "blindzone."

The function thus usually does not become "visible" until the relation with the self object is somehow broken. When we establish a relationship with a new self object, the relationship connection can "lock in place" in a powerful way. An example of this phenomenon is powerful transference.

A potential problem for the self occurs when a self object is needed but is not accessible. This is called a frustration. Kohut called the contrast of this an **optimal frustration**. Kohut considered that the "skillful analyst will conduct the analysis according to the principle of optimal frustration." Suboptimal frustrations are like Freud's trauma concept, or to problem solution in the oedipal phase.

So, how does his treatment work in reality?

It is the empathic process of understanding and explaining that allows the treatment to go forward and the self to acquire the missing structures. He says it's a three step process:

1. First, there is the analysis of defense and resistance against the emergence of the new editions of the self object transference.

2. Second, there is the unfolding of the various self object transferences and their working through.

3. Third, there is the making possible the establishment of an empathic intuneness between the self and the self object on a more mature adult level.

In other words, self psychology does not view the mature self as achieving an ideal state of "separation-individuation," as certain object relations theory would suggest. But it does maintain that even the mature self continues to have a need for mirroring, idealizing, and twin ship self object experiences

Kohut's theories are complicated. One critic referred to his book *The Analysis of the Self* as "breathtakingly unreadable."

Some critics argue that Kohut simply seems to blame parental deficit for all childhood difficulties. He sees unempathic everywhere just like Freud sees sex everywhere. But today his theories are better interpreted and self psychology offers important insights to twenty-first-century clinicians.

ALBERT ELLIS (1913-2007)

"The best years of your life are the ones in which you decide your problems are your own. You do not blame them on your mother, the ecology, or the president. You realize that you control your own destiny"

Rational Emotive Behavior Therapy
Cognitive Revolutionary Paradigm Shift
Cognitive Behavior Therapies

Sex Without Guilt

Albert Ellis was an American psychologist who is best known for developing Rational Emotive Behavior Therapy (REBT). He is also one of the originators of the cognitive revolutionary paradigm shift in psychotherapy and the founder of cognitive-behavioral therapies.

By the 1960s, Ellis had come to be seen as one of the founders of the American sexual revolution. Based on a 1982 professional survey of USA and Canadian psychologists, he was considered as the second most influential psychotherapist in history after Carl Rogers and ahead of Sigmund Freud.

Ellis was born to a Jewish family in Pittsburgh, Pennsylvania, USA, on the 27 September 1913. Although born in Pittsburgh he was raised in New York. He was the eldest of three children. His father was a businessman who spent much of his time travelling. His mother suffered from a bi-polar disorder. Neither demonstrated much affection for their children and they had to fend a lot for themselves. Ellis spent his youth looking after his younger siblings.

When the Great Depression struck, all three children worked to help support the family. As a child Ellis was quite sickly and suffered numerous health problems like kidney disease, and tonsillitis which led to a severe streptococcal infection requiring emergency surgery. Between the age of five and seven he was hospitalized seven times. His parents divorced when he was twelve. Growing up he was acutely shy, particularly around women. When he was nineteen he forced himself to speak with one hundred women over a period of a month in the Bronx Botanical gardens. Even then he was showing signs of thinking like a cognitive-behaviorist therapist. Despite his efforts he still failed to secure a date. He was later to say that the experience desensitized himself to his fear of rejection by women.

In junior high school Ellis decided he wanted to be the next Great American Novelist. He had his life worked out. He planned to study accounting in high school and college, make enough money to retire at thirty, and write without the pressure of financial need.

The Great Depression put an end to his dream but he did succeed in making it to college and in 1934 earned a degree in business administration from the City University of New York. His first venture in the business world was a pants-matching business which he started with his younger brother. They scoured the New York garment auctions for pants to match their customer's still-usable coats. In 1938, he became the personnel manager for a gift and novelty firm.

In his spare time he wrote short stories, plays, novels, comic poetry, essays and nonfiction books. By the time he was twenty eight, he had finished twenty full-length manuscripts, but had not succeeding in having a single one published. Realizing that he had no future in fiction he turned to non-fiction and began writing around the sexual revolution.

He had a talent for this, so much so that friends and acquaintances began asking him for advice. Ellis then realized he had a talent not just for writing non-fiction but also for counselling.

In 1942 he returned to college and entered the clinical-psychology program at Columbia. He started a part-time private practice in family and sex counseling soon after he received his master's degree in 1943. He continued on to obtain his Ph.D. while practicing as a psychologist possibly because there was no licensing of psychologists in New York at that time.

He began publishing articles even before receiving his Ph.D. By the time he received his doctorate he had decided that Freud's psychoanalysis was the deepest and most effective form of therapy. He sought additional training in psychoanalysis and then began to practice classical psychoanalysis.

In the late 1940s he taught at Rutgers and New York University, and was the senior clinical psychologist at the Northern New Jersey Mental Hygiene Clinic. He also became the chief psychologist at the New Jersey Diagnostic Center and then at the New Jersey Department of Institutions and Agencies. Later, he began a Jungian analysis and program of supervision with Richard Hulbeck, a leading analyst at the Karen Horney Institute. Shortly afterwards, his support for psychoanalysis began to diminish.

Ellis found that when he saw clients only once a week or even every other week, they progressed as well as when he saw them daily. He decided to take a more active role, interjecting advice and direct interpretations as he did when he was counseling people with family or sex problems. He noticed that his clients improved quicker with this type of therapy than when he used passive psychoanalytic procedures.

And remembering that before he underwent analysis, he had worked through many of his own problems by reading and practicing the philosophies of Epictetus, Marcus Aurelius, Spinoza and Bertrand Russell, he began to teach his clients the principles that had worked for him. From the late 1940s onwards, Ellis worked on REBT (Rational Emotive Behavioral Therapy).

By 1955, Ellis had given up psychoanalysis entirely, and instead was concentrating on changing people's behavior by confronting them with their irrational beliefs and persuading them to adopt rational ones.

This role was more to Ellis' taste, for he could be more honest with himself. "When I became rational-emotive," he said, "my own personality processes really began to vibrate." He now began calling himself a rational therapist, advocating a new more active and directive type of psychotherapy.

In 1955, he presented Rational Therapy (RT) a therapy in which the therapist sought to help the client understand, and act on the understanding that his personal philosophy contained beliefs that contributed to his own emotional pain. RT stressed actively working to change a client's self-defeating beliefs and behaviors by demonstrating their irrationality, self-defeatism and rigidity. Soon he was teaching his new techniques to other therapists.

By 1957, Ellis formally set out the first cognitive behavior therapy by proposing that therapists help people adjust their thinking and behavior as the treatment for emotional and behavioral problems.

In 1959 he published *How to Live with a Neurotic*, and the following year presented a paper on his new approach at the American Psychological Association (APA) convention in Chicago. But his ideas did not go down as well as he had hoped. Despite the fact that his approach emphasized cognitive, emotive, and behavioral methods, his strong cognitive emphasis only provoked the nearly the entire psychotherapeutic establishment with the possible exception of the followers of Adler.

When his approach failed to take off with others he set up his own institute, *The Institute for Rational Living*, in 1959. By 1968, it was chartered by the New York State Board of Regents as a training institute and psychological clinic.

So what exactly is REBT?

First of all it is pronounced Rebt and not rebbit. It is a form of psychotherapy and a philosophy of living based on the premise that whenever we become upset, it is not the events taking place in our lives that upset us; it is the beliefs that we hold that cause us to become depressed, anxious, enraged, etc.

This was not a new idea. It was first articulated by Epictetus around 2,000 years ago: "Men are disturbed not by events, but by the views which they take of them."

According to REBT we all want to be happy, whether we are alone or with others; we want to get along with others, especially with one or two close friends; we want to be well informed and educated; we want a good job with good pay; and we want to enjoy our leisure time. Most of us would agree with that. But life doesn't allow us to have what we want. When our goals are thwarted, we can respond in ways that are healthy and helpful, or we can react in ways that are unhealthy and unhelpful. Ellis and REBT posit that our reaction to having our goals blocked is determined by our beliefs.

To illustrate this, Ellis developed a simple format to teach people how their beliefs cause their emotional and behavioral responses. It is called the ABC format. It works like this:

A. Something happens.

B. You have a belief about the situation.

C. You have an emotional reaction to the belief.

For example:
A. Your wife wrongly accuses you of having an affair and threatens to leave you.

B. You believe, "She has no grounds to accuse me. She's so wrong!"

C. You feel angry.

If you had held a different belief, your emotional response would have been different:

A. Your wife wrongly accuses you of having an affair.

B. You believe, "I must not let her believe that. It would ruin our marriage and be unbearable."

C. You feel anxious.

The ABC model shows that A does not cause C. It is B that causes C. In the first example, it is not your wife's false accusation and threat that make you angry; it is your belief that she has no grounds to accuse you.

In the second example, it is not her accusation and threat that make you anxious; it is the belief that you must not lose your wife, and that losing your wife would be unbearable.

Ellis also wrote about the three basic musts. Although we all express ourselves differently, according to REBT, the beliefs that upset us are all variations of three common irrational beliefs. Each of the three common irrational beliefs contains a demand. This demand may be about ourselves, other people, or the world in general.

These beliefs are known as "**The Three Basic Musts**."

The first is that I must do well and win the approval of others for my performances or else I am no good.

The second is that other people must treat me considerately, fairly and kindly, and in exactly the way I want them to treat me. If they don't, they are no good and they deserve to be condemned and punished.

The third is that I must get what I want, when I want it; and I must not get what I don't want. It's terrible if I don't get what I want, and I can't stand it. The first belief often leads to anxiety, depression, shame, and guilt. The second belief often leads to rage, passive-aggression and acts of violence. The third belief often leads to self-pity and procrastination.

REBT states that it is the demanding nature of the beliefs that causes the problem. If the beliefs were less demanding and more flexible this would lead to healthy emotions and helpful behaviors.

The goal of REBT is to help people change their irrational beliefs into rational beliefs. Changing beliefs is the real work of therapy and is achieved by the therapist disputing the client's irrational beliefs.

REBT posits that although we all think irrationally from time to time, we can work at eliminating this. While it's unlikely that we can ever entirely eliminate the tendency to think irrationally we can reduce the frequency, the duration, and the intensity of these irrational beliefs by developing three insights:

1. We don't merely get upset but mainly upset ourselves by holding inflexible beliefs.

2. No matter when and how we start upsetting ourselves, we continue to feel upset because we cling to our irrational beliefs.

3. The only way to get better is to work hard at changing our beliefs.

REBT is generally considered to be effective and efficient at reducing emotional pain. When Albert Ellis created REBT in the 1950s he met with much resistance from others in mental health. But today it is one of the most widely-practiced therapies throughout the world.

In the original version of his book *Sex Without Guilt*, Ellis wrote that religious restrictions on sexual expression are often needless and harmful to emotional health. Later in his life he described himself as a probabilistic atheist by which he meant that while he acknowledged that he wasn't certain there was no God, he believed the probability a God exists was so small that it was not worth his or anyone else's attention.

But while his personal atheism and humanism remained consistent, his views about the role of religion in mental health changed over time. Ellis was careful to state that REBT was independent of his atheism, noting that many skilled REBT practitioners are religious, including some who are ordained ministers. In his later days, he significantly toned down his opposition to religion.

In the mid-1990s, Ellis changed the name of his psychotherapy and behavior change system from Rational Therapy and then Rational-Emotive Therapy to Rational Emotive Behavior Therapy. His reason for doing this was to stress the interrelated importance of cognition, emotion and behavior in his therapeutic approach.

Despite serious ill health Ellis never stopped working often up to sixteen hours a day. Towards the end this was carried out with the assistance of his wife, Australian psychologist Debbie Joffe Ellis. In April 2006 he contracted pneumonia, and spent more than a year shuttling between hospital and a rehabilitation facility. He eventually returned to his residence on the top floor of the Albert Ellis Institute where he died on the 24 July, 2007 with his wife at his bedside. In his lifetime he had authored and co-authored more than eighty books and well over one thousand articles.

A recent book by Dr. Jim Byrne entitled *A Wounded Psychotherapist Albert*

Ellis's Childhood (2014) claims that Ellis was seriously harmed by parental neglect when he was a young child and that this had two negative impacts upon him. Firstly, he developed an insecure attachment style. Byrne says that this is illustrated by Ellis's own description of his relationship with his first real love, Karyl, and that this stayed with him throughout his life.

Secondly, he became significantly amoral. He admitted to indulging in serious frotteurism (the sexual misconduct of rubbing up against women) on the New York subway system with strange women when he was a teenager.

Byrne argues that some of the effects of his insecure attachment style and his amoralism had negative effects upon the theory of REBT. For example: (a) his inaccurate belief that 'virtually all' humans demand that they be loved by all significant others all of the time; and: (b) his failure to recognize that people need to use 'should-&-must-language' in order to retain a moral code: I must not steal; I should not harm others; etc.

Albert Ellis is credited (at least he credits himself) with inventing cognitive-behavioral therapy (CBT), the most widely practiced and popular of all psychotherapy approaches today. By his own lights, he beat Aaron Beck, the "other" inventor of CBT, to the punch by a few years.

Both Beck and Ellis departed radically from the dominant psychoanalytic approach by asserting that childhood events were largely irrelevant to the emotional problems of adults. Instead, they focused on changing the self-defeating beliefs (usually automatic) that kept people stuck in their own emotional morass.

Ellis maintained that his version of CBT, called Rational Emotional Behavior Therapy (REBT), differed from Beck's because it isn't just a clinical approach, but a realistic and rational philosophy of life, based on unconditional acceptance of oneself, of others, and of the world as it really is. The huge popularity of CBT, and that of REBT, owes much to Ellis's never-ending self-promotion.

JEROME BRUNER (1915-

"How one conceives of education, we have finally come to recognize, is a function of how one conceives of

the culture and its aims, professed and otherwise"

Cognitive Psychology
Educational Psychology

J erome S. Bruner is one of the best known and influential psychologists of the twentieth century and a prominent player in the so called 'cognitive revolution.'

But it is probably as an educator that his influence has been especially felt. His best selling books *The Process of Education* (1960) and *Towards a Theory of Instruction* (1966) are regarded as classics in the field of education and his work on the social studies program *Man: A Course of Study* is a landmark in curriculum development.

More recently Bruner has come to be critical of the 'cognitive revolution' and has looked to the building of a cultural psychology that takes proper account of the historical and social context of participants.

He developed these arguments in his 1996 book *The Culture of Education* with respect to education in general and schooling in particular. Along with Jean Piaget, Bruner's work on perception, learning, and memory in young children has hugely influenced the American educational system.

Jerome Seymour Bruner was born on the 1 October 1915 in New York. His parents, Herman and Rose Bruner, were Polish immigrants. His father was a watch maker and when he died when Jerome was only twelve his mother worked extra hard to bring him up.

Jerome was sent to university and in 1937 received a bachelor's degree in psychology from Duke University. He went on to complete a masters there before transferring to Harvard from which he received his doctorate in psychology in 1941.

During World War II, he served on the Psychological Warfare Division researching social psychological phenomena. In 1945, he returned to Harvard as a psychology professor and was heavily involved in research relating to cognitive psychology and educational psychology.

In 1970, Bruner left Harvard to teach at the University of Oxford in England. He returned to the United States in 1980 to continue his research in developmental psychology. In 1991, Bruner joined the faculty at New

York University where he taught how psychology affects legal practice. Throughout his career, Bruner has been awarded honorary doctorates from Yale and Columbia, as well as colleges and universities in Sorbonne, Berlin, and Rome. He is a Fellow of the American Academy of Arts and Sciences.

In the 1940s, Jerome Bruner together with Leo Postman, worked on the ways in which needs, motivations, and expectations influence perception. They explored perception from a functional orientation. Bruner also began investigating the role of strategies in the process of human categorization, and more generally, the development of human cognition. This interest in cognitive psychology led to a particular interest in the cognitive development of children and just what the appropriate forms of education might be.

In 1960 he published *The Process of Education* which greatly influenced the generation of a range of educational programs and experiments in the 1960s. He also became involved in the design and implementation of the influential MACOS project. This project which included Howard Gardner, sought to produce a comprehensive curriculum drawing upon the behavioral sciences.

The curriculum famously aimed to address three questions:

(a) What is uniquely human about human beings?

(b) How did they get that way?

(c) How could they be made more so?

MACOS was attacked by conservatives claiming that it was difficult to implement. The educational tide had begun to move away from more liberal and progressive thinkers like Jerome Bruner.

In the 1960s Bruner developed a theory of cognitive growth. Unlike Piaget, Bruner looked to environmental and experiential factors and maintained that intellectual ability developed in stages through step-by-step changes in how the mind is used.

Influenced by writers like Lev Vygotsky he began to be critical of the intrapersonal focus he had taken, and the lack of attention paid to social and political context.

After he went to Oxford he continued his research into questions of agency in infants and began a series of explorations of children's language. Later he became critical of the 'cognitive revolution' and began to argue for the building of a cultural psychology. This 'cultural turn' was then reflected in his work on education which can be seen in his 1996 book: *The Culture of Education.*

But it was his 1960 book *The Process of Education* that had a direct impact on policy formation in the United States. Its view of children as active problem-solvers who are ready to explore 'difficult' subjects while being out of step with the dominant view in education at that time, struck a chord with many. The book contained four key themes:

1. The role of structure in learning and how it may be made central in teaching:
Bruner argued that the approach taken should be a practical one.

2. Readiness for learning:
Here the argument is that schools have wasted a great deal of people's time by postponing the teaching of important areas because they are deemed 'too difficult'.

3. Intuitive and analytical thinking:
Here Bruner notes how experts in different fields appear 'to leap intuitively into a decision or to a solution to a problem' and looked to how teachers and schools might create the conditions for intuition to flourish.

4. Motives for learning:
'Ideally', Jerome Bruner writes, interest in the material to be learned is the best stimulus to learning, rather than such external goals as grades or later competitive advantage.'

Bruner wrote two 'postscripts' to *The Process of Education: Towards a theory of instruction* (1966) and *The Relevance of Education* (1971) in which he put forward his evolving ideas about the ways in which instruction actually affects the mental models of the world that students construct, elaborate on and transform.

Bruner's reflections on education in *The Culture of Education* (1996) show the impact of the changes in his thinking since the 1960s. He now placed his work within a thorough appreciation of culture. It also takes Bruner well beyond the confines of schooling.

Jerome S. Bruner has had a profound effect on education. His influence can be summed up by his one time student Howard Gardner who has commented: "Jerome Bruner is not merely one of the foremost educational thinkers of the era; he is also an inspired learner and teacher. His infectious curiosity inspires all who are not completely jaded. Individuals of every age and background are invited to join in. Logical analyses, technical dissertations, rich and wide knowledge of diverse subject matters, asides to an ever wider orbit of information, intuitive leaps, pregnant enigmas pour forth from his indefatigable mouth and pen. In his words, 'Intellectual activity is anywhere and everywhere, whether at the frontier of knowledge or in a third-grade classroom'. To those who know him, Bruner remains the Compleat Educator in the flesh."

JAMES BUGENTAL (1915-2008)

"Without awareness, we are not truly alive"

Existential-Humanistic Therapy
Humanistic Psychology

James F. T. Bugental was a leading psychotherapist and a founding father, with Abraham Maslow and others, of humanistic psychology or "the third force." He was also the creator, along with Rollo May, of existential-humanistic psychotherapy.

James Frederick Thomas Bugental was born on Christmas day in 1915 in Fort Wayne, Indiana, America. He moved frequently as a child, and lived at various times in Ohio, Illinois, Michigan, and California. His upbringing proved challenging due to frequent moves, and the personal and financial setbacks of his parents.

He earned his doctorate from the Ohio State University in 1948 where he was influenced by Victor Raimy and George Kelly. His dissertation, *An Investigation of the Relationship of the Conceptual Matrix to the Self-concept* (1948), expressed his early interest in authenticity and identity.

In 1953 he resigned from the psychology faculty of UCLA to set up with Alvin Lasko, the first group practice of psychotherapy called Psychological Service Associates. Later they were joined by Tom Greening, Gerard Haigh, Bill Zielonka, and Harris Monosoff.

His group were heavily influenced by Rollo May's publication *Existence* in 1958 leading him and his colleagues to develop existential psychotherapy further. They brought Rollo May to Los Angeles for a training seminar. Bugental's germinal book *The Search for Authenticity* (1965) grew out of these encounters.

Later, Bugental with Abraham Maslow and others, cofounded the *Journal of Humanistic Psychology* and the Association for Humanistic Psychology in 1961. In 1963 his landmark article in *The American Psychologist* called "Humanistic Psychology: A New Breakthrough" presented the fundamental assumptions of humanistic psychology to the discipline.

The **humanistic psychology** perspective is summarized by five core principles or postulates of humanistic psychology as set out in Bugental's *The Search for Authenticity* (1965). The five basic principles of humanistic psychology are:

1. Human beings, as human, supersede the sum of their parts. They cannot be reduced to components.

2. Human beings have their existence in a uniquely human context, as well as in a cosmic ecology.

3. Human beings are aware and are aware of being aware i.e., they are conscious. Human consciousness always includes an awareness of oneself in the context of other people.

4. Human beings have some choice and, with that, responsibility.

5. Human beings are intentional, aim at goals, are aware that they cause future events, and seek meaning, value, and creativity.

It should be pointed out that while humanistic psychology is a specific division within the American Psychological Association (Division 32), humanistic psychology is not so much a discipline within psychology as a perspective on the human condition that informs psychological research and practice.

With the advent of *The Search for Authenticity*, Bugental inspired a new generation to consider and apply **the existential approach** first translated and popularized in America by Rollo May.

While May elaborated existential-humanistic theory and social analysis, Bugental stressed their living application to practice. Among his signal contributions are:

A. his articulations of therapeutic presence;

B. the various "presses" or valences that optimize therapeutic presence; and,

C. the challenge to translate therapeutic presence into an authentic and responsible life.

In his later years Bugental presented his work at over 250 universities, colleges, hospitals, and clinics. He received the 1991 Pathfinder Award of the Association for Humanistic Psychology and an honorary degree in 1993 from Saybrook Graduate School, where he was a central figure. Numerous trainees emerged from his tutorials, including Myrtle Heery, Kirk Schneider, Orah Krug, and Nader Shabahangi, who went on to co-found, at Jim's instigation, the Existential-Humanistic Institute (EHI) and the International Institute for Humanistic Studies (IIHS).

More recently, Bugental's work has been extended to a new generation with the publication of an edited collection by Kirk Schneider titled *Existential-Integrative Psychotherapy* (2008) and an APA monograph by Kirk Schneider and Orah Krug called *Existential-Humanistic Therapy*.

He died on the 17 September 2008.

HANS JüRGEN EYSENCK (1916 – 1997)

"There thus appears to be an inverse correlation between recovery and psychotherapy; the more psychotherapy, the smaller the recovery rate"

Intelligence
Psychological Science

Hans Eysenck was a German born British educated psychologist noted for his polarizing and forthright views who developed a distinctive dimensional model of personality based on factor-analytic summaries and biogenetic processes.

Eysenck managed to join descriptive statistics with physiological experimentation, collapsing the distinction between pure and applied science. He was an outspoken advocate of the biogenetic basis of individual differences in intelligence and personality. He was also a lifelong critic of psychoanalytic psychotherapy. He was the author of eighty-five books and more than one thousand scientific papers. He was also a renowned popularizer of psychological science.

He was born in Berlin on the 4 March 1916 to a Catholic father, Eduard Eysenck who was a stage performer in a nightclub. His mother was Silesian-born film star Ruth Werner known as Helga Molander. Eysenck was an only child. Soon after he was born his parents separated, and he was raised by his Jewish maternal grandmother.

Eysenck completed his secondary schooling at Prinz-Heinrichs-Gymnasium in Berlin in 1934. However, his ambiguous ethnic background left him with a difficult choice: He could either toe the National Socialist line or emigrate.

His mother and her *de facto* partner, Jewish film producer, Max Glass, had already fled to France. Eysenck chose to join them, spending a few months in Dijon in the summer of 1934. He then travelled to London the following August.

Meanwhile his father remained in Berlin and joined the Nazi Party in May 1937, much to Hans's disgust. Eysenck was later to say: "My hatred of Hitler and the Nazis, and all they stood for, was so overwhelming that no argument could counter it."

Because of his nationality he found it difficult to gain employment in London. He undertook bridging courses at Pitman's College in London in the winter of 1934–1935. He then applied to study physics at University College London, but lacking the necessary prerequisites, he opted instead for psychology.

After taking his degree in 1938, Eysenck remained at University College, rapidly completing a Ph.D. on the experimental analysis of aesthetic preferences, supervised by Cyril Burt. As the war escalated Eysenck completed his doctorate and just managed to avoid internment.

Eventually, he secured a position at the Mill Hill Hospital in Northern London in June 1942. Headed by the imposing psychiatrist Aubrey Lewis, Mill Hill functioned as the relocated Maudsley psychiatric hospital. Afterwards he headed up the new Institute of Psychiatry (IoP) in London which was really his first and only job until his retirement in 1983.

In 1938 Eysenck married Canadian graduate student Margaret Davies. Their one child, Michael, was born in 1944 and went on to become a notable psychologist. However, his marriage didn't last. He later became a British citizen. Eysenck's first and most important book. *Dimensions of Personality* (1947) outlined two personality factors of neuroticism (N) and introversion-extraversion (I-E), creating an inverted "T" grid with an I-E base and an N vertex.

Eysenck believed that two common psychiatric diagnoses, dysthymia and hysteria, were the introverted and extraverted manifestations of a highly neurotic personality. Eysenck deliberately contrasted these continuums with the discrete typologies of psychiatry and attempted to clear up the confusing and speculative trait lists of personality psychology.

In 1952 *The Scientific Study of Personality* introduced a third factor, psychoticism (P), again constructed around the idea that psychotic disorders differed in terms of introversion-extraversion.

In his seminal work, *The Dynamics of Anxiety and Hysteria*, (1957) he argued that I-E was related to a simplified version of Pavlov's notion of excitation and inhibition, while N was vaguely linked with anxiety drive strength. This allowed him to connect personality differences with conditioned learning.

Eysenck posited that introverts were far more responsive than extroverts, learning quicker, better, and for longer periods. As a consequence, introverts also tended to have a more developed sense of morality and a greater capacity for academic achievement.

His 1967 book, *The Biological Basis of Personality*, developed his theory and now said that I-E was linked to cortical arousal levels in the brain stem's activation systems. Learning was now seen as an interaction between external stimulation and internal activation levels, with introverts and extroverts having characteristically different optimal bandwidths.

Essentially, Eysenck was an interactionist rather than a reductionist, who believed that behavior was the sum effect of genetic endowment and environment. In the mid-1960s he controversially likened conscience to a conditioned reflex suggesting that extroverts were slower to develop socially acceptable behavior. Needless to say these suggestions were not well received.

In 1959 he introduced the Maudsley Personality Inventory (measuring I-E and N) which then became the Eysenck Personality Inventory and later with the help of second wife, Sybil Rostal, the 1975 version was renamed the **Eysenck Personality Questionnaire**.

These inventories became some of the most widely used of their type in the world and served as valuable research tools for those researching Eysenck-related topics.

Eysenck also played a major role in clinical psychology in Britain and was a key promoter of behavior therapy. In the early 1950s, he argued for a research-based clinical discipline that put science ahead of social need and was critical of the rapid development of clinical psychology in America. He attacked the reliability of psychiatric diagnosis and the validity of projective tests like the Rorschach.

In his 1952 article, *"The Effects of Psychotherapy: An Evaluation,"* he famously questioned the efficacy of talk psychotherapy and over the years, his dislike of psychoanalysis deepened. He called it insular and imprecise and not properly empirically tested. He became the leading anti-Freudian in Britain.

A new type of therapy was needed. The emerging Behavior therapy seemed to be perfectly in tune with Eysenck's perspective of the detached clinical scientist. Behavior therapy was less talk and more a targeted course of remedial training summed up by Eysenck's pithy 1959 slogan: "Get rid of the symptom and you have eliminated the neurosis."

By late 1958 Eysenck began to advocate openly that psychologists practice behavioral treatment. But behavior therapy proved vulnerable to the radical social critiques of the period and such therapists were obliged to soften their style. Diagnosis and directed therapy gave way to helping the patients help themselves.

While psychoanalysts learned to ignore his attacks, Eysenck helped ensure that clinical psychology became a more accountable, empirically based practice. However, his vision of clinical psychology as the research-based application of learning principles has been swamped by a more diverse, service-oriented profession wielding a hybrid variety of humanistic and cognitive-behavioral techniques. Eysenck would concede that cognitive factors were important, but he re-described them in a manner which suggested that behavior therapy always allowed for them.

Eysenck believed that intellectual differences were 80 percent heritable. Later in his life he played a key role in attempts to increase intelligence with vitamins and at one stage he controversially suggested that nutritional factors may account for race differences.

In his lifetime, Eysenck's popular paperbacks and media appearances turned him into a celebrity making him the People's Psychologist in 1960s Britain. But his uncompromising three-dimensional view of personality was always countered by more complex descriptive systems in America like Raymond Cattrell's sixteen personality factors.

Despite this, Eysenck was the most influential post war psychologist but only in Britain. He never received the attention he deserved in America and was largely ignored in his own country of Germany. Regarded by mainstream psychologists as too controversial it should be pointed out that his reputation derived in part from his involvement in issues which were already controversial. He died in 1997.

VIRGINIA SATIR (1916-1988)

Satir Model
Family Therapy

Virginia Satir was an American visionary family therapist, whose Satir Model continues to inform and influence the work of individual, family and group practitioners seeking to facilitate a greater sense of vitality and inner peace for clients.

She established professional training groups in the Satir Model around the world: the Middle East, Asia, Western and Eastern Europe, Central and Latin America, and Russia. She believed that people are capable of continued growth, change and new understanding.

Her initial purpose was to improve relationships and communication within the family unit. Ultimately her work grew to be accepted as applicable to all human communication and growth, within a person, a family, a community or a company. She remained a leading force for human growth and family therapy until her death in 1988.

Virginia Satir was born on the 26 June 1916 at the family farm in Neillsville, Wisconsin, in America. She was followed 18 months later by twins: Russell and Roger. Then in 1921 Edith was born, followed two years later by Ray. Being the eldest she felt a sense of responsibility for her siblings, and cared for them during their years growing up.

Her grandparents, on both sides, were born in Germany between 1870 and 1875. Both sets of grandparents came from a privileged socioeconomic class and married working-class men. Her father, Oscar Alfred Reinnard Pagenkopf, was the youngest of thirteen children. He was a farmer and had very little formal education. One quality he instilled in her was the importance of honesty.

Her mother, Minnie Happe Pagenkopf, came from a family of seven children. She realized the importance of education and insisted the family move to the city when Virginia, the eldest, started high school in 1929. Her mother was a Christian Scientist and when Virginia became ill at the age of five her mother refused to bring her to a doctor.

Her father finally took her to hospital where they discovered that her appendix had ruptured. She remained in hospital for several months. Despite this unfortunate experience, she enjoyed a happy family life.

Virginia began reading when she was three and enjoyed a thirst for knowledge. Virginia was enrolled at South Division High School in Milwaukee. She finished school in 1932 when she was sixteen. She then attended Milwaukee State Teachers College now University of Wisconsin. Working while studying in order to pay her way she graduated in 1936 with a B.A. in Education. The following year she started graduate school.

In 1941, she married a young soldier called Gordon Rodgers, While he was away at war she finished her masters at the University of Chicago in 1943. She divorced in 1949. She married again this time to Norman Satir. This marriage lasted from 1951 to 1957. It was during this second marriage that Virginia adopted Mary and Ruth as she was unable to have children of her own.

How could someone who was unable to sustain a normal healthy marriage be so successful in helping others? Virginia is quoted as saying: "Had I known back then what I know today, we would have had a lot of different things happening. But I didn't know. You always look back with hindsight, and hindsight is wonderful for writing Ph.D. papers, but not very good for life."

After teaching she went into social work. She entered private practice. By 1955 she was working with Dr. Calmest Gyros at the Illinois Psychiatric Institute, spreading the idea of working not just with patients but with their families as well. She moved to California, where together with Don Jackson and Jules Riskin, she founded the Mental Health Research Institute in Menlo Park.

In 1964 she began visiting Esalen Institute, in Big Sur, California and later became one of the first Directors of Training, overseeing the Human Potential Development Programs.

At the core of Virginia Satir's philosophy was a profound respect for human life and the potential of each person: "Human beings are a marvel, also a treasure, and indeed a miracle. My approach, the **Human Process Validation Model** is based on the premise that all we manifest at any point in time represents what we have learned, consciously, implicitly, cellularly. Our behavior reflects what we have learned. Learning is the basis of behavior. To change behavior, we need to have new learning. To accomplish new learning, we need a motive, a purpose, a nurturing context, and a trust in something from the outside to help us."

In 1964 Virginia published her first book, *Conjoint Family Therapy*, followed immediately by *Peoplemaking*. She became a pioneer of family therapy and was increasingly in demand all over the United States and abroad. In her workshops, she taught people practical things about themselves, communication, families, and communities.

She used humor and made pictures by asking people to stand or sit in a certain way to demonstrate feelings externally. Using these tools of sculpting and role playing, she was able to create a safe place so that people could open themselves to new experiences.

In 1970 she began the International Human Learning Resources Network (IHLRN) under the name *Beautiful People*. In 1977 Virginia founded The Avanta Network, later called *Avanta*, The Virginia Satir Network. She used these networks to develop various opportunities for reaching out to individuals, families, and other mental health workers.

In her final book, *The Third Birth*, she said that the **first birth** comes when an ovum and sperm find each other and unite.

The **second birth** is when we came out of the womb. This is probably one of the most startling changes we will ever undergo. We are coming from a place where it is dark. In this darkness, we hear the sounds of the internal organs working.

It is a place where the temperature is even and the context is water. From there we move to a place where it is light and sounds are completely different, the temperature is most uneven, and the water is found only in the bath, once a day.

The **third birth** is when we become our own decision-makers. Some people call this being mature. It occurs when we take charge of our life, stand on our own feet. Taking charge of this process of developing our uniqueness and becoming a responsible and responsive human, among our other human beings on this planet, is a vital stage of growth. Everyone who has lived has made the first two births, but according to Virginia relatively few have made the third.

Virginia Satir died from cancer at the age of 72. Today Satir Centers and Institutes are operating all over the world. In particular, *Avanta* carries on her work with a current and ever-evolving scope. Since she founded *Avanta* in 1977, it has been a forum for developing ideas, techniques, skills and training.

Through national and international conferences, workshops and training efforts, as well as the efforts of individual members, *Avanta* has used the inspiration and drive that Virginia Satir inspired to reach thousands of people worldwide.

Satir often integrated meditations and poetic writing into both her public workshops and writings. One of her most well-known works, *I Am Me*, was written by Satir in response to a question posed by an angry teenage girl:

"I am me
In all the world, there is no one else exactly like me
Everything that comes out of me is authentically me
Because I alone chose it – I own everything about me
My body, my feelings, my mouth, my voice, all my actions,
Whether they be to others or to myself – I own my fantasies,
My dreams, my hopes, my fears – I own all my triumphs and
Successes, all my failures and mistakes Because I own all of
Me, I can become intimately acquainted with me – by so doing
I can love me and be friendly with me in all my parts – I know
There are aspects about myself that puzzle me, and other
Aspects that I do not know – but as long as I am
Friendly and loving to myself, I can courageously
And hopefully look for solutions to the puzzles
And for ways to find out more about me – However I

Look and sound, whatever I say and do, and whatever
I think and feel at a given moment in time is authentically
Me – If later some parts of how I looked, sounded, thought
And felt turn out to be unfitting, I can discard that which is
Unfitting, keep the rest, and invent something new for that
Which I discarded – I can see, hear, feel, think, say, and do
I have the tools to survive, to be close to others, to be
Productive to make sense and order out of the world of
People and things outside of me – I own me, and
therefore I can engineer me – I am me and I AM OKAY"

Of all the brilliant psychologists referenced in this book Virginia Satir is in a class of her own. For many therapists, she is the special one. She was different from her peers. For a start, her height at six foot was augmented by both her her three-inch heels and several inches of bouffant hair-do. Her hallmark was her extraordinary sensitivity to the nonverbal aspects of communication like height differentials, distance, voice, tone, eye contact, posture, touch, and movement.

She believed that if she could help her clients see, hear, and feel more, their personal and interpersonal resources would lead them to their own solutions. Readers of this book are urged to watch the videos of her seminars which capture Satir's genius better than anything she ever wrote.

But Satir's real power was her ability to work in many styles at once. Her sessions incorporated essential elements of strategic, structural, systemic, intergenerational, and experiential family therapy into a distinctive whole. She believed the cognitive approach to self-differentiation was insufficient. She believed that meaningful change meant involving the whole person, reaching out to them on as many levels as possible.

Like a strategic therapist, she emphasized obtaining specific descriptions of the family's presenting problem from family members. But she insisted that the presenting issue itself was seldom the real problem; rather, how people coped with the issue created the problem.

She incorporated in her work the structuralists' insistence upon giving people an experience of change within the therapy hour, believing words change people only if they're supported by the full experience of what the words mean.

She used family sculpting to get her clients to enact their interactional difficulties so that she could get a clearer picture of exactly what was going on. But in addition to her concern with the here and now, she recognized the enormous influence of people's experiences in their families of origin.

How does her therapy work?

In her own words: "It is simply a question of life reaching out to life. As a therapist, I am a companion. I try to help people tune into their own wisdom. Of course, all this doesn't fit much of a psychotherapeutic theory."

BRENDA MILNER (1918-

"The thing that has driven me my whole life is curiosity. I am incredibly curious about the little things I see around me"

Neuropsychology

British born Canadian based neuropsychologist Brenda Milner is regarded as the "founder of neuropsychology." Milner has contributed a vast amount of research to the field.

She continues to work at the age of 95. She is currently a professor at McGill University's Department of Neurology and Neurosurgery as well as a professor of psychology at the Montreal Neurological Institute. At present, Milner's work is partly focused on how the left and right hemispheres of the brain interact as well as the study of neural pathways involved in the learning of language. The many honors she has received for her work include the prestigious Gairdner Award and the Order of Canada.

She was born Brenda Langford on the 25 July, 1918, in Manchester, England. Her father was a musical critic, journalist, and teacher and her mother was a singing student. However, Brenda herself had no interest in music. She attended Withington Girls' School and went on to Newnham College, Cambridge, first to read mathematics and then psychology under Oliver Zangwill.

In 1937 she graduated with a B.A. in experimental psychology. It is to the brilliant Zangwill that she owes her first interest in human brain function. Zangwill began postgraduate research with Frederic Bartlett, Cambridge's first Professor of Experimental Psychology who had an extraordinarily powerful effect on the shape of British academic psychology.

After her graduation, Milner was awarded a Sarah Smithson Research Studentship which allowed her to attend Newnham for the following two years. Because of the War, the Cambridge Psychological Laboratory, under Bartlett's leadership, was diverted to applied research in the selection of aircrew.

Milner's job was to devise perceptual tasks for future use in selecting aircrew. She was also part of a team which sought to distinguish fighter pilots from bomber pilots using aptitude tests.

After receiving her masters in 1944, she married electrical engineer Peter Milner and emigrated to Canada where Peter had been invited to work with physicists on atomic research. Milner then became a Ph.D. candidate in psychophysiology at McGill University, under the direction of the Donald Olding Hebb.

In 1950, Hebb gave Milner an opportunity to study the behavior of epileptic patients treated with focal ablation of brain tissue with Wilder Penfield at the Montreal Neurological Institute. In 1952, she received her Ph.D. in experimental psychology. In 1954 she published an article in the McGill University Psychological Bulletin called *Intellectual Function of the Temporal Lobes* in which she reviewed animal studies of neural function and compared it to human neuroscience work.

She asserted that temporal lobe damage can cause emotional and intellectual changes in humans and lower primates thus discouraging several neurosurgeons from completing surgeries on human beings that could negatively impact their lives.

Milner was a pioneer in the field of memory and studied the effects of damage to the medial temporal lobe on memory. She systematically described the deficits in the most famous patient in cognitive neuroscience who was originally known only by his initials, H.M.

Born in February 1926, Henry Molaison suffered from intractable epilepsy causing partial seizures for many years and then several tonic-clonic seizures after his sixteenth birthday. In 1953 he was referred to William Beecher Scoville, a neurosurgeon at Hartford Hospital.

Scoville localized Molaison's epilepsy to his left and right medial temporal lobes (MTLs) and suggested surgical resection of the MTLs as a treatment. In 1953, Molaison's bilateral medial temporal lobe resection was surgically removed.

His hippocampi appeared entirely nonfunctional because the remaining 2 cm of hippocampal tissue appeared atrophic and because the entire entorhinal cortex, which forms the major sensory input to the hippocampus, was destroyed. Some of his anterolateral temporal cortex was also destroyed. However, the surgery was successful in its primary goal of controlling his epilepsy.

But following the surgical procedure, he suffered from severe anterograde amnesia. Although his working memory and procedural memory were intact, he could not commit new events to his explicit memory. According to some scientists, Molaison was impaired in his ability to form new semantic knowledge. He also suffered moderate retrograde amnesia.

He could not remember most events in the one to two period before surgery, nor some events up to eleven years before. This meant that his amnesia was temporally graded. However, his ability to form long-term procedural memories was intact; thus he could, for example, learn new motor skills, despite not being able to remember learning them.

In the early stages of her work with H.M., Milner wanted to completely understand his memory impairments. She was able to show that the medial temporal lobe amnestic syndrome is characterized by an inability to acquire new memories and an inability to recall established memories from a few years immediately before damage, while memories from the more remote past and other cognitive abilities, including language, perception and reasoning were intact.

Her study led her to speculate that there are different types of learning and memory, each dependent on a separate system of the brain. She indeitied two two different memory systems; episodic memory and procedural memory. From this and other cases she discovered that "bilateral medial temporal-lobe resection in man results in a persistent impairment of recent memory whenever the removal is carried far enough posteriorly to damage portions of the anterior hippocampus and hippocampal gyrus."

This finding introduced the concept of multiple memory systems within the brain and stimulated an enormous body of research. Milner is the Dorothy J. Killam Professor at the Montreal Neurological Institute, and a professor in the Department of Neurology and Neurosurgery at McGill.

AARON BECK (1921-

"When married people develop such an intense but inappropriate fixation to somebody other than their mate, they may be driven to jeopardize or even destroy a reasonable marital relationship. In the heat of passion, they seem incapable of attaching any real weight to the potentially disastrous consequences of their infatuation, the possible breakup of their marriage. They cannot "turn off" their infatuation even if they want to! Yet, when enough time has elapsed without their seeing "the other woman (or man)," they generally find that their infatuation dies down"

Cognitive Therapy
Clinical Depression
Children's Depression Inventory

Aaron Temkin Beck is an American psychiatrist who is

regarded as the father of cognitive therapy and one of the world's leading researchers in psychopathology. He has been credited with shaping the face of American psychiatry.

The American Psychologist has called him "one of the five most influential psychotherapists of all time." His pioneering theories are widely used in the treatment of clinical depression. Beck is also responsible for the development of self-report measures of depression and anxiety including the Beck Depression Inventory (BDI), the Beck Hopelessness Scale, the Beck Scale for Suicidal Ideation (BSS), the Beck Anxiety Inventory (BAI), and Beck Youth Inventories.

His creation of cognitive therapy and the BDI is one of the most widely used instruments for measuring depression severity. He is the President Emeritus of the non-profit Beck Institute for Cognitive Behavior Therapy and the Honorary President of the Academy of Cognitive Therapy, an institution which certifies qualified cognitive therapists. Beck was born on the 18 July 1921 in Providence, Rhode Island, USA, the youngest child of four siblings to Russian Jewish immigrants.

He graduated from Brown University in 1942 before transferring to Yale Medical School from which he received his M.D. in 1946. Following his graduation from medical school he served as assistant chief of neuropsychiatry at Valley Forge Army Hospital in the United States Military.

In 1954 he became an instructor at the University of Pennsylvania (Penn). It was here, in the early 1960s that he developed cognitive therapy. Prior to this he had studied and practiced psychoanalysis. But as he researched and performed experiments to test psychoanalytic concepts of depression he was shocked to discover that his experiments did not validate its fundamental precepts.

Following this discovery he embarked on an investigative journey to find other ways of conceptualizing depression. He found that patients suffering from depression experienced streams of negative thoughts that seemed to arrive spontaneously. He called these automatic thoughts, and categorized them into negative ideas about themselves, the world, and the future.

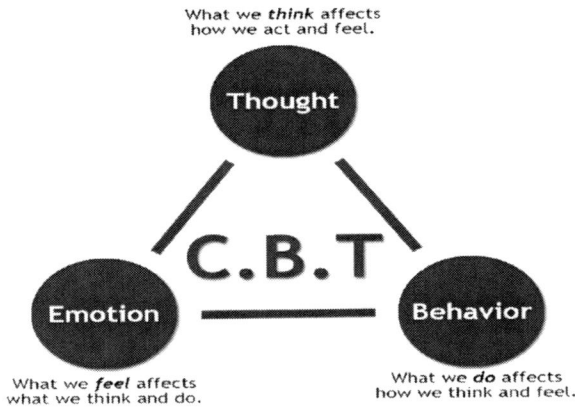

What we *think* affects how we act and feel.

Thought

C.B.T

Emotion

Behavior

What we *feel* affects what we think and do.

What we *do* affects how we think and feel.

He found that if patients could identify and evaluate these thoughts they would be able to think more realistically. This would make them feel better emotionally and behave more functionally. His research led him to believe that ideas in CBT explained that different disorders were associated with different types of distorted thinking which has a negative effect on our behavior irrespective of the type of disorder.

He posited that successful interventions would educate a person to understand and become aware of their distorted thinking, and would allow them challenge its effects. He also discovered that frequent negative automatic thoughts reveal a person's core beliefs which are formed over lifelong experiences. Essentially, we "feel" these beliefs to be true.

Beck's approach is similar to Albert Ellis in that it emphasizes recognizing and changing negative thoughts and maladaptive beliefs. He believed that negative thoughts underlie mental disorders and he was particularly keen to find out why people suffered with depression. He identified two mechanisms that he thought were responsible for it, Errors in Logic and Cognitive Triad.

The first was **Errors in Logic,** that is faulty information processing. The second was what he called the **Cognitive triad**. Patients have negative views about the world which lead to negative views about the future which lead to negative views about themselves. It become a vicious circle.

In addition, Beck identifies a number of **illogical thinking processes**:

Selective Attention:
Seeing only the negative features of an event;

Magnification:
Exaggerating the importance of undesirable events; and,

Overgeneralization:
Drawing broad negative conclusions on the basis of a single insignificant event.

These illogical thought patterns are self-defeating, and can cause great anxiety or depression for the individual. His system of therapy is very like Ellis's, but has been most widely used in cases of depression. Hollon and Beck (1994) found that patients suffering from depression who are treated with Beck's approach improve significantly more than those who receive no treatment and about the same as those who receive biological treatments. Beck's Cognitive therapy has also been successfully applied to panic disorders and other anxiety disorders.

Today this type of psychotherapy is used to treat a wide range of disorders including not only depression and bipolar disorders, but also eating disorders, drug abuse, anxiety disorders, personality disorders, and many other medical conditions with psychological components.

Some of his more recent work focused on cognitive therapy for schizophrenia, borderline personality disorder, and for patients who are repeat suicide attempters.

Beck has also collaborated with others to develop new therapies. He worked with Maria Kovacs, in the development of the Children's Depression Inventory, which is a psychological assessment that rates the severity of symptoms related to depression and/or dysthymic disorder in children and adolescents.

Beck's research was also the inspiration for Martin Seligman to refine his own cognitive techniques and exercises, and later work on learned helplessness.

Learned helplessness is a behavior in which an organism forced to endure aversive, painful or otherwise unpleasant stimuli, becomes unable or unwilling to avoid subsequent encounters with those stimuli, even if they are escapable. The theory states that clinical depression and related mental illnesses may result from a perceived absence of control over the outcome of a situation.

Beck has been described as one of the "Americans in history who shaped the face of American Psychiatry." If all therapists today are at least a little bit Rogerian, it's probably true that most of them are also a little bit Beckian.

Cognitive therapy as he originally called it, emerged quietly and unobtrusively on the scene in the 1960s, invented more or less simultaneously and independently by Aaron Beck and Albert Ellis. Forty years on it's a hugely successful therapy called CBT or cognitive-behavioral therapy.

The genius of Beck's method was not only its brevity and effectiveness, but its easily replicable methodology, which lent itself readily to clinical trials. Beck not only developed a systematic model of brief therapy based on the notion that distorted thinking sustains depression and anxiety, but also perfected an empirically testable clinical technique.

Beck was one of the first to have his clients sit up and face him (rather than lie down on the couch), so he could see their expressions and body language, and asked them what they were thinking.

All responded by saying things like, "I'm stupid," or "I'm boring," or "I'm a terrible failure." This constant drip of negativity poisoned their entire existence. Becks says that when he focused on these negative thoughts, clients got better fairly soon, in ten or twelve sessions. From these almost incidental beginnings, a mighty empire grew.

Supporters of CBT have often been criticized for giving short shrift to all the old virtues of therapy, like compassion, empathy, and the like. Not Beck, however.

He is recorded as saying: "Therapists who are good at the technical end of cognitive therapy fall flat on their faces when it comes to the more complex case. Empathy, sensitivity, considerateness, together with the ability to put them together with technical aspects, is the combination needed."

So, perhaps, Aaron Temkin Beck, the father of cognitive therapy, the most "mental" of therapies, is secretly another Rogerian!

SALVADOR MINUCHIN (1921-

Structural Family Therapy

Salvador Minuchin is a family therapist, born in Argentina who developed structural family therapy, a method of psychotherapy which addresses problems in functioning within a family.

Salvador Minuchin was the eldest of three born to the children of Russian-Jewish immigrants. He was born and raised in San Salvador, Entre Ríos, a closely knit small Jewish community in rural Argentina. His father had been a prosperous businessman until the Great Depression forced his family into poverty.

In high school, he decided he would help juvenile delinquents after hearing his psychology teacher discuss the philosopher Jean-Jacque Rousseau's ideas that delinquents are victims of society.

At eighteen, Minuchin entered university as a medical student. In 1944, while a student, he became active in the leftist political movement opposing the dictator Juan Peron, who had taken control of Argentina's universities. Minuchin was jailed for three months. Upon graduation in 1946, he began a residency in pediatrics and took a subspecialty in psychiatry. In 1948, as Minuchin was opening a pediatric practice, the state of Israel was created and immediately plunged into war. He moved to Israel and joined its army, where he treated young Jewish soldiers who had survived the Holocaust.

Minuchin emigrated to America in 1950 to study psychiatry. He worked with psychotic children at Bellevue Hospital in New York City as a part-time psychiatric resident. Minuchin also worked at the Jewish Board of Guardians where he lived in its institutional housing with twenty disturbed children. His training there was psychoanalytic, which did not seem compatible with his work with the children.

Minuchin married Patricia Pittluck, a psychologist, and emigrated to Israel in 1951. There he co-directed five residential institutions for disturbed children. Most of them were orphans of the Holocaust and Jewish children from Asia and the Middle East. Here, he first began to work therapeutically with groups instead of individuals.

Between 1954 and 1958, Minuchin trained at the William Alanson White Institute of Psychoanalysis in New York City. He went there because the Institute supported the ideas of Harry Stack Sullivan, who created interpersonal psychiatry and stressed the importance of interpersonal interaction.

As he was training there, he began practicing family therapy at the Wiltwyck School for Boys, a school for troubled youth and juvenile delinquents. Slowly, he began to believe that he needed to see a client's family. In his experience, seeing them alone, as per psychoanalysis, was not an effective treatment technique.

Minuchin and a number of other professionals began working as a team to develop approaches to family therapy. These youths at the Wiltwyck School and their families tended not to be very introspective, so Minuchin and his team focused on communication and behavior, and developed a therapy approach in which the therapist is very active, making suggestions and directing activities.

In 1965, Minuchin, his wife, and their two children moved to Philadelphia, where he became, at the same time, Director of Psychiatry at Children's Hospital of Philadelphia, Director of the Philadelphia Child Guidance Clinic, and Professor of Child Psychiatry at the University of Pennsylvania School of Medicine. During this time, he began working therapeutically with children with psychosomatic illnesses. Research with these children and families indicated that family therapy could help these patients improve, and that maladaptive family patterns were partly to blame for these illnesses.

During the 1960s and 1970s, Minuchin became interested in the larger social world in which families are embedded. He and his group started studying communities and social service agencies. In one project, he and his colleagues, under an intensive program, trained minorities from the community to be family therapists. However, Minuchin struggled to understand family dynamics.

He explored what other family therapists and colleagues in the social sciences were doing, and drew on those that seemed to work. He found Gregory Bateson's systems theory (a system is comprised of interdependent parts that mutually affect each other) to go a long way in explaining family dynamics. Minuchin was also influenced by Nathan Ackerman, a child analyst who began to look at the interpersonal aspects of the family unit, and the ways individual behavior relates to that unit.

In 1975, Minuchin retired from his position as Director of the Philadelphia Clinic. He then served as Director Emeritus of the Clinic until 1981 at which time he established Family Studies, Inc., in New York City, an organization to teach family therapists.

Minuchin left the University of Pennsylvania, Philadelphia in 1983, when he joined New York University School of Medicine as a Research Professor. He retired in 1996 and currently lives in Boca Raton, Florida.

Minuchin has contributed to numerous professional journals and coauthored numerous books, many of which explore the effects of poverty and socials systems on families.

He is best known for founding Structural Family Therapy (SFT) a method of psychotherapy that addresses problems in functioning within a family. SFT therapists strive to enter, or "join", the family system in therapy in order to understand the invisible rules which govern its functioning, map the relationships between family members or between subsets of the family, and ultimately disrupt dysfunctional relationships within the family, causing it to stabilize into healthier patterns. Minuchin believes that pathology rests not in the individual, but within the family system.

SFT utilizes, not only a special systems terminology, but also a means of depicting key family parameters diagrammatically. Its focus is on the structure of the family, including its various substructures. In this regard, Minuchin is a follower of systems and communication theory, since his structures are defined by transactions among interrelated systems within the family.

He subscribes to the systems notions of wholeness and equifinality, both of which are critical to his notion of change. An essential trait of SFT is that the therapist actually enters, or "joins", with the family system as a catalyst for positive change. Joining with a family is a goal of the therapist early on in his or her therapeutic relationship with the family. Structural and Strategic therapy are important therapeutic models to identify as many therapists use these models as the bases for treatment.

Each model has its own approach using different ways in conceptualizing a problem and developing treatment plans that support the goals stated for therapy. In addition, theory-based treatment plans are the source for goal development and treatment options by identifying the presenting problem and social influences.

Both these models use similar approaches and define goals with various therapeutic processes that begin with the building of therapist and client relationship. In addition, diversity and theory are identified as a major component in choosing a theory that addresses diversity issues.

So what is the aim of this model?

It's aim is to prevent sequences from repeating and it does this by interrupting the family's covert hierarchical structure. This includes the distribution of power shifting to others to by changing the style of interaction.

However, structural therapy is the opposite and works on altering the dysfunctional structure by promoting growth and encouragement in individuals for the building of family support.

In addition, goals of family structure are to alter the dynamics and provide new alternative ways in solving problems and interactions. This includes subsystems that influence the way each member interacts with each other.

Members that have trouble in solving family problems require a change in structure, implementing some order and organization. This includes realignment or the altering of behaviors in the family structure by working with each member finding ways to improve interaction. Minuchin's goal is to promote a restructuring of the family system along more healthy lines.

He tries to accomplish this by entering the various family subsystems, "continually causing upheavals by intervening in ways that will produce unstable situations which require change and the restructuring of family organization. Therapeutic change cannot occur unless some pre-existing frames of reference are modified, flexibility introduced and new ways of functioning developed."

To accelerate such change, Minuchin manipulates the format of the therapy sessions, structuring desired subsystems by isolating them from the remainder of the family.

He does this either by the use of space and positioning (seating) within the room, or by having non-members of the desired substructure leave the room (but stay involved by viewing from behind a one-way mirror).

The aim of such interventions is often to cause the unbalancing of the family system, in order to help them to see the dysfunctional patterns and remain open to restructuring.

He believes that change must be gradual and taken in digestible steps for it to be useful and lasting. Because structures tend to self-perpetuate, especially when there is positive feedback, Minuchin asserts that therapeutic change is likely to be maintained beyond the limits of the therapy session.

One variant or extension of his methodology can be said to move from manipulation of experience toward fostering understanding. When working with families who are not introspective and are oriented toward concrete thinking, Minuchin will use the subsystem isolation—one-way mirror technique to teach those family members on the viewing side of the mirror to move from being an enmeshed participant to being an evaluation observer.

This is effected by him joining them in the viewing room and pointing out the patterns of transaction occurring on the other side of the mirror. While Minuchin doesn't formally integrate this extension into his view of therapeutic change, it seems that he is requiring a minimal level of insight or understanding for his subsystem restructuring efforts to "take" and to allow for the resultant positive feedback among the subsystems to induce stability and resistance to change.

Like any theory, structural family therapy is not without its critics. It met with criticism from many feminists, who argued that this type of theory focused more on issues of power between different generations, rather than focusing more on issues of power that take place between relationships inside the current generation, for example, spousal abuse.

In addition to this criticism, it has also been said that this kind of therapy only involves members of a nuclear family and ignores the interaction of other factors such as: extended family, social institutions, and neighbors.

Recruited by the Philadelphia Child Guidance Center and working with people like Cloe Madanes and Jay Haley, he created the template for the emerging field of family therapy as set out in his classic 1974 text, *Families and Family Therapy.*

Minuchin could size up a family in three minutes, then in rapid succession, he'd mock, reassure, charm, annoy, encourage, congratulate, and confront them, ordering them around, joking with them, touching them, and moving them from chair to chair.

He'd throw them off-balance by looking bored, smoking a cigarette, until suddenly he'd hammer a point home with high intensity, crowing in delight.

It could be fun to watch but does it really work? Many therapists seem to think so.

ALBERT BANDURA (1925-

*"People who believe they have the power to exercise some
measure of control over their lives are healthier, more
effective and more successful than those who lack faith
in their ability to effect changes in their lives"*

Social Learning Theory
Bobo Doll Studies
Self Efficacy

Albert Bandura is a psychologist best known for his *Social Learning Theory*, the 1961 Bobo Doll Studies, Observational Learning and the theoretical construct of Self Efficacy.

But he has been responsible for contributions to many fields of psychology, including social cognitive theory, therapy and personality psychology. He was also instrumental in the transition between behaviorism and cognitive psychology. Social learning theory is how people learn through observing others, like for example, students imitating their teacher. Self-efficacy, believing in yourself, is "the belief in one's capabilities to organize and execute the courses of action required to manage prospective situations." In the famous 1961 Bobo Doll Experiment Bandura studied aggression and non-aggression in children.

Canadian by birth Albert Bandura was born on the 4 December 1925 and raised in Mundare, a town of four hundred inhabitants, in the western province of Alberta. He was the last and only son in a family of six children.

His family were of Ukrainian descent. The name bandura refers to a Ukrainian 60-stringed musical instrument. His unique limitations in early education experiences would prove formative to his subsequent view of learning as an essentially social and self-directed experience.

Prior to college he only ever had two teachers. Referring to this time he once said: "The students had to take charge of their own education. . . .Very often we developed a better grasp of the subjects than the overworked teachers." Despite their lack of educational resources approximately 60% of

Bandura's class went on to pursue degrees at various levels which was unprecedented for that farming community. Bandura's view on this was that "The content of most textbooks is perishable, but the tools of self-directedness serve one well over time." In 1946 he attended the University of British Columbia and enrolled in some psychology classes to fill time slots. He became so fascinated by the subject that he pursued it as his major.

After graduating in just three years, he went on to graduate school at the University of Iowa. The school had been home to Clark Hull and other psychologists including Kenneth Spence and Kurt Lewin. While the program took an interest in social learning theory, Bandura felt that it was too focused on behaviorist explanations.

He earned his M.A. degree in 1951 and his Ph.D. in clinical psychology in 1952 from the University of Iowa. He married Virginia Varns in 1952. The following year he joined Stanford University and remained there all his academic life.

In 1959 Noam Chomsky published his criticism of B.F. Skinner's book *Verbal Behavior*. According to Chomsky, pure stimulus-response theories of behavior could not account for the process of language acquisition.

It was this argument that contributed significantly to psychology's cognitive revolution. Within this context, Albert Bandura studied learning processes that occurred in interpersonal contexts and were not adequately explained by theories of operant conditioning or existing models of social learning.

Bandura believed that "the weaknesses of learning approaches that discount the influence of social variables are nowhere more clearly revealed than in their treatment of the acquisition of novel responses." At that time Skinner's explanation of the acquisition of new responses relied on the process of successive approximation. This required multiple trials, reinforcement for components of behavior, and gradual change.

Meanwhile, Julian Rotter's theory proposed that the likelihood of a behavior occurring was a function of the subjective expectancy and value of the reinforcement. Bandura believed that because this model assumed a hierarchy of existing responses it did not account for a response that had not yet been learned.

He began to conduct studies of the rapid acquisition of novel behaviors via social observation. The most famous of these studies was the Bobo doll experiments in which he studied children's behavior after watching an adult model act aggressively towards a Bobo doll.

A Bobo doll (not to be confused with a Barbie doll) is an inflatable toy that is about 5 feet tall and is usually made of a soft durable vinyl or plastic. The Bobo doll was most often painted to look like a clown. The doll was designed to be bottom-weighted so that if it were hit, it would fall over then immediately lift back up to a standing position. It first came on the market in the 1960s once in the form of *Yogi Bear.*

There are different variations of the experiment. The most notable experiment measured the children's behavior after seeing the model get rewarded, get punished, or experience no consequence for beating up the bobo doll.

The bobo doll experiment is the empirical demonstration of Bandura's social learning theory which claims that people learn through observing, imitating, and modeling. The theory posits that people not only learn by being rewarded or punished itself (behaviorism), they can learn from watching somebody being rewarded or punished, too (observational learning).

The keys tenets of **social learning theory** are as follows:

1. Learning is not purely behavioral; rather, it is a cognitive process that takes place within a social context.

2. Learning can occur by observing a behavior and by observing the consequences of the behavior (vicarious reinforcement).

3. Learning involves observation, extraction of information from those observations, and making decisions about the performance of the behavior (observational learning or modeling). Thus, learning can occur without an observable change in behavior.

4. Reinforcement plays a role in learning but is not entirely responsible for learning.

5. The learner is not a passive recipient of information. Cognition, environment, and behavior all mutually influence each other (reciprocal determinism).

One important application of social learning theory has been in the treatment and conceptualization of anxiety disorders. The classical conditioning approach to anxiety disorders began to go out of favor in the late 1970s as researchers began to question its underlying assumptions. Social learning theory helped salvage learning approaches to anxiety disorders by providing additional mechanisms beyond classical conditioning that could account for the acquisition of fear. At the age of 82, Albert Bandura was awarded the Grawemeyer Award for psychology. He is known as one of the most influential psychologists of our time.

WILLIAM GLASSER (1925-2013)

"What happened in the past that was painful has a great deal to do with what we are today, but revisiting this painful past can contribute little or nothing to what we need to do now"

Choice Theory
Reality Therapy

William Glasser was an American psychiatrist who developed Choice Theory and Reality Therapy. He believed in personal choice, personal responsibility and personal transformation.

He was considered controversial by mainstream psychiatrists who focus instead on classifying psychiatric syndromes as "illnesses" and who often prescribe medications to treat mental disorders. Glasser didn't agree with such medications believing instead that the patient may not be mentally ill at all but might simply be acting out of unhappiness. He also argued that conventional psychotherapy had failed to work and that a new type of psychotherapy was necessary.

Glasser was born on the 11 May 1925, in Cleveland, Ohio, to Ben and Betty Glasser. His father repaired clocks for a living. While he related well to his father he endured a difficult relationship with his mother.

While he was unremarkable at school in 1945 he earned a B.Sc. in chemical engineering and began work as a chemical engineer for Lubrizol. Later he was drafted into the US Army and spent time testing German poisonous gasses.

He then entered Western Reserve University completing a doctorate in

Clinical Psychology. In 1949 he entered Medical School and in 1954 began a psychiatric residency as a ward doctor at the Brentwood Veterans. Two years later he worked as a psychiatrist for the Ventura School for Delinquent Girls before entering private practice.

Originally he was influenced by William Powers' "Control Theory." In 1965 he published Reality Therapy. He was married to the same lady, Naomi, for 46 years and following her death from cancer he married a co-worker, Carleen Floyd. He died in August 2013.

In **Choice Theory** Glasser believed that the vast majority of our problems stem from unhappy relationships: "If we are not sick, poverty stricken or suffering the ravages of old age the major human problems we struggle with … are caused by unsatisfying relationships."

He identified five basic needs that we all have which he classified as Survival; Love and Belonging; Freedom; Power, and Fun. Unlike Maslow's needs which are hierarchical, Glasser's needs are linear. We are, at all times during our life, behaving to meet those needs. But we don't always behave effectively. So what really drives us is figuring out what we want.

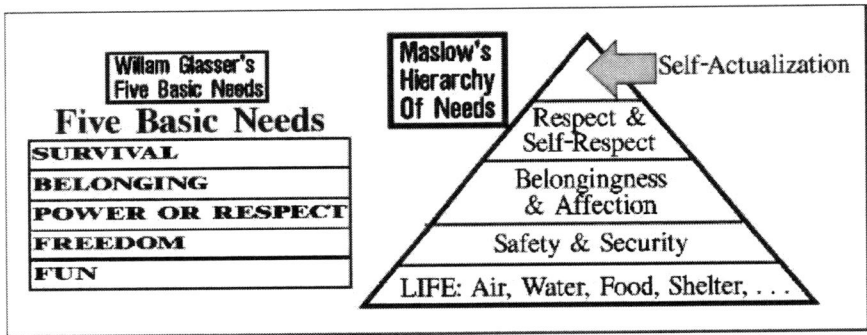

Glasser introduced the concept of the **Quality World**; the personal picture album of all the things, people, ideas, and ideals that we have discovered increase the quality of our lives.

While the five Basic Needs are the general motivation for our behavior and describe what we need, the Quality World is the specific motivation which sets out how we meet those needs. The Basic Needs are universal; the Quality World unique.

Choice Theory advocates that **control** is bad. Control destroys relationships. The only person we should really control is ourselves.

Everybody needs a certain amount of control but when we forget that the other person in our relationship also has a need for control then that will result in conflict. Therefore we need to negotiate, compromise and co-operate in order to achieve harmony.

Another key concept is **Total Behavior**. All we can do is behave; all we can give another person is information; and, the only person whose behavior we can control is our own. To get what we want we behave. When we behave four things are happening: we are doing; we are feeling; we are thinking, and something is going on in our bodies. He calls these four components Total Behavior.

Choice Theory can be applied to individuals, business and education. Two keys concepts, Control and Total Behavior, are worthy of consideration here.

In the concept of control Glasser gives examples of how in education we punish our children and in business coerce our employees in an effort to make them do things; basically, to make them conform to do what we want them to do. Punishing a child for not doing their homework or an employee for not performing a task well enough is not the solution. It actually causes resentment, entrenchment and makes relationships worse.

The concept of Total Behavior illustrates one of the fundamentals at the core of Choice Theory - doing something. If we change what we do we can change how we feel. If we change how we feel we can get what we want.

Cl: "My wife won't speak to me because I forgot our anniversary."
Co: "But you can speak to her.

Cl: "I'm so depressed I can't motivate myself to get out of bed never mind going to work"
Co: "Don't go to work, yet, but maybe you could think about getting out of bed, having a shower."

When we have done something, like getting out of bed and showering, we might feel differently; we may then think differently. Eventually, we might actually do something differently. This type of behavior effects positive change. These are the obvious strengths of Choice Theory, effecting positive change.

Its application can replace the Seven Deadly Habits of external control psychology, that is, criticizing, blaming, complaining, nagging, threatening, punishing and bribing, with seven caring habits that focus on the autonomy of the individual, that is, supporting, encouraging, listening, accepting, trusting, respecting and negotiating differences.

But the Theory is not without its weaknesses and limitations. Human beings do more than just behave which begs the question as to whether the theory is somewhat simplistic in its approach.

Not all of us know the best choices to make. For example, in its educational application students need guidance to make the right choices.

The theory also ignores any type of biological or chemical root cause for mental or psychological problems. A person, for example, suffering from a bi-polar disorder, is not always able to take control of their own behavior. A client's ability to change may be adversely affected by a chemical imbalance. Should we ignore the possible benefits of requesting them to take blood tests?

Counselling has come a long way from the days of drugging and leeching, through psychoanalysis up to modern day therapies such as Choice Theory. Today the relationship between counsellor and client involves an equal, positive, non-judgmental, accepting professional contract.

The key concepts of Glasser's Choice Theory, the Five Basic Needs, the Quality World, the necessary dilution of Control, Total Behavior have all greatly enhanced that contract.

The core of his theory is the act of "doing" and with it, positive change. His replacement of the seven deadly habits of external control with seven caring habits is hugely beneficial.

Glasser has certainly given us a new way forward, a new alternative to traditional concepts in psychotherapy. And while his theory if far from perfect it has provided and continues to provide a major contribution.

R. D. LAING (1927-1989)

"There is a great deal of pain in life and perhaps the only pain that can be avoided is the pain that comes from trying to avoid pain"

Psychosis and Mental Illness

Ronald David Laing (sometimes Lang) was a Scottish psychiatrist and psychoanalyst who contributed greatly to what we now now about psychosis and mental illness.

He is famous for his radical views, influenced by existential philosophy, on the causes and treatment of mental illness. His views were contrary to the psychiatric orthodoxy of the time in that Laing took the expressions of his patients as representing valid descriptions of lived experience or reality rather than as symptoms of some separate or underlying disorder. Although he is often associated with the anti-psychiatry movement he maintained that he was merely a non-conformist.

Ronald David Laing was born on the 7 October 1927 the only child of David Park MacNair Laing an electrical engineer with the RAF and Amelia Glen Kirkwood. They were a middle class Presbyterian family. Ronald spent his early life in Govanhill, Glasgow. He attended Sir John Neilson Cuthbertson Public School and after four years transferred to Hutchesons' Grammar School. He had a classical education and enjoyed reading and music.

He was emotionally distant from his mother who was "a bit odd" and Ronald had his first 'existential crisis' at the age of five when his parents revealed to him that there was no Santa Claus. His childhood has been described as materially privileged and emotionally bleak.

He was elected as a Licentiate of the Royal Academy of Music in 1944, and an associate in April 1945. He read numerous works of philosophy while still at school, including Freud, Marx, Nietzsche and especially Kierkegaard.

Between 1945-1951 he attended Glasgow University to study medicine. Having failed his final exam he eventually qualified on the re-sit. Shortly afterwards he joined the army for two years where he worked as a psychiatrist. It was here he met his first wife nurse Anne Hearne whom he married after she became pregnant. Soon he was questioning traditional treatments for psychiatric remedies like medication, electroshock, and insulin coma therapy and preferred instead to talk to his patients.

After leaving the army, he returned to Gartnavel Hospital in Glasgow to complete his psychiatric training. In 1956 he transferred to London and worked at the Tavistock Clinic in London where he met John Bowlby, Marion Milner, D. W. Winnicott and Charles Rycroft. He remained at the Tavistock Institute until 1964.

In 1960, Laing qualified as a psychoanalyst and set up a private practice at 21 Wimpole Street, London. He began to experiment with drugs, especially LSD. In the same year he published *The Divided Self An Existential Study of Madness and Sanity* which focused on the application of Existential/phenomenological ideas to the so-called 'schizoid condition'. It was the first of many books.

In fact, between 1957-64 he wrote or co-wrote six highly influential books which would ultimately establish his growing reputation as a force to be reckoned with in the psychological field. The books also made him famous.

In 1962 he began an affair with a *Daily Express* journalist called Sally Vincent.

By 1967, Laing's public persona of guru and prophet culminated with his controversial book called *The Politics of Experience*. During this period Laing completed his first family and he and Anna were blessed with five children. But as his fame and public life grew his family and private life crumbled.

Soon afterwards he was instrumental in forming the charity *The Philadelphia Association* whose purpose was to provide true asylum for those people in such states of distress that they would otherwise receive treatment in a more traditional psychiatric hospital.

In his personal life his first marriage broke up and he began an affair with a young German woman, called Jutta Werner with whom he would eventually have three more children.

In 1970 he published a book called *Knots* which became a highly successful book and acted as a transition for him to enter the more literary world of poetry.

At this juncture Kingsley Hall the clinic set up by the charity closed. Laing decided to take a year off and travelled to Sri Lanka and India devoting himself to Theravedic Buddhist meditation. After his return from the east, he discovered that things had changed.

A new *Philadelphia Association* had evolved with new members and new ambitions. In addition, an 'R.D. Laing industry' had emerged with a number of published secondary books in which the various authors jostle amongst themselves to talk about what R.D. Laing really meant and said.

So Laing decided on a major lecture tour of the U.S. When he returned his interests began to crystallize around the politics of the birth process and the importance of intrauterine life. Inspired by the work of American psychotherapist Elizabeth Fehr, Laing began to develop a team offering 'rebirthing workshops' in which one designated person would choose to re-experience the struggle of trying to break out of the birth canal represented by the remaining members of the group who surround him/her.

This culminated in the publication of *The Facts of Life* (1976) but was denied the same critical acclaim of some of his previous works. By the late 1970s his new interests had taken him more into the realm of humanistic psychology. Meanwhile, the gulf between himself and those of his colleagues, Heaton, Chriss and Haya Oakley, Paul Zeal, widened. His colleagues were more interested in a philosophically informed type of psychoanalysis begins to widen.

But the real turning point in the life of R. D. Laing came in 1980 when shortly after the death of one of his friends, Hugh Crawford, Laing attended a conference in Saragossa, Spain where, his wife had a short affair with a German lawyer. This was the same conference at which he met an American psychologist, Roberta Russell, who would eventually publish a book about him entitled *R. D. Laing and Me: Lessons in Love*. After this, he broke with his own charity and helped form a new one with Kevin O'Sullivan called *St. Oran's Trust*.

His second marriage disintegrated and he began a relationship with Marguerita Romayne--Kendon. They moved to the United States in 1986 and returned to a small town in Austria in 1988. At this stage a number of incidents fueled by alcoholism and clinical depression led to his "resignation" from the General Medical Council.

He ultimately died of a heart attack at 61 while playing tennis in the south of France. Laing fathered six sons and four daughters by four different women. In 2008, one son, Adrian, said it was ironic that his father became well known as a family psychiatrist, when, in the meantime, he had nothing to do with his own family.

A strong, complex, uncompromising genius, what did R. D. Laing ever do for mental health? Laing believed that the erratic behavior and seemingly confused speech of people undergoing a psychotic episode were ultimately understandable and identifiable. He saw them as an attempt to communicate worries and concerns. He stressed the role of society, and particularly the family, in the development of madness.

He argued that individuals can often be put in impossible situations, where they are unable to conform to the conflicting expectations of their peers. This causes them to experience what he called a 'lose-lose situation' and immense mental distress. For him madness was an expression of this distress, and should be valued as a cathartic and transformative experience.

This idea was in stark contrast to the psychiatric orthodoxy of the time and even today.

Psychiatrist and philosopher, Karl Jaspers, in his book *General Psychopathology* (1913), had posited that the content of madness, and particularly of delusions, were 'un-understandable'. Jaspers argued that they were therefore not worthy of consideration except as a sign of some other underlying primary disorder.

But Laing valued the content of psychotic behavior and speech as a valid expression of distress. He believed that if a therapist can better understand the person they can begin to make sense of the symbolism of their madness, and therefore start addressing the concerns which are the root cause of their distress.

Laing never denied the existence of mental illness. He simply viewed it in a radically different light from his contemporaries. He believed madness could be a transformative expedition during which the process of undergoing mental distress was compared to a shamanic journey. The traveler could return from the journey with important insights, and may even have become a wiser and more grounded person as a result.

Some believe that Laing's most enduring and practically beneficial contribution to mental health, is his co-founding and chairmanship of the *Philadelphia Association*. Contrary to popular belief Laing was not anti-psychiatry; he never denied the value of treating mental distress. He simply sought to challenge the core values of contemporary psychiatry which considered mental illness as primarily a biological phenomenon of no intrinsic value, a view which is still held today.

He was, however, critical of psychiatric diagnosis and argued that diagnosis of a mental disorder contradicted accepted medical procedure. His objection was because diagnosis was made on the basis of behavior or conduct, and examination that traditionally precede diagnosis of viable pathologies like broken bones happened only after the diagnosis of mental disorder.

Laing abandoned quantitative research into mental illnesses in favor of qualitative research. He attempted a kind of phenomenology of madness in an effort to express what it's like to have a mental illness. His aim was to recognize within the "patient" the problems of living in the light of the existential paradoxes that are common to humanity.

He may have effected no cures but at least he engaged with his patients in a way that helped him better understand their problems. For this he should be afforded the highest praise.

IRVIN YALOM (1931-

"Only the wounded healer can truly heal"

Group Therapy
Existential Psychotherapy
The Theory and Practice of Group Psychotherapy **(1970)**

Irvin Yalom is an American psychiatrist and best selling author of both fiction and non-fiction books. He has been a major figure in psychotherapy ever since he wrote *The Theory and Practice of Group Psychotherapy* (1970).

The book now in its fifth edition has sold over 700,000 copies and has been translated into over twenty languages. It is regarded as the definitive book on Group Therapy and has been widely used as a text for training therapists. He is also America's best known theorist and practitioner of existential psychotherapy. Yalom's writing on existential psychology centers on what he refers to as the four "givens" of the human condition: isolation, meaninglessness, mortality and freedom. He has written extensively about the ways in which the human person can respond to these concerns either in a functional or dysfunctional fashion.

Yalom co-founded the Irvin D. Yalom Institute of Psychotherapy which he co-directs with Professor Ruthellen Josselson, the aim of which is to advance his approach to psychotherapy. This approach involves the unique combination of integrating more philosophy into the psychotherapy and can be considered as psychosophy.

But it's undoubtedly his works of fiction about psychotherapy that have made him world famous. He has written several best-selling fiction books on psychotherapy including *Love's Executioner, Momma and the Meaning of Life, When Nietzsche Wept, Lying on the Couch*, and *The Schopenhauer Cure*. He experiments with different writing styles.

In *Everyday Gets a Little Closer* Yalom invited a patient to co-write about the experience of therapy. The book has two distinct voices which are looking at the same experience in alternating sections. Yalom's works have been used as collegiate textbooks and standard reading for psychology students.

He intended them as pedagogical works, books of teaching stories and a new genre, the teaching novel. His new and unique view of the patient/client relationship has been added to curriculum in psychology programs at such schools as John Jay College of Criminal Justice in New York City.

He was born on the 13 June 1931 in Washington into a family of Russian immigrants. His parents came from a small village named Celtz near the Polish border. They ran a grocery store on 1st Street and Seaton Place. Uneducated, they were consumed with economic survival.

As his parents worked long hours in the store Yalom spent much of his childhood reading books in the flat above the store. They lived in the middle of a poor, black neighborhood. Life on the streets was often perilous; even getting to and from the local library could be hazardous.

After graduating from high school, he attended George Washington University from which he graduated in 1952 with a B.A. He then attended Boston University School of Medicine. He qualified as a medical doctor in 1956 and went to complete his internship at Mount Sinai Hospital in New York and his residency at the Phipps Clinic of Johns Hopkins Hospital in Baltimore. He then completed two years of Army service at Tripler General Hospital in Honolulu, before he began his academic career at Stanford University. Yalom has continued to maintain a part-time private practice and has produced several video documentaries on therapeutic techniques.

He is married to Marilyn Yalom a feminist author and historian. She is a senior scholar at the Clayman Institute for Gender Research at Stanford University. They have four children.

A consummate storyteller Yalom frequently recounts the tale of his first therapy encounter. The first patient to whom he was assigned was a lesbian whom he was to see twice a week for twelve weeks. Yalom says he knew nothing about psychiatry or therapy, and certainly nothing about lesbianism. In the introduction to The Yalom Reader he writes:

"What could I possibly offer her? All I could do, I ultimately decided, was to allow her to be my guide and to explore her world as best I could. Her previous experience with men had been horrendous, and I was the first of my sex to listen, respectfully and attentively, to her. Her story touched me. I thought about her often between our meetings, and over the weeks we developed a tender, even loving, relationship."

He told those assembled for a presentation of the case how the woman improved rapidly after the sessions and the loving feelings they had developed. Afterwards, Yalom was highly praised for his approach. He then realized that patients can be fully known and understood only from their stories and from the relationship they form with a therapist.

Yalom believes that most psychodynamic therapies don't go nearly deep enough. For him, the universality of death, requires a certain humility in the therapist. So rather than maintaining the distinction between "us" (the healers) and "them" (the afflicted), Yalom prefers to think of therapists and patients as "fellow travelers . . . all in this together, [with] no therapist and no person immune to the inherent tragedies of existence."

If you ask Yalom how an "existential therapist" should operate he will tell you that the most important antidote to existential despair is full-blooded human engagement and commitment, the lack of which probably brings most patients into therapy in the first place.

In the prologue to Love's Executioner he says that engagement is where therapists must direct their efforts, not that engagement provides the rational answer to questions of meaning, but it makes these questions irrelevant. If he had a motto it might be "Let the patient matter to you." He has often said and written that nothing the therapist does takes precedence over building a trusting relationship with a patient.

Yalom says that he finds psychiatry endlessly intriguing and that he has approached all of his patients with a sense of wonderment at the story that will unfold.

He believes that a different therapy must be constructed for each patient because each has a unique story.

As he matured this attitude moved him farther and farther from the center of professional psychiatry, which he claims is now so fiercely driven by economic forces in precisely opposite directions, namely accurate de-individualizing (symptom-based) diagnosis and uniform, protocol-driven, brief therapy for all. In a 2008 interview published in Psychotheraphy.net in 2009, Ruthellen Josselson, asked him about the future of psychotherapy. This is what he had to say:

"I do feel there is a pendulum swinging, even in psychiatry. I do hear about more programs starting to introduce therapy again. Many contemporary therapists are trained in manualized mechanical modes, all of which eschew the authentic encounter.

After some years of practice, however, a great many of these therapists come to appreciate the superficiality of their approach and yearn for something deeper, something more far-reaching and lasting. At this time therapists enter postgraduate therapy training programs or supervision.

Or they learn by entering their own therapy. And I can assure you they never never seek a therapist who practices mechanical, behavioral or manualized therapy. They go in search of a genuine encounter that will recognize the challenge inherent in facing the human condition."

On the website In Therapy in March 2009 Dr. Ryan Howes asked him several questions relating to his approach to therapy the first being how he would respond to a new clients who asks: "What should I talk about?"

"Well, nobody really quite says that to me, but I generally start my sessions with: 'tell me what ails?' But if they're very anxious and have not seen a therapist before and they need a little help I'll give them a little structure and say: 'well, until you get comfortable let me get some demographic information about you' and start to ask them questions about their past and their situation in the world, who they live with.

I rarely get through a first session without trying to find out what they do with their 24 hour day. 'Give me a typical day.' That usually gives me a good look at their interpersonal contacts and how their life is peopled and also about their sleep patterns and their dreams. So that's one device that I'll usually put into first sessions."

He also asked him what mistakes therapist make that hinder the therapeutic process? "You know, I think everybody I've seen has come from some other therapy, and almost invariably it's very much the same thing: the therapist is too disinterested, a little too aloof, a little too inactive. They're not really interested in the person, he doesn't relate to the person.

All these things I've written so much about. That's why I've made such a practice really, over and over to hammer home the point of self-revelation and being more of yourself and showing yourself. Every book I write I want to get that in there."

He also said that therapists need to have a long experience in personal therapy to see what it's like to be on the other side of the couch and see what they find helpful or not helpful. And if possible, therapists should get into therapy at different stages of their life with different kinds of therapists just to sample a bit. When he was asked if he thought psychotherapy was dying he had this to say:

"I think it's in definite trouble. But I think there will always be people around ... really want to help. I can't imagine the desire for self-understanding is going to disappear. I have a hunch that certain trends come in various waves. Certainly CBT is so much in vogue right now.

Someone's got to do some more research, but I would really like to know: when a CBT therapist really gets distressed, who does he go see? I just have a strong sense it's not another CBT therapist. I think he wants to go out and search for somebody who's wise and can help him explore deeper levels. If you come across the data let me know. I certainly see a lot of them in therapy."

INSOO KIM BERG (1934-2007)

"In the 1970s and in early 1980s, a startling discovery was made that almost every problem contains an element of solutions"

Solution Focused Brief Therapy

Insoo Kim Berg was a Korean-born American psychotherapist. She was a pioneer of solution focused brief therapy. She influenced the fields of psychotherapy, consulting, supervision and coaching with concepts such as resource-orientation and brief therapy.

In 1978 she co-founded the Brief Family Therapy Center (BFTC) in Milwaukee with her husband Steve de Shazer. She is the author of ten highly acclaimed books. When she died in 2005 the rights to BFTC were transferred to the Solution Focused Brief Therapy Association.

Insoo Kim Berg was born on the 25 July 1934 in Korea into a wealthy pharmaceutical manufacturing family. On the instructions of her parents she became a pharmacy major at Ewha Woman's University in Seoul. In 1957 she emigrated to America to continue her studies at the University of Wisconsin in Milwaukee, where she graduated with a B.Sc., a Master of Science (M.Sc.), and a social work (MSSW) degree. With her background in pharmacy and chemistry, she worked at the medical school and published articles on stomach cancer research.

She then decided to change her focus to social work because she wanted to help people. She developed an interest in psychotherapy. She completed her post-graduate studies at the Family Institute of Chicago, the Menninger Foundation, and the Mental Research Institute (MRI) in Palo Alto, California, where John Weakland was her mentor. At the MRI she also met her future husband, Steve de Shazer.

She began her treatment in social work with family therapy but soon found the process too slow. In an interview with Victor Yalom and Bart Rubin in Psychotherapy.net in 2003 she said: "I realized that it was just not helping the families, not helping the clients. I pretty much worked with working class families. I don't understand all of it, since I come from a fairly financially well off family background, but I felt so comfortable working with working class families. They're not interested in "insights" or "growth," or "development." They're interested in getting the problem out of the way."

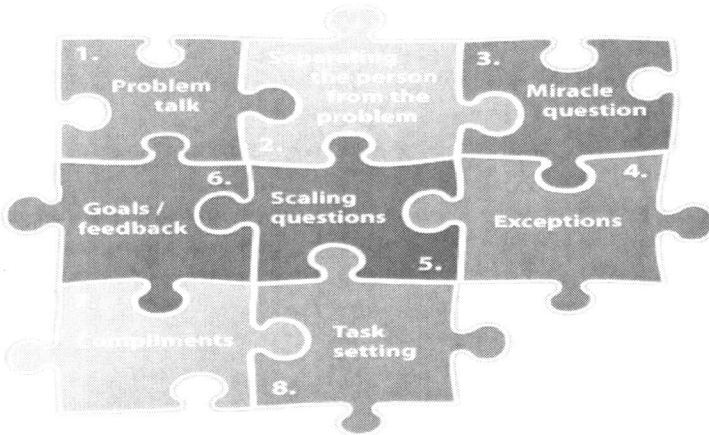

But the type of therapy she was using wasn't working for them or her: "Here I was using a very psychoanalytically-oriented family therapy model with these clients. It was such a bad fit. It wasn't working very well. So I had some phenomenal failures with families, which disturbed me terribly; I wasn't used to failing. Academically, all my life I had been successful, and here I was with all this education and I felt like I was such a failure. I couldn't stand it."

She then became influenced by Jay Haley's writings. "It just blew me away. Because I was raised as a Presbyterian. I read the Bible many times, because that's one of the things you do when you're a Korean Presbyterian! Anyway, Jay Haley had this article called, "Power Tactics of Jesus Christ."
She then persuaded her future husband Steve de Shazer to join her and she began a new type of therapy which she describes as a solution focused model. Their initial goal was to create a Midwest MRI, in Milwaukee and to see how it went from there.

So, what is solution focused therapy?

Insoo tells us how **solution focused therapy** works: "Instead of problem solving, we focus on solution-building. Which sounds like a play on words, but it's a profoundly different paradigm. We're not worrying about the problems. We discovered that there's no connection between a problem and its solution. No connection whatsoever.

Because when you ask a client about their problem, they will tell you a certain kind of description; but when you ask them about their solutions, they give you entirely different descriptions of what the solution would look like for them. So a horrible, alcoholic family will say, "We will have dinner together and talk to each other. We will go for a walk together."

So, how did she propose that their clients would get from A to B because that would vary considerably from person to person. Isoo's solution was to ask the Miracle Question. This is the quickest way to solve the problem.

So what is the **miracle question**?

"Suppose a miracle happens overnight, tonight, when you go to bed. And all the problems that brought you here to talk to me today are gone. Disappeared. But because this happens while you were sleeping, you have no idea that there was a miracle during the night. The problem is all gone, all solved.

So when you are slowly waking up, coming out of your sleep, what might be the first, small clue that will make you think, 'Oh my gosh. There must have been a miracle during the night. The problem is all gone?'" And that's the beginning of it.

People start to tell you, and they add more and more descriptions. "How could your husband tell that there was a miracle for you during the night? What about your children? What would your colleagues do?" You keep expanding the social context wider and wider."

Basically what she is saying here is that they can start to visualize some concrete steps that could get them to a better place and find a solution. Then they must ask themselves what they need to do to get this process started. So, the question the reader will ask is why haven't they done this before they came to their therapist?

Insoo says that the difference is that the therapist is asking them about their own plan. It is not the therapist's agenda for the client, but the client's plan. They didn't even know they had a plan. In fact, according to Insoo most don't when they first come to therapy.

They usually tell their therapist that they have no idea what to do. And then in the process of talking, they start to gradually, through this building process, develop a blueprint to put all the pieces together and find a solution. Basically, she says, the clients have the bits and pieces all along, they just haven't figured out yet how to put them together.

An extremely hard working person, Insoo Kim Berg took obvious pleasure in her work and rarely took a day off. In her personal life, she enjoyed a wide range of physical activities including daily walks, yoga, stretching exercises, and gardening. She enjoyed well-written novels, healthy well-prepared food and listening to classical music. She was widely recognized as a profoundly gifted clinician with an impressive intellect. She held an abiding compassion for and deeply caring attitude to her clients and friends. Insoo Kim Berg passed away suddenly in Milwaukee, Wisconsin on the 10 January, 2007 at the age of 72. Her husband, Steve de Shazer, died sixteen months earlier in September 2005 in Vienna, Austria.

DONALD MEICHENBAUM (1940-

The Melissa Institute
Cognitive Behavioral Modification (CBM)

Cognitive Behavior Modification: An Integrative Approach (1977)

Donald Meichenbaum is one of the founders of Cognitive Behavioral Modification and has been voted one of the ten most influential psychotherapists of the century.

As an expert in the treatment of PTS, he has lectured throughout North and Central America, Israel, Japan, and the former Soviet Union. He is the author and co-author of numerous books including: *Cognitive Behavior Modification: An Integrative Approach*, which is considered a classic in its field.

Donald Meichenbaum was born on the 10 June 1940 in New York City. He received his undergraduate degree in psychology from City College of New York, then moved to Illinois to pursue graduate studies at the University of Illinois.

Originally, he thought he would become an industrial psychologist, but took a research assistantship at a local psychiatric hospital. Fascinated by the patients, he decided to study clinical psychology instead.

In 1966 the University of Waterloo offered him a position and because he wanted to work with Richard Walters, he was happy to accept. Unfortunately, Walters died soon after he arrived. Nevertheless he stayed there for 33 years until he retired in 1998.

In the 1950s, behaviorism, the area of psychology which focuses entirely on behavior and not at all on what happens in the brain, was the prevailing method in psychotherapy. However, in the 1960s and 1970s, the development of computers as a metaphor for the mind, along with some interesting findings by Jean Piaget, Noam Chomsky and others stemmed the area of psychology that deals with attention, memory, concept-formation, and problem solving: cognitive psychology.

The "Cognitive Revolution", as it was called, sparked new interest in psychological disorders and how to treat them. In 1977 Meichenbaum published *Cognitive-behavior Modification: An Integrative Approach*, a technique which puts patients in charge of their own psychotherapy by modifying what they say to themselves, their so-called 'inner dialogue'.

Meichenbaum's interest in people's ability to control their thoughts led him to an interest in anger. What turns anger into violence? Why doesn't all anger result in violence? Is there a specific type of person or way of thinking that is more likely to result in violence?

Meichenbaum was intrigued by all of these questions, and through years of research, found that indeed some thought patterns are more likely to result in violence than others. Over the last forty years, he has written several books about post-traumatic stress, inner dialogues, and most recently the educational potential of children with fellow psychologist Andrew Biemiller.

He helped open The Melissa Institute in Miami, Florida, a think tank for preventing violence in schools. The Institute is named after a victim of violence in the local community. Meichenbaum is married with four children.

Meichenbaum is one of the main developers of cognitive behavior modification, more commonly known today as Cognitive-Behavioral Therapy or CBT. Cognitive behavior modification initially grew out of integrating the clinical concerns of cognitive semantic therapists with behavior technology in the mid-20th century.

As it evolved, he came to view cognitive behavior modification as an integrative, biopsychosocial approach that draws on aspects of many different orientations, including the constructive/narrative emphases on clients' stories, their cultural context, and their strengths and resources.

Meichenbaum describes his approach as one that is sensitive to the interconnection between thoughts, feelings, behavior and resultant consequences.

Primarily through psychoeducation, he empowers clients to identify their own agency in their emotional and behavioral experiences and to develop skills to manage how their thoughts, feelings and behaviors interact and influence one another. By developing self-awareness, performing experiments and monitoring themselves, clients can shift their beliefs about themselves and about the world.

Cognitive-behavioral therapy comprises a variety of procedures, such as cognitive restructuring, stress inoculation training, problem solving, skills training, relaxation training and others. Meichenbaum uses these procedures to help clients recognize and develop strengths and coping skills which they can then generalize and apply to different aspects of their life.

One of the most important tasks of the therapist involves creating and maintaining a therapeutic relationship that is genuine, empathic, nonjudgmental and supportive, and using that relationship as a foundation from which to nurture a sense of hope. From a CBT perspective, the relationship supports the client's key therapeutic goals: developing coping skills, taking credit for changes and relapse.

Although Meichenbaum does not utilize the concepts of transference and countertransference per se, his psychoeducational approach relies on talking openly with the client about all data relevant to the client's efforts to build skills for relapse prevention, including data about the client's experience of the therapist and the therapist's experience of the client.

CBT can be tailored to many different populations including children and adolescents, trauma survivors, developmentally delayed individuals, people with traumatic brain injuries and their families and many others. The therapist chooses from many different techniques and procedures to meet the specific cultural, developmental and diagnostic needs of whatever population is being addressed. Virtually any set of clients can benefit from a CBT approach, modified to meet that group's unique needs.

In an interview in Psychotherapy.net Meichenbaum explained how the Melissa Institute came about. Melissa was a young lady who grew up in Miami and she was attending Washington University in St. Louis. One day she was car jacked and murdered.

One of his areas of specialization was research into the impact of trauma. A friend of Melissa's parents read his handbook and attended one of his workshops. She put him in touch with Melissa's parents and with Dr. Suzanne Keeley, they established an Institute in Melissa's name.

The Melissa Institute is designed to bridge the gap between scientific findings and public policies, clinical and educational practices. Meichenbaum says it is designed to "give psychology away" in an effort to reduce violence and to treat victims of violence. It is not a direct service Institute. Instead, it provides services in three areas.

First, it provides graduate student scholarships in support of doctoral dissertation work in the areas of violence prevention and treatment of victims.

Second, it provides training and education in the form of workshops and conferences. They hold an annual May conference and conduct other trainings for various members of the community, as well as school children (e.g., on bullying).

Third, and most importantly, The Institute provides consultation to various public agencies in the area of violence prevention.

JOHN GOTTMAN (1942-

Marriage Counselling
Gottman Method Couple's Therapy
The Seven Principles for Making Marriage Work (2000)

John Gottman is an American mathematician-turned-psychologist known for his work on marital stability and relationship analysis through scientific direct observations.

With his wife, Julie Schwartz, he heads up both the non-profit Relationship Research Institute and a therapist training entity The Gottman Institute. In 2007 he was recognized as one of the top ten most influential psychologists of the last quarter century.

Gottman was born on the 26 July 1942 in the Dominican Republic to Orthodox Jewish parents. His father was a rabbi in pre-World War Two Vienna. He was educated in a Lubavitch yeshiva elementary school in Brooklyn. He and his wife Julie currently live in Washington state and have one child called Moriah. In the mid 1980s John Gottman fitted out a studio apartment in Seattle to record ordinary couples interact. The media dubbed the studio the "love lab."

It was here that Gottman filmed couples in their most ordinary moments, playing solitaire, talking, kissing, arguing, watching TV, cooking, and joking. Sometimes he asked them to discuss an area of conflict and strapped monitors to their chests to record their heart rates. Other times he he sat them on spring-loaded platforms to record fidgeting.

He studied all types of couples including newlyweds, abusive couples, people who shout, and people who didn't. He used an elaborate coding system while he tracked flickering facial expressions, sighs, clammy hands, and rolling eyes. He followed couples for more than two decades to see who got divorced, who established parallel lives, and who stayed together (happily or not). Later he converted his data into numbers.

Gottman believes by extracting information from these figures he can predict future divorces with a 91% accuracy simply by analyzing seven different variables during a couple's five-minute disagreement. His findings made him famous. Some commentators now believe that most of what we know today about marriage and divorce comes from his research.

He examined more than 3,000 couples. From this examination he discovered that most fought, and that even those who were the most happily married never resolved 69% of their conflicts. He believes that what is crucial to the longevity of a marriage, isn't whether a couple fight. It is how they fight.

He calls couples whose marriages survive well the "masters of marriage." These are wives who raised issues gently and bring them up sooner rather than later. His findings showed that neither husbands nor wives regularly became so upset with each other that their heart rates rose above 95 beats a minute, and these couples broke rising tension with jokes, reassurance, and distractions. Gottman found that 80% of complaints come from wives, but successful husbands don't play king or cross their arms in response. His research showed that it wasn't just how couples fought that mattered, but how they made up.

Couples that learned to reconcile successfully after a fight had marriages that became more stable over time. Those heading for divorce responded to each other's bids to clear the air only 33% of the time, while the happy couples' response rate was 80%.

In 1994, Gottman and his wife, Julie, combined their expertise to start a science-based couples therapy. In 1998 they began advanced training for therapists. By 2004, 4,000 couples had gone through their workshops or clinic. By 2006, more than 3,000 therapists had taken a basic training workshop with them in the Gottman Method Couples Therapy described as a mix between classic therapeutic skills and scientific dispassion. Three levels of professional training are generally delivered through intensive two-day seminars to help therapists to:

A. Learn how to integrate research-based methods and inspire transformation in their work with couples;

B. Identify the communication patterns, friendship basis, and conflict management dynamics that characterize enduring intimate relationships; and,

C. Discover a roadmap for helping couples to compassionately manage their conflicts, deepen their friendship and intimacy, and share their life purpose and dreams.

In his most famous book *The Seven Principles for Making Marriage Work* (2000), Gottman discusses behaviors that he has observed in marriages that are successful and those that are detrimental to marriage. He outlines seven principles that will reinforce the positive aspects of a relationship and help marriages endure during the rough moments.

The **seven principles** Gottman sets out are for the partners to enhance their love maps; nurture fondness and admiration; turn toward each other instead of away; let their partner influence them; solve their solvable problems; overcome gridlock; and create shared meaning. In 2013 he published a follow-up to this book called *What Makes Love Last?*

1. Enhancing Love Maps:
A "love map" is that part of your brain where you store all the relevant information about your spouse's life. This includes their history, worries, hopes, fears, goals and aspirations and the facts and feelings of their world.

Gottman says that happily married couples use their love maps to express not only their understanding of each other, but their fondness and admiration as well.

2. Nurturing Fondness and Admiration:
This involves meditating a bit on one's partner and what makes one cherish him or her. Exercises the book suggests for doing this include thinking about incidents that illustrate characteristics one appreciates in one's partner; talking about the happy events of the past; and completing a 49-item "Seven-Week Course in Fondness and Admiration".

3. Turning Toward Each Other:
This means connecting with your partner; being there for each other during the minor events in each other's lives; and responding favorably to your partner's bids for attention, affection, humor or support.

4. Accepting Influence:
Essentially, this means power sharing. We need to make our spouse a partner in the decision-making process. We need to take on board their opinions and feelings.

5. Solving Solvable Problems:
Gottman's model for conflict resolution suggests that we should soften up

the start by which he means beginning the discussion without criticism or contempt, making a straightforward comment about a concern and expressing one's need in a positive fashion; learning to make and receive repair attempts which he identifies as statements or actions that prevent negativity from escalating out of control; efforts the couple makes to deescalate the tension during a touchy discussion; soothing oneself and one's partner; compromising; and being tolerant of each other's faults.

6. **Overcoming Gridlock**:

Gridlock occurs when a conflict makes one feel rejected by one's partner. They keep going on about it but make no headway, finally becoming entrenched in their positions and are unwilling to compromise. When they discuss the subject, they end up feeling more frustrated and hurt. Their conversations about the problem are devoid of humor, amusement, or affection.

This entrenchment results in them vilifying each other resulting in polarization and less of a willingness to compromise. This then leads to disengagement. Gottman states that the only thing that couples need to get out of entrenchment is motivation and a willingness to explore the hidden issues that are really causing the gridlock.

7. **Creating Shared Meaning**:

This is the spiritual dimension to marriage that has to do with creating an inner life together. It involves a culture rich with symbols and rituals, and an appreciation for the spouses' roles and goals that link them, that lead them to understand what it means to be a part of the family they have become.

When the marriage enjoys a shared sense of meaning, then conflict is much less intense and perpetual problems are less likely to lead to gridlock.

In an interview in Psychotherapy.net in July 2000 it was put to him that many couple's therapists, recommend "active listening" and "I messages," which is pretty much the bedrock or the history of couples therapy in America.

Virginia Satir and Carl Rogers advocated these approaches so why is he critical of them? Gottman said he used to recommend it. Bernard Guerney took it from Carl Rogers' client-centered therapy. Carl Rogers would be accepting and understanding and genuine and the client theoretically would grow and develop and open up. So each member of the couple could then be a therapist to the other person?

But suggesting that the same thing could be applied to marriages is a big leap because, first of all, there's a hierarchical relationship between therapists and client. The client is paying, the therapist isn't. paying.

Usually the client is complaining about somebody else, so it's very easy for the therapist to say: "Oh, that's terrible what you have to put up with, your mother is awful, or your husband, or whatever it is. I really understand how you feel." But in marriages, it's different because now you're the target, and your partner is saying: "You're terrible," and you're supposed to be able to empathize and be understanding.

Gottman says that he found in their research that hardly anybody does that, even in great marriages. When somebody attacks you, you attack back. Gottman also said that he wasn't against empathy, he just didn't think that active listening is a very good tool for accomplishing it.

He went on to explain it in the following terms: "Let's say my wife is really angry with me because I repeatedly haven't balanced the checkbook and the checks bounce. I keep saying: "I'm sorry, and I'll try not to do it again." So finally she gets angry and confronts me in a therapy session.

What would it accomplish if I say: "I hear what you're saying, you're really angry with me, and I can understand why you're angry with me because I'm not balancing the checkbook." That's not going to make her feel any better, I still haven't balanced the damned checkbook! So I've got to really change - real empathy comes from going: "You know, I understand how upset you are. It really hurts me that I'm messing up this way, and I've got take some action." Real empathy comes from feeling your partner's pain in a real way, and then doing something about it."

Gottman goes on to say that couples heading for divorce take the problem and they put it on their partner: "The problem is you, and your personality, your character; you're a screw-up." That's an attack, and that's the fundamental attribution error that everybody's making: "I'm okay, you're the problem, you're not okay." So then their partner responds defensively and denies responsibility and says: "You're the problem; I'm not the problem."

Gottman says is what the masters do is they say: "We've got this problem. Let's take a look at it, let's kick it around. How do you see it? I see it this way, and we kick it around." And all of a sudden I can have empathy for your position because you're telling me what you contribute to the problem.

Research indicates that therapists using this approach can decisively stop their clients from what the Gottmans call "The Four Horsemen of Marital Apocalypse" which are contempt, criticism, defensiveness, and stone-walling.

More than thirty pen-and-paper questionnaires are methodically administered to each partner before therapy begins. Videotaping and heart-monitoring are standard parts of the therapy. The dispassion, structure, and authority of the approach eases and contains the discouragement and chaos often generated by couples in trouble.

Gottman's theories are not without criticism but can they really work? It's still too early to know how many of Gottman's "love lab" couples were affected by Gottman himself and by being research subjects. Replication by others will decide Gottman Method's ultimate effectiveness, but it will take several years of such replication to garner further useful data.

Results so far are promising, but at this stage, we must leave it for time to tell.

MARTIN SELIGMAN (1942-

"The very good news is there is quite a number of internal circumstances under your voluntary control. If you decide to change them, and be warned that none of these changes come without real effort, your level of happiness is likely to increase lastingly"

Positive Psychology
Learned Helplessness

Martin Seligman is an American psychologist and educator who is famous for Positive Psychology and its efforts to scientifically explore human potential as well as his theory of learned helplessness.

Seligman is the director of the University of Pennsylvania's Positive Psychology Center. He has authored over twenty books and 250 scholarly publications.

He is regarded as the leading authority in fields of resilience, depression, optimism, and pessimism. He is the recipient of the American Psychological

Society's William James Fellow Award and the James McKeen Cattell Fellow Award. He lectures worldwide to educators, mental health professionals, and parents. He has written columns on such far-flung topics as education, violence, happiness, and therapy.

Martin E. P. "Marty" Seligman was born on the 12 August, 1942 in Albany, New York. He was educated at a public school and at The Albany Academy. He earned a bachelor's degree in philosophy at Princeton University in 1964. He had to choose between three offers from various universities. They included a scholarship to study analytic philosophy at Oxford University, animal experimental psychology at the University of Pennsylvania and finally an offer to join Penn's bridge team. Seligman chose to attend the University of Pennsylvania to study psychology.

He earned his Ph.D. in psychology at University of Pennsylvania in 1967. He plays bridge, and finished second in one of the three major North American pair championships, the Blue Ribbon Pairs (1998), and has won over fifty regional championships. He has seven children, four grandchildren, and three dogs. Seligman and his second wife, Mandy, live in a three-story mansion once occupied by Eugene Ormandy, the conductor of the Philadelphia Orchestra..

In *Authentic Happiness* (2002), he explains that his journey towards this new field in psychology started off in a study on learned helplessness in dogs. During the course of the study, he noticed that, in spite of numerous configurations, some dogs would not quit and did not "learn" helplessness.

This intrigued and excited the self-proclaimed pessimist and he drew parallels between dogs and learned helplessness with depression in humans. This shaped his work and he has since become one of the most often-cited psychologists not only in positive psychology but psychology in general.

In 1967 Seligman began his foundational experiments and theory of "learned helplessness" at the University of Pennsylvania. The experiments were an extension of his interest in depression. Purely by accident, Seligman and colleagues discovered that the conditioning of dogs led to outcomes that were opposite to the predictions of B.F. Skinner's behaviorism.

They developed the theory further and discovered that learned helplessness was a psychological condition in which a human being or an animal has learned to act or behave helplessly in a particular situation.

This was usually after experiencing some inability to avoid an adverse situation and this occurred even when it actually has the power to change its unpleasant or even harmful circumstance.

Seligman saw a similarity with severely depressed patients. He argued that clinical depression and related mental illnesses result in part from a perceived absence of control over the outcome of a situation. In later years, alongside Abramson, Seligman reformulated his theory of learned helplessness to include attributional style.

Seligman worked with Christopher Peterson to create what they describe as a 'positive' counterpart to the Diagnostic and Statistical Manual of Mental Disorders (DSM). While the DSM focuses on what can go wrong, Character Strengths and Virtues is designed to look at what can go right. In their research they looked across cultures and across millennia to attempt to distill a manageable list of virtues that have been highly valued from ancient China and India, through Greece and Rome, to contemporary Western cultures.

Their list includes **six character strengths** which they identify as follows:

Wisdom/knowledge;
Courage;
Humanity;
Justice;
Temperance;
Transcendence.

Each of these has three to five sub-entries; for instance, temperance includes forgiveness, humility, prudence, and self-regulation. The authors do not believe that there is a hierarchy for the six virtues; no one is more fundamental than or a precursor to the others. Seligman wrote an account of the **good life**, which consisted of five elements under the acronym PERMA:

Positive emotion:
Tunable by writing down, every day at bed time, three things that went well, and why.

Engagement:
Tunable by preferentially using one's highest strengths to perform the tasks which one would perform anyway.

Relationships:

Tunable, but not in a way that can be explained briefly.

Meaning:
Belonging to and serving something bigger than one's self.

Achievement:
Determination is known to count for more than IQ

Although the term itself was first used by Abraham Maslow it is Seligman who is the pioneer of Positive Psychology. This is not only because he created a systematic theory about why happy people are happy, but because he uses the scientific method to explore it.

Seligman used extensive questionnaires to discover that the most satisfied, upbeat people were those who had discovered and exploited their unique combination of "signature strengths," such as humanity, temperance and persistence. This vision of happiness combines the virtue ethics of Confucius, Mencius and Aristotle with modern psychological theories of motivation.

Seligman's conclusion is that **happiness has three dimensions** that can be cultivated:

the Pleasant Life;
the Good Life; and,
the Meaningful Life.

The Pleasant Life is realized if we learn to savor and appreciate such basic pleasures as companionship, the natural environment and our bodily needs. We can remain pleasantly stuck at this stage or we can go on to experience the Good Life.

The Good Life is achieved through discovering our unique virtues and strengths, and employing them creatively to enhance our lives. According to modern theories of self-esteem life is only genuinely satisfying if we discover value within ourselves. Yet one of the best ways of discovering this value is by nourishing our unique strengths in contributing to the happiness of our fellow humans.

The Meaningful Life is the final stage and the stage in which we find a deep sense of fulfilment by employing our unique strengths for a purpose greater than ourselves.

The strength of Seligman's theory is that it reconciles two conflicting views of human happiness, the individualistic approach and the altruistic approach. The former emphasizes that we should take care of ourselves and nurture our own strengths, while the latter tends to downplay individuality and emphasizes sacrifice for the greater purpose.

Although Maslow helped to call attention to humanistic psychology, which focused on human strengths and potential rather than neuroses and pathologies, he was an intuitively inspired theorist. He simply didn't have methodologically sound, empirical evidence to support his theories.

The new generation of psychologists such as Seligman, Ed Diener and Mihaly Csiskzenmihalyi are working to scientifically study the effects of positive emotions and the ways in which they affect health, performance and overall life satisfaction.

More importantly, their studies seem to indicate that happiness can be taught and learned. In fact, according to Seligman, we can experience three kinds of happiness:

1) Pleasure and gratification,
2) Embodiment of strengths and virtues and
3) Meaning and purpose.

Each kind of happiness is linked to positive emotion but from his quote at the beginning of the article, you can see that in his mind there is a progression from the first type of happiness of pleasure/gratification to strengths/virtues and finally meaning/purpose.

Seligman provides a mental "toolkit" to achieve what he calls the pleasant life by enabling people to think constructively about the past, gain optimism and hope for the future and, as a result, gain greater happiness in the present.

Among Seligman's tools for combating unhappiness with the past is gratitude and forgiveness. Seligman refers to American society as a "ventilationist society" that "deems it honest, just and even healthy to express our anger."

He notes that this is often seen in the types of therapy used for issues, problems and challenges. In contrast, Seligman extols the East Asian tendency to quietly deal with difficult situations. He cites studies that find that those who refrain from expressing negative emotions and in turn use different strategies to cope with the stresses of life also tend to be happier. When looking to the future, Seligman recommends an outlook of hope and optimism.

After making headway with these strategies for dealing with negative emotions of the past and building hope and optimism for the future, Seligman recommends breaking habituation, savoring experiences and using mindfulness as ways to increase happiness in the present.

"Many studies have shown that positive emotions are frequently accompanied by fortunate circumstances. I'm talking here about such things as health, longer life, and large social networks. For example, one study observed nuns who were, for the most part, leading virtually identical lifestyles. It seemed that the nuns who expressed positive emotions more intensely and more frequently in their daily life lived longer than many of the nuns who clearly did not."

Another study used high school yearbook photos of women to see if the ultimate expression of happiness (a smile) might also be used as an indicator as to how satisfied they might be 20 years later. When surveyed, those who were photographed with genuine, "Duchenne" smiles were more likely to find themselves, in their mid-life, married with families and involved in richer social lives.

Accordingly, Seligman's point is that positive emotions are frequently paired with happy circumstances. And while one might be tempted to assume that happiness causes positive emotions, Seligman asks if it's possible that positive emotions cause happiness. If so, what does this mean for our life and our happiness?

Seligman's learned helplessness experiments have been heavily criticized for their deliberate mistreatment of animals. In particular, critics argued that inflicting electrical shocks upon dogs at random intervals, until the dogs reached a helpless state in which they did not escape the shocks even when given the opportunity to do so was cruel and unacceptable.

It has been asserted that under current ethical standards for humane treatment of animals, Seligman's learned helplessness experiments could not be performed today.

Others have criticized Positive Psychology in more general terms claiming that it is intentionally oblivious to the stark realities of life. And though Seligman ventures into the area of pleasure and gratification through his research in the area of positive emotion, there is much more to his work beyond this. In his study of the Good Life and the Meaningful Life, positive psychology endeavors to assist people acquire the skills so that they can effectively deal with problems of life in ever fuller, deeper ways.

MARSHA LINEHAN (1943-

"They put me in a four-walled room
But left me really out
My soul was tossed somewhere askew
My limbs were tossed here about"

Dialectical Behavior Therapy

Marsha Linehan is an American psychologist and the creator of Dialectical Behavior Therapy, a psychotherapy that combines behavioral science with Buddhism concepts like acceptance and mindfulness.

She is a Professor of Psychology, Adjunct Professor of Psychiatry and Behavioral Sciences at the University of Washington in Seattle and Director of the Behavioral Research and Therapy Clinics. Marsha Linehan was born in Tulsa, Oklahoma on the 5 May 1943.

She had a problematic childhood. She eventually told her story in public for the first time before an audience of friends, family and doctors at the Institute of Living, the Hartford clinic where she was first treated for extreme social withdrawal at age of seventeen. Linehan told the shocked assembled audience that she first arrived at the Institute of Living on the 9 March, 1961, and quickly became the sole occupant of the seclusion room on the unit known as Thompson Two.

This room was used for the most severely ill patients. The staff saw her as such. She had continuously self-harmed, burning her wrists with cigarettes, slashing her arms, her legs and her midsection. The seclusion didn't help. Her urge to die deepened so she did the only thing she could do in that small room. She banged her head hard against the wall and floor to make it all stop. Speaking of the incident she said: "My whole experience of these episodes was that someone else was doing it; it was like 'I know this is coming, I'm out of control, somebody help me; where are you, God?" I felt totally empty, like the Tin Man; I had no way to communicate what was going on, no way to understand it."

How did she get to this stage? Her childhood provided few clues. The third of six children, she was a excellent student who excelled at pianoforte. Her father was an oilman and her mother was a home-maker. Everything seemed normal but it wasn't. Marsha felt deeply inferior to her attractive and accomplished siblings. No one knew what she was going through until she was bedridden with headaches in her senior year of high school.

Then a local psychiatrist recommended that she be admitted to the Institute of Living. She was diagnosed with schizophrenia; dosed with Thorazine and Librium; given hours of psychoanalysis; and strapped her down for electroshock treatments. It didn't help. Soon she was back in seclusion on the locked ward.

Twenty six months of hospitalization brought no cure. In fact, the resultant medical care only made matters worse. She herself determined that any real treatment would have to be based not on some theory but on facts. What was the precise emotion, that led to which thought, that led to the latest gruesome act.? She needed to know this in order to break that chain. She decided that she would have to teach a new behavior. As she said: "I was in hell, and I made a vow: when I get out, I'm going to come back and get others out of here."

In 1968 Linehan graduated from Loyola University Chicago with a B.Sc. in psychology. She earned her M.A. in 1970 and her Ph.D. in clinical psychology the following year. After Loyola she began her predoctoral internship at The Suicide Prevention and Crisis Service in Buffalo, New York.

During this time she served as an adjunct assistant professor at University at Buffalo, The State University of New York. She completed her Post-Doctoral fellowship in Behavior Modification at Stony Brook University and then returned to Loyola to serve as an adjunct professor until 1975.

Between 1973-1977 she served as an Assistant Professor in Psychology at The Catholic University of America in Washington, D.C. from 1973 to 1977.

She claims that in 1967 she had a religious experience in a small Catholic chapel in Chicago that changed her life. She described it as follows: "One night I was kneeling in there, looking up at the cross, and the whole place became gold, and suddenly I felt something coming toward me. It was this shimmering experience, and I just ran back to my room and said, 'I love myself.' It was the first time I remembered talking to myself in the first person. I felt transformed."

Linehan went on to create Dialectical Behavior Therapy (DBT). DBT is a therapy designed to help people change patterns of behavior that are not effective. It helps people increase their emotional and cognitive regulation by learning about the triggers that lead to reactive states. It helps to assess which coping skills to apply in the sequence of events, thoughts, feelings and behaviors that lead to the undesired behavior.

That basic idea, radical acceptance, as she now calls it, became increasingly important as she began working with patients, first at a suicide clinic in Buffalo and later as a researcher. She believed that real change was possible.

The emerging discipline of behaviorism taught that people could learn new behaviors; that acting differently can eventually alter underlying emotions from the top down. But deeply suicidal people have tried to change a million times and it wasn't working. Something had to change. Linehan thought that the only way to get through to them was to acknowledge that their behavior actually made sense.

Linehan decided to focus on two seemingly opposed principles that could form the basis of a treatment:

1. acceptance of life as it is, not as it is supposed to be; and,

2. the need to change, despite that reality and because of it.

The only way to know for sure whether she had something more than a theory was to test it scientifically in the real world. "I decided to get super suicidal people, the very worst cases, because I figured these are the most miserable people in the world, they think they're evil, that they're bad, bad, bad, and I understood that they weren't. I understood their suffering because I'd been there, in hell, with no idea how to get out."

Linehan chose to treat people with a diagnosis that she would have given herself at seventeen years of age: borderline personality disorder, a poorly understood condition characterized by neediness, outbursts and self-destructive urges, often leading to cutting or burning. Linehan found that the tension of acceptance could at least keep people in the room.

In turn, the therapist accepts that given all this, cutting, burning and suicide attempts make some sense. Finally, the therapist elicits a commitment from the patient to change his or her behavior, a verbal pledge in exchange for a chance to live: "Therapy does not work for people who are dead" is one way she puts it.

Yet even as she climbed the academic ladder she knew that acceptance and change weren't enough. She knew that her own emerging approach to treatment, now called D.B.T., would also have to include day-to-day skills. She borrowed from other behavioral therapies and added elements, like opposite action, in which patients act opposite to the way they feel when an emotion is inappropriate; and mindfulness meditation, a Zen technique in which people focus on their breath and observe their emotions come and go without acting on them.

Researchers tracked the progress of hundreds of borderline patients at high risk of suicide who attended weekly dialectical therapy sessions and found that those who learned Linehan's approach made far fewer suicide attempts, were hospitalized less often and were much more likely to stay in treatment.

D.B.T. contains four modules; Mindfulness, Distress Tolerance, Emotion Regulation, and Inter-personal Effectiveness.

Mindfulness is one of the core concepts behind all elements of DBT. It is in fact a foundation for the other skills taught in DBT, because it helps individuals accept and tolerate the powerful emotions they may feel when challenging their habits or exposing themselves to upsetting situations

As of 2015 Linehan remains unmarried and lives with her adult adopted Peruvian daughter Geraldine and her son-in-law in Seattle, Washington.

JON KABAT-ZINN (1944-

"You can't stop the waves, but you can learn to surf"

Mindfulness Based Stress Reduction

Jon Kabat-Zinn is Professor of Medicine emeritus at the University of Massachusetts Medical School and creator of Mindfulness-based stress reduction (MBSR).

He has been a student of Buddhist teachers such as Thich Nhat Hanh and Zen Master Seung Sahn. His practice of yoga and studies with Buddhist teachers led him to integrate their teachings with those of science. The curriculum started by Kabat-Zinn at University of Massachusetts Medical Center has produced nearly 1,000 certified MBSR instructors who are in nearly every state in the US and more than 30 countries.

Corporations such as General Mills have made it available to their employees or set aside rooms for meditation. Kabat-Zinn believes that his program of mindfulness can help people cope with stress, anxiety, pain, and illness. His stress reduction program is offered by medical centers, hospitals, and health maintenance organizations all over the world.

Jon Kabat-Zinn was born Jon Kabat in New York City on the 5 June 1944 to Jewish parents, Elvin and Sally Kabat His father was a biomedical scientist and his mother a painter. In 1971 he graduated from Haverford College and went on to earn a Ph.D. in molecular biology from the Massachusetts Institute of Technology.

Although he was born into the Jewish faith and was trained in Buddhist principles he grew up with beliefs which he said were more a fusion of science and art rather than Jewish.

He says he was first introduced to meditation by Philip Kapleau, a Zen missionary who came to speak at MIT while Kabat-Zinn was a student. He later studied at the Insight Meditation Society and eventually also taught there.

In 1979 he founded the Stress Reduction Clinic at the University of Massachusetts Medical School, where he adapted the Buddhist teachings on mindfulness and developed the innovative Stress Reduction and Relaxation Program.

He subsequently renamed the structured eight-week course Mindfulness-Based Stress Reduction (MBSR). Later also removed the Buddhist framework and eventually downplayed any connection between mindfulness and Buddhism, preferring instead to put MBSR in a scientific context.

His secular technique combines meditation and Hatha yoga in helping patients cope with stress, pain, and illness by using what is called "moment-to-moment awareness." In 1991 he published his breakthrough book *Full Catastrophe Living: Using the Wisdom of Your Body and Mind to Face Stress, Pain, and Illness* which set out detailed instructions for the technique.

Two years later his work in the Stress Reduction Clinic was featured in Bill

Moyers's PBS special Healing and the Mind. The program catapulted him into the headlines. In 1994 Kabat-Zinn's second book, titled *Wherever You Go, There You Are*, became a national bestseller. The success of the book was instrumental in the opening towards the latter part of the 1990s of many MBSR clinics throughout America. They operated either as standalone centers or as part of a hospital's holistic medicine program.

So, what exactly is MBSR and how effective is it on psoriasis, pain, anxiety, brain function, and immune function?

MBSR has been described as "a group program that focuses upon the progressive acquisition of mindful awareness, of mindfulness". Essentially it is a mindfulness-based program designed initially to assist people with pain and a range of conditions and life issues that were difficult to treat in a hospital setting.

It employs a combination of mindfulness meditation, body awareness, and yoga to help people become more mindful. Clinical research has shown evidence of certain beneficial effects such as stress reduction, relaxation, and improvements to quality of life. However, the program does not help prevent or cure any disease. Its roots are in spiritual teachings. The program itself is secular. How does it work?

The MBSR program is an eight-week workshop taught by certified trainers that entails weekly group meetings, homework, and instruction in three formal techniques: mindfulness meditation, body scanning and simple yoga postures. Body scanning is the first prolonged formal mindfulness technique taught during the first four weeks of the workshop. It entails quietly lying on one's back and focusing one's attention on various regions of the body, starting with the toes and moving up slowly to the top of the head. The basis of MBSR is "moment-to-moment, non-judgmental awareness."

Has the technique been empirically tested? In 2003 a total of fifty two papers were published examining the technique. By 2012 this had risen to 477 with over one hundred randomized controlled trials by the end of 2014. However some of the quality of the research has been criticized as being unscientific. According to Cancer Research UK, while some evidence has shown MBSR may help with symptom relief and improve quality of life, there is no evidence it helps prevent or cure disease.

In 2013 the American Heart Association in writing about alternative approaches to lowering blood pressure concluded that meditation techniques other than Transcendental Meditation, including MBSR, are not recommended in clinical practice to lower blood pressure. Despite this, it is generally accepted that MBSR may have a small beneficial effect helping with the depression and psychological distress associated with chronic illness. There is no evidence of long-term benefit but low-quality evidence of a small short-term benefit.

In, *Wherever You Go, There You Are* (1994) he shares his insights into the practice of meditation as a means to reduce stress. He discusses the different philosophies behind meditation and different techniques for practice. He also describes different meditation techniques. Two visualization techniques called The Mountain Meditation and The Lake Meditation are worth consideration.

Kabat-Zinn believes that in order to be mindful we need to focus on three aspects of our life:

1. Being honest with ourselves – we must be honest about what is happening to us internally and externally, mentally and physically, right now;

2. Being non-judgmental; and

3. Living fully present in each moment. By this he means not basing your thoughts on either the past or the future.

His views on honesty are particularly relevant. He says that we often create different ways to lie to ourselves. This may be to justify our anger at not getting something we think we deserve, or to cushion our emotions after a hurtful experience. Sometimes those lies can shape our self-identity. These lies are actually judgments about ourselves. He believes that they obstruct us in being mindful and honest.

Jon Kabat-Zinn believes that best way to achieve mindfulness is through meditation and he specifically emphasizes his two visual meditation techniques, the Mountain Meditation and the Lake Meditation. Here are the instructions for the Mountain Meditation which I have adapted to give you an idea of what is involved but to achieve the real effect you should buy his books. The purpose of the mountain meditation is to become grounded and access our inner strength and stability when faced with stressful and challenging circumstances, both internal and external. We should then follow these steps:

1. Sit down in a comfortable position on the floor or in a chair.

2. After following your breath for a few moments, imagine in vivid detail-the most beautiful mountain you know of and resonate with. Envision its various details and stable, unmoving presence grounded in the earth.

3. After a few minutes of developing and holding this clear image in your mind, imagine bringing the mountain inside yourself and becoming the mountain.

4. Imagine yourself sitting in stillness and in calm, simply observing and resting unwavering as the various weather patterns, storms, and seasons pass before you.

5. Just as a mountain endures constant changes and extremes, we also experience various thoughts, emotions and life challenges.

6. Imagine viewing these experiences as external, fleeting and impersonal events, akin to weather patterns.

7. Feel yourself unwavering and rooted in stillness amidst the constant change of your internal and external experience.

This meditation is designed to last about twenty minutes but can be shortened or extended based on the practitioner's preference. Kabat-Zinn claims that these meditations can help an individual to apply mindfulness to their daily life, which in turn can bring about positive change in reactions, emotion and behavior. This will lead to a more satisfying and fuller life. For more information on mindfulness, meditation, and Jon Kabat-Zinn's buy the book *Wherever You Go, There You Are.*

JOHN TEASDALE

Mindfulness Based Cognitive Therapy

John Teasdale has worked as a research scientist, funded by the Medical Research Council, first in the Department of Psychiatry, University of Oxford, then in the Cognition and Brain Sciences Unit, Cambridge.

His research has investigated basic psychological processes and the application of that understanding to the relief of emotional disorders. For many years, this research involved the exploration of cognitive approaches to understanding and treating major depression. Teasdale is one of the pioneers of cognitive therapy research in the United Kingdom.

More recently, the findings of earlier research have been applied to the development and evaluation of mindfulness-based cognitive therapy.

He has received a Distinguished Scientist Award from the American Psychological Association, and has been elected Fellow of both the British Academy and the Academy of Medical Sciences. He is currently retired, pursuing personal interests in practicing and teaching meditation and mindfulness training.

In 1991, alongside Phil Barnard, Teasdale developed a theory of the mind he called **interacting cognitive subsystems**. This model argues that the mind can operate in multiple modes, each of which is responsible for processing new information on both an intellectual and cognitive level.

From this theory mindfulness-based cognitive therapy grew. Developed by John Teasdale, Zindel Segal, and Mark Williams, mindfulness-based cognitive therapy is based on the mindfulness-based stress reduction program designed by Jon Kabat-Zinn.

Teasdale studied cognitive therapies for years and developed MBCT as a viable and effective form of treatment for the prevention of depression relapse. MBCT combines traditional cognitive behavioral therapy with mindfulness and other contemplative approaches.

Like meditation, MBCT helps a person learn to accept emotions and thoughts in a nonjudgmental way, in order to identify them more clearly. By gaining awareness of and control over one's thoughts, a person struggling with depression can work to counteract automatic negative thoughts. MBCT also strives to help participants avoid ruminating on negative emotions rather than simply ignoring unpleasant feelings. The therapy places a strong emphasis on not judging oneself or one's thoughts.

Conducted in a group setting over the course of eight weekly sessions, MBCT has a strong focus on practice. Every course lasts two hours, and after five weeks, participants attend a day-long course. Participants also do homework such as guided meditations, thought logs, and other tools designed to promote mindfulness.

Some therapists have begun using this approach with other disorders, such as schizophrenia, but there has not been much clinical research on MBCT's effectiveness with other mental health issues, outside of depression. For the treatment of depression, MBCT is an empirically validated approach.

John Teasdale received his first degree in psychology from the University of Cambridge. Subsequently, he studied for his Ph.D. in abnormal psychology, and trained as a clinical psychologist, at the Institute of Psychiatry, University of London, where he then taught for a number of years.

After working as a National Health Service clinical psychologist in the University Hospital of Wales, he began a thirty year period of full-time research, supported by the Medical Research Council, first in the Department of Psychiatry, University of Oxford, subsequently in the MRC Cognition and Brain Sciences Unit, Cambridge.

The continuing focus of this research has been the investigation of basic psychological processes and the application of that understanding to the relief of emotional disorders. Initially this involved the development and evaluation of behavioral therapies for anxiety disorders, subsequently the exploration of cognitive approaches to understanding and treating major depression, and, most recently, the development of mindfulness-based cognitive therapy, a program that is effective in substantially reducing future risk of major depression through an integration of mindfulness training and cognitive approaches.

John Teasdale has published more than a hundred scientific papers and chapters, and co-authored three books. His colleague, Mark Williams, is a Professor of Clinical Psychology and Wellcome Principal Research Fellow at the University of Oxford. He holds a joint appointment in the Department of Psychiatry and the Department of Experimental Psychology. He is a Fellow of the British Psychological Society, the Academy of Medical Sciences and the British Academy. He was educated at Stockton Grammar School, Stockton-on-Tees, and at the University of Oxford. He is currently working on how autobiographical memory biases and deficits affect current and future vulnerability. He is an ordained priest of the Church of England.

FRANCINE SHAPIRO (1948-

EMDR

Francine Shapiro is an American psychologist who founded and

developed EMDR, a form of psychotherapy for resolving the symptoms of traumatic and other disturbing life experiences.

EMDR is an abbreviation for "Eye Movement Desensitization". This form of psychotherapy is now recommended as an effective treatment for trauma in the Practice Guidelines of the American Psychiatric Association, and those of the Departments of Defense and Veterans Affairs.

Shapiro is a Senior Research Fellow Emeritus at the Mental Research Institute in Palo Alto, California, Executive Director of the EMDR Institute in Watsonville, CA, and founder and President Emeritus of the EMDR Humanitarian Assistance Programs, a non-profit organization that coordinates disaster response and low fee trainings worldwide.

She is a recipient of the International Sigmund Freud Award for distinguished contribution to psychotherapy, the American Psychological Association Trauma Division Award for Outstanding Contributions to Practice in Trauma Psychology, and the Distinguished Scientific Achievement in Psychology Award presented by the California Psychological Association.

Shapiro has served as advisor to a wide variety of trauma treatment and outreach organizations and journals. She has been an invited speaker at psychology conferences worldwide and has written and co-authored more than sixty articles, chapters, and books about EMDR.

Shapiro was educated at Brooklyn College, City University of New York where she obtained a B.A. in 1968 and an M.A. in 1974 in English Literature. In 1974, while employed full-time as an English teacher, she was diagnosed with cancer. Her post-recovery experiences shifted her attention from literature to the writings of Norman Cousins and others who investigated the effects of stress on the immune system.

She spent the following few years participating in numerous workshops and programs that explored various stress reduction and self-care procedures. During that time she enrolled in the Professional School of Psychological Studies in San Diego and began her dissertation on the beneficial effect of eye movements and the development of procedures to utilize them in clinical practice. In 1988 she received her Ph.D. and the following year her was published in the Journal of Traumatic Studies.

So, what exactly is EMDR?

It is a relatively new controversial treatment that is growing in popularity. Empirical studies have found that EMDR is highly effective with post traumatic stress (PTSD). However, the research on the role of the eye movements is conflicting; some studies equate the eye movements to the REM stage of sleep. The results of EMDR as a treatment for other mental health conditions are mixed, and some insurance plans will only cover EMDR for trauma and posttraumatic stress.

EMDR uses an eight stage-based treatment protocol to reduce the symptoms of trauma.

History taking:
The therapist conducts an evaluation of the client's current symptoms and history.

Preparation:
The therapist explains the process and helps the client to establish stress reduction skills to be used throughout the process as necessary.

Assessment:
The therapist asks the client to identify some aspect of the trauma to serve as a target for change. The client rates the target for how disturbing it is, on a scale of 0–10. The client will also select a positive cognition and rate this for how true it feels on a scale of 1–7.

Desensitization:
A client is encouraged to focus on the target during brief sessions of bilateral stimulation, consisting of rapid tones, taps, or eye movements. The client will again rate the level of disturbance with each session until the level is rated at zero.

Installation:
The therapist asks the client to rate the positive cognition identified in phase three to see if it has changed. Bilateral stimulation continues until the positive cognition is rated at seven, completely true.

Body scan:
The client checks in with his or her body to reveal whether any tension associated with the traumatic event may linger. Bilateral stimulation continues as needed to reduce the distress.

Closure:
The therapist conducts a final check-in. If anything is left unprocessed, the

therapist and client discuss ways to contain and manage the distress between sessions.

Re-evaluation:
The next session begins here. The therapist reviews the previous session(s) and the client assesses the level of disturbance and evaluates the positive cognition. If anything was left incomplete, the desensitization process begins again.

So, how did Shapiro discover this therapy?

She says that she discovered the effects of the eye movements that are now used in EMDR therapy one day as she was taking a walk. She noticed that disturbing thoughts she had been having had disappeared and when she brought them back they didn't have the same "charge."

She was puzzled since she hadn't done anything deliberately to deal with them. So she started paying careful attention and noticed that when that kind of thought came up, her eyes started moving rapidly in a certain way and the thoughts shifted out of consciousness. When she brought them back they were less bothersome.

As a result of this experience she started doing it deliberately and found the same results. Then she experimented with about seventy people. During that time she developed additional procedures to achieve consistent effects.

She tested the procedures in a randomized study that was published in the *Journal of Traumatic Stress* in 1989. Then she continued the development of the procedures and published a textbook on EMDR therapy in 1995.

What does an EMDR entail for a client suffering from PTSD? EMDR therapy is an eight-phase approach. It begins with a history-taking phase that identifies the current problems and the earlier experiences that have set the foundation for the different symptoms, and what is needed for a fulfilling future. Then a preparation phase prepares the client for memory processing. The memory is accessed in a certain way and processing proceeds with the client attending briefly to different parts of the memory while the information processing system of the brain is stimulated.

Brief sets of eye movements, taps or tones are used for about thirty seconds during which time the brain makes the needed connections that transform the "stuck memory" into a learning experience and take it to an adaptive resolution. New emotions, thoughts and memories can emerge.

What is useful is learned, and what is now useless (the negative reactions, emotions and thoughts) is discarded. A rape victim, for example, may begin with feelings of shame and fear, but at the end of the session report: "The shame is his, not mine. I'm a strong resilient woman."

How does EMDR help clients process problematic experiences? There are very few research-supported trauma treatments. The other two besides EMDR that are best known ask the client to describe the memory in detail because it is necessary for the therapy procedures that are used.

In one of these, Prolonged Exposure therapy, the clients are asked to describe the memory in detail two to three times during the session as if reliving it. The rationale for this treatment is that "avoidance" is causing the problem to persist and the clients need to learn that they can experience the disturbance without going crazy or being overwhelmed. For the same reasons, they are also asked to listen to recordings of the event for homework and visit places they previously avoided in order to allow the disturbance to abate.

The other form of treatment is Cognitive Processing Therapy. This asks clients for details of the event in order to determine what negative beliefs they hold so they can be challenged and changed. This is done during sessions and with homework.

EMDR therapy is different to both of these approaches. In EMDR therapy, the emphasis is on allowing the information processing system of the brain to make the internal connections needed to resolve the disturbance. So, the person only needs to focus briefly on the disturbing memory as the internal associations are made. Researchers have published articles setting out how the eye movements in EMDR therapy seem to link into the same processes that occur during rapid eye movement (REM) sleep. This is the time that dreams take place and the brain processes survival information.

According to the theory, the memory is then transferred from episodic memory, which holds the emotions, physical sensations and beliefs that were stored at the time of the original event, into semantic memory networks. This is the place where the person has "digested" the experience so that the accurate personal meaning of the life event has been extracted and those negative visceral reactions no longer exist.

In an EMDR session you can observe these connections being made as learning rapidly takes place through the internal connections.

Shapiro includes in her books a wide range of self-help techniques that will allow people to

(a) manage stress;

(b) change their emotions, physical sensations and negative thoughts in the present;

(c) help get rid of negative intrusive images;

(d) identify situations that trigger these kinds of reactions and help prepare for them in advance; and

(e) identify the unprocessed memories that are causing the negative reactions.

Additional techniques include ones taught to Olympic athletes to achieve peak performance. These can also help people prepare for future challenges such as presentations, job interviews and social situations.

EMDR seems to be most effective in relation to treatment for PTSD in that it is supported by more than twenty randomized studies and is recognized as an effective trauma treatment worldwide by organizations such as the US Department of Defense and the American Psychiatric Association.

Three EMDR studies have reported an 84-100 percent remission of PTSD from a single trauma in the equivalent of three 90-minute reprocessing sessions. So, while complex PTSD, such as from pervasive childhood trauma, will definitely need more extensive treatment than three sessions, in most cases it doesn't take long for the client to derive benefit. It's not like some versions of talk therapy where change is not expected to be apparent for many months, or even years.

Is EMDR useful in situations other than those involving PTSD? Recent research has shown that certain types of life experiences can cause more PTSD symptoms than major trauma. It has also been documented that negative childhood experiences can cause later problems.

EMDR therapy addresses the life experiences that set the foundation for a wide range of clinical complaints involving negative emotions, physical sensations, thoughts, beliefs, behaviors and relationship difficulties. It also incorporates procedures to address future concerns and challenges.

Further research and development will ultimately determine the true effectiveness of Shapiro's innovative therapy but for now it seems to becoming increasingly more popular.

KIRK STROSAHL

ACT

Kirk D. Strosahl, is cofounder of acceptance and commitment therapy (ACT), a cognitive behavioral approach that has gained widespread adoption in the mental health and substance abuse communities.

Strosahl works as a practicing psychologist at Central Washington Family Medicine, a community health center providing health care to medically underserved patients. He also teaches family medicine physicians in how to use the principles of mindfulness and acceptance in general practice. Strosahl lives in a vineyard in Zillah, Washington.

In 1973 he received a B.Sc. in Psychology from Colorado University Boulder. In 1977 he received his master in Clinical Psychology from Purdue University Lafayette, Indiana. Four years later he received his doctorate from the same university. He then took his post doctoral internship at American Lakes V. A. Medical Center Tacoma, Washington.

Between 1981 to 1984 he was research associate professor at the University of Washington Seattle. After this he was Staff Psychologist and Research and Evaluation Coordinator, Division of Behavioral Health Services at Group Health Cooperative of Puget Sound. In 1999 he moved to Mountainview Consulting Group Moxee, where he remains as Principal and Research and Training Director.

Originally called Comprehensive Distancing, ACT or Acceptance and Commitment Therapy is a form of clinical behavior analysis used in psychotherapy.

It was developed by Strosahl, Steven C. Hayes and Kelly G. Wilson in the late 1980s. It is an empirically-based psychological intervention that uses acceptance and mindfulness strategies mixed in different ways with commitment and behavior-change strategies, to increase psychological flexibility.

ACT is based on relational frame theory (RFT), a comprehensive theory of language and cognition that is an offshoot of behavior analysis.

But ACT differs from traditional cognitive behavioral therapy in that rather than trying to teach people to better control their thoughts, feelings, sensations, memories and other private events, ACT teaches them to "just notice," accept, and embrace their private events, especially previously unwanted ones. ACT helps the individual get in contact with a transcendent sense of self known as "self-as-context". Self-as-Context is the you that is always there observing and experiencing and yet distinct from one's thoughts, feelings, sensations, and memories.

The aims of ACT is to help the individual clarify their personal values and to take action on them, bringing more vitality and meaning to their life in the process. ACT assumes that the psychological processes of a normal human mind are often destructive and that psychological suffering is usually caused by experiential avoidance, cognitive entanglement, and resulting psychological rigidity all of which leads to a failure to take needed behavioral steps. The model can be summarized in the FEAR:

Fusion with your thoughts
Evaluation of experience
Avoidance of your experience
Reason-giving for your behavior

And the healthy alternative is to ACT:

Accept your reactions and be present
Choose a valued direction
Take action

ACT commonly employs six core principles to help clients develop psychological flexibility:

Cognitive Defusion:
These are learning methods to reduce the tendency to reify thoughts, images, emotions, and memories.

Acceptance:
This involves allowing thoughts to come and go without struggling with them.

Contact with the present moment:
We must have awareness of the here and now, experienced with openness, interest, and receptiveness.

Observing the self:
This requires accessing a transcendent sense of self, a continuity of consciousness which is unchanging.

Values:
We must discover what is most important to one's true self.

Committed action:
We need to set goals according to values and carry them out responsibly.

ACT is considered an empirically validated treatment by the American Psychological Association. It holds the status of "Modest Research Support" in depression and "Strong Research Support" in chronic pain. It is also listed as evidence-based by the Substance Abuse and Mental Health Services Administration of the United States federal government which has examined randomized trials for ACT in the areas of psychosis, work site stress, and obsessive compulsive disorder, including depression outcomes.

But it is still relatively new in the development of its research base. However, it has shown preliminary research evidence of effectiveness in randomized trials for a variety of problems including chronic pain, addictions, smoking cessation, depression, anxiety, psychosis, workplace stress, diabetes management, weight management, epilepsy control, self-harm, body dissatisfaction, eating disorders, burn out, and several other areas.

ZINDEL SEGAL (1956-

Mindfulness Based Cognitive Therapy

Zindel Segal is currently a professor of psychiatry at the University of Toronto. He is also the head of the Cognitive Behavior Therapy Clinic of the Mood and Anxiety Disorders Program at the Centre for Addiction and Mental Health (CAMH).

Segal's career has focused on the prevention and treatment of depression. Segal developed mindfulness-based cognitive therapy (MBCT) with Mark Williams and John Teasdale in an effort to help people avoid relapse after a major depressive episode.

Segal has received the Hope Award from the Mood Disorders Association of Ontario, as well as the Douglas Utting Prize for his work and insight into treatment for depression. Mindfulness-based cognitive therapy (MBCT) incorporates elements of conventional cognitive behavioral therapy with mindfulness meditation and was inspired by Jon Kabat-Zinn's mindfulness-based stress reduction program (MBSR).

Rather than encouraging people to change their thoughts, MBCT attempts to teach people to think differently about their thoughts. Like other contemplative approaches, MBCT helps people learn to focus on their thoughts without judgment and to consider how some habitual thoughts can trigger a downturn in mood. Instead of attempting to eliminate negative thoughts altogether, people are encouraged to learn how to move from negative thoughts to positive ones without dwelling on unpleasant emotions.

Segal originally developed MBCT to prevent relapse in patients experiencing depression, but has expanded the approach to include a wide variety of psychiatric symptoms. MBCT is an empirically validated approach to therapy and the treatment of depression, and several studies have found it to be effective.

Zindel Segal was born in Lutsk, Ukraine, in 1956. He received his B.A. (Hons) from McGill University in 1978, his M.A. from Queen's University in 1979, and Ph.D. in Psychology from Queen's in 1983.

Segal is author of more than ten books and 150 scientific publications including *Mindfulness Based Cognitive Therapy* and *The Mindful Way Workbook*, a patient guide for achieving mood balance in everyday life.

In his 2014 TEDx talk, *The Mindful Way Through Depression*, he discusses the effectiveness of Mindfulness-Based Cognitive Therapy (MBCT) in treating depression. He continues to advocate for the relevance of mindfulness-based clinical care in psychiatry and mental health.

Zindel Segal, Mark Williams and John Teasdale developed Mindfulness-Based Cognitive Therapy (MBCT) for helping people not relapse into depression. Over time research has shown the positive impact MBCT has in relapse depression. For those unable to attend a workshop Segal and Sona Dimidjian developed a new online program called Mindful Noggin that can bring MBCT to you anywhere and anytime.

The program is a digital version of Mindfulness Based Cognitive Therapy, called Mindful Mood Balance (MMB). The program was developed for patients who wanted to learn the core practices of MMB but didn't have access to an in-person group. It provides a way to learn the core practices of MBCT in a highly experiential, immerse context. The various interactivities, video clips and expert guidance for patients in Mindful Mood Balance could provide the same type of focal training to support therapists who may be providing MBCT or offering elements of the model to their clients.

Their emphasis is on supporting mindful affect regulation and extending its availability beyond the cushion to the everyday moments of people's lives. They have also developed a companion program called the Three Minute Breathing Space.

The **Three Minute Breathing Space** or 3MBS is a mini meditation that Segal designed to bring the perspective of the more formal and longer practice of mindfulness into our often, very busy lives. What clients learn is the intentional and flexible engagement of two types of attention; one that is open and another that is focused.

1. In the first step of the 3MBS, the emphasis is on **Awareness**, especially recognizing and acknowledging one's current experience.

2. The second step emphasizes **Gathering**, particularly by bringing the attention to the sensations of the breath in a particular place in the body.

3. The third step is about **Expanding** the awareness into the body as a whole using the particular sensations of the breath as an anchor, while opening to the range of experience that is present.

Segal says that the movement of attention in the 3MBS can be seen as following the path of an hourglass. It starts with a wide opening, moving to a narrow throat and expanding once again at a wide base. Because it's simple, brief and accessible, you can take a 3MBS wherever and whenever you remember to do so.

Segal says that the 3MBS is really the spine of the MBCT program. The thing about the 3MBS training is that the training starts with embedding this practice in your own life, so that it can be understood from the inside. With this foundation in place, the program supports introducing 3MBS to your clients, leading mindfulness practices with your clients, conducting inquiry and recording mindfulness practices to support your clients' home practice.

They developed it in response to what many therapists who have attended in person MBCT workshops and were asking for, continued support and engagement with a learning community and help in implementing and refining newly acquired skills.

You can buy the program online.

BARBARA FREDRICKSON (1964-

Positive Psychology
Broaden and Build Theory of Positive Emotion

Barbara Lee Fredrickson is an American psychologist and currently the Kenan Distinguished Professor of Psychology at the University of North Carolina at Chapel Hill, who conducts research in emotions and positive psychology.

Her main work is related to her broaden-and-build theory of positive emotions. This theory suggests that positive emotions lead to novel, expansive, or exploratory behavior, and that, over time, these actions lead to meaningful, long-term resources such as knowledge and social relationships.

In 2009 she published a book called *Positivity*, a general-audience book that draws on her own research and that of other social scientists. In 2013, she published *Love 2.0*, which discusses the supreme emotion of love, micro-moments of connection as well as how love can affect your biological and cellular make-up over time.

Fredrickson earned her Ph.D. from Stanford University in 1990. She was a professor at the University of Michigan for ten years before moving to the University of North Carolina at Chapel Hill. Her mentors include Robert Levenson and Laura Carstensen.

The concept of specific-action tendencies (the idea that emotions prepare the body both physically and psychologically to act in particular ways) is central to many existing theories of emotion. For example, fear causes an urge to escape while anger creates the urge to attack. But emotions like joy and gratitude don't seem as useful as fear or anger.

The urge to act and the facial expressions produced by positive emotions are not as specific or as obviously relevant to survival as those sparked by negative emotions. If positive emotions didn't promote our ancestors' survival in life-threatening situations, then what good were they? How did they survive evolutionary pressures?

In order to solve this puzzle, Barbara Fredrickson, developed the Broaden-and-Build Theory of Positive Emotions. In this theory she explains the mechanics of how positive emotions were important to survival. According to Fredrickson, positive emotions expand cognition and behavioral tendencies. The theory questions if all emotions really lead to specific action tendencies. It argues that positive emotions increase the number of potential behavioral options. Instead, emotions should be cast as leading to changes in "momentary thought-action repertoires".

The expanded cognitive flexibility evident during positive emotional states results in resource building and such building becomes useful over time. Even though a positive emotional state is only momentary, the benefits last in the form of traits and social bonds that endure into the future. The implication here is that positive emotions have inherent value to human growth and development. Accordingly, the cultivation of these emotions will help people lead fuller lives.

In Fredrickson's research, randomly assigned participants watched movies that induced positive emotions like as amusement and contentment, negative emotions such as fear and sadness, or no emotions at all. Compared to people in the other conditions, participants who experience positive emotions show heightened levels of creativity, inventiveness, and "big picture" perceptual focus. Other studies showed a role in the development of long-term resources.

In a 2005 paper, co-written by Marial Losada, they argued that precise values of an individual's emotional positivity-to-negativity ratio exist, outside of which they will fail to flourish. They used nonlinear dynamics modelling, taken from fluid dynamics, to derive these values.

This use was strongly criticized by other researchers, namely, Nicholas Brown, Alan Sokal, and Harris Friedman. In 2013 they pointed out numerous fundamental mathematical errors in this study, in an article published in *American Psychologist*, the same journal in which Fredrickson's original findings were published in eight years earlier.

Their article sought to completely discredit Frederickson's theory. Fredrickson later agreed that the mathematical modelling is "questionable", but firmly stood by the more general idea that a high emotional positivity-to-negativity ratio is beneficial.

In another area Fredrickson and others hypothesize that positive emotions undo the cardiovascular effects of negative emotions. When people experience stress, they demonstrate symptoms like increased heart rate, higher blood sugar, and other adaptations optimized for immediate action. If they do not regulate these changes once the stress is over, they can be subject to illnesses like coronary disease. Research indicates that positive emotions help people who were previously under stress relax back to their physiological baseline.

Past research has shown that anger, fear and sadness each elicit distinct responses in the autonomic nervous system. In direct contrast, the positive emotions appeared to have no distinguishable autonomic responses. Positive emotions do not themselves generate cardiovascular reactivity. They quell any existing cardiovascular reactivity caused by negative emotions. To put this another way, a prior state of negative emotional arousal may be a necessary backdrop to illuminate the cardiovascular impact of positive emotions.

If you assume, as most emotion theorists do, that the cardiovascular reactivity sparked by certain negative emotions prepares the body for specific actions, Fredrickson's broaden-and-build theory suggests that positive emotions can speed recovery from, or undo, this cardiovascular reactivity. It can also return the body to mid-range levels of activation suitable for pursuing a wider range of behavioral options.

In one study they presented participants with an acute stressor telling them that they had to give a public speech. As they prepared for this speech their bodies exhibit increased sympathetic nervous system activation. After a minute or so of this heightened state of arousal, the participants were told that they didn't have to give the speech at all.

All they had to do was view a randomly assigned video clip that generates a positive or negative emotion, or a state of neutrality. Researchers measured the amount of time it took each person to recover from their anxiety about the possible speech. Results indicated that positive emotions led to a quicker return to a resting state than neutral or negative emotions. This is called the **undoing effect**.

In other work, Fredrickson has researched social and environmental cues that can carry sexist messages and enhance stereotypical gender differences. She discovered that when women were randomly assigned a dress in a way that calls attention to their bodies, they show impaired performance on a math task and were literally more likely to "throw like a girl". What this research suggested was that drawing attention to women's bodies also activated stereotypical beliefs about their gender.

Fredrickson has also contributed to research for the Objectification Theory which posits that women internalize an outsider's point of view when viewing themselves and their bodies. She posits that this objectification of women's bodies may be a contributory factor to the high prevalence of mental health risks that women suffer.

In 2000, Fredrickson received the American Psychological Association's inaugural Templeton Prize in Positive Psychology for her work on the broaden-and-build theory. Or the past sixteen years her work has been supported by grants from the National Institute of Health.

In 2008 she received the Society of Experimental Social Psychology's Career Trajectory Award. In 2013 she was awarded the inaugural Christopher Peterson Gold Medal which is the highest honor bestowed by the International Positive Psychology Association.

It appears that Barbara Fredrickson has a lot more to offer to the field of psychology.

GALLERY

THE ORIGINALS

SIGMUND FREUD

ALFRED ADLER

E.L.THORNDIKE

CARL JUNG

JOHN B WATSON

MELANIE KLEIN

ANNA FREUD

MARGARET MAHLER

BRENDA MILNER

MARSHA LINEHAN

INSOO KIM BERG

OTTO RANK

W.R. FAIRBAIRN

JACOB MORENO

HARRY STACK SULLIVAN

MARGARET MAHLER

S.H. FOULKES

ERICH FROMM

CARL ROGERS

MILTON ERICKSON

B.F. SKINNER

ABRAHAM MASLOW

ROLLO MAY

ERIC BERNE

MURRAY BOWEN

HEINZ KOHUT

ALBERT ELLIS

JEROME BRUNER

JAMES BUGENTAL

HANS JURGEN ESYENCK

VIRGINIA SATIR

AARON BECK

SALVADOR MINUCHIN

ALBERT BANDURA

J.D.LAING

WILLIAM GLASSER

IRVIN YALOM

DONALD MEICHENBAUM

JOHN GOTTMAN

MARTIN SELIGMAN

JON KABAT ZINN

JOHN TEASDALE

FRANCINE SHAPIRO

KIRK STROSAHL

ZINDEL SEGAL

BARBARA LEE FREDRICKSON

ABOUT THE AUTHOR

David Elio Malocco was born in Dundalk, County Louth, Ireland. His father was born in Casalattico in Frosinone in Italy and his mother was born in Monaghan in Ireland. He was educated at the Christian Brothers School in Dundalk and his parents later sent him to St. Patrick's College in Cavan where they hoped he would be ordained as a Roman Catholic priest. But he chose law and business instead.

He received his Bachelor of Civil Law degree from University College Dublin and spent fifteen years as a criminal lawyer before taking a second degree at the Open University, Milton Keynes in England where he obtained a first class honors degree in Psychology majoring in Cognitive Development.

In 1991 he realized a personal ambition and moved to New York where he studied film direction, production and writing for film at New York University. Since then he has written numerous screenplays in several genre and has written, produced and directed numerous shorts and three feature films, Virgin Cowboys, Magdalen and Jack Gambel: The Enigma.

He later studied creative writing at Oxford University and is presently completing a qualification as a psychotherapist at the Institute for Integrative Counselling and Psychotherapy in Dublin. He is a graduate member of the British Psychological Society and a member of the American Criminology Society.

He has written several books on true crime and forensic science. The books were motivated by dual diplomas he had taken. The first was in the Psychology of Criminal Profiling and the second in Forensic Science specializing in crime scene analysis. His publications include:

Who's Who Serial Killers: The Top 100;
Murder for Profit: They Killed for Money;
Sexual Psychopaths: British Serial Killers;
Serial Sex Killers: Real American Psychos;
Wicked Women;
I am a Cannibal: A Study of Anthropophagy;
The World's Worst Serial Killers;

Criminal Profiling: A Basic Introduction;
The Beatles Conspiracy: John, Paul, George, Ringo and Bill!;
Forensic Science: Crime Scene Analysis.
Psychotherapy: The Top 50 Theorists and Theories is his eleventh book and the first in the series called Student Guides Simplified.

His next book is a discussion on the crime of murder and those who make a living from killing others. It features evidence from crime scene analyses and is sub-titled How to Commit the Perfect Murder.

David is a lifelong supporter of Liverpool Football Club and enjoys filmmaking, writing, drinking wine, cooking and rescuing abandoned and abused dogs.

His current project is to set up a charity for people suffering from mental health issues as he believes that everyone should be entitled to access psychotherapy even if they can't afford it.

Further information can be obtained by visiting his website davidemalocco.com

Forthcoming books in the Student Guides Simplified library include:
A Brief History of Psychology: Important Timelines (March 2015)
Psychotherapy: Approaches and Theories (April 2015)

CPSIA information can be obtained at www.ICGtesting.com
Printed in the USA
LVOW11s1454240416

485094LV00003B/192/P